Heroes
Who Live On

Published by

CE National, Inc.
P.O. Box 365
Winona Lake, IN 46590

©2002 by CE National, Inc.

Requests for information should be addressed to:
        CE National, Inc.
        P.O. Box 365
        Winona Lake, IN 46590-0365
        (574) 267-6622
        www.cenational.org

    ISBN # 0-9722278-2-2

Writers/Editors: Robert Cover, Sr.; Holly Jones; Viki Rife

Cover design and sketches: Mallory Nixon

Contents

Acknowledgments

We would like to thank the friends and relatives of our "heroes" who contributed information, photos, and encouragement for this project. It would be impossible to list all of them, but they know who they are. We trust that each of you knows how much we appreciate your contribution to this book.

We want to also thank Ed Lewis, Executive Director of CE National, for his conviction that this project was worthwhile and his commitment to seeing it done.

Thank you, also, to the CE National Children's Cabinet for their encouragement and support, and to the many children's workers whose enthusiasm for this idea spurred this project along.

Most of all we want to thank our Lord, who knows what it takes to make a hero.

Preface

This book has been born of the conviction that children can learn character through the example of others. The individuals chosen for this book did not set out to be heroes. They were just ordinary people who listened to a higher calling and who chose a higher way. They touch our lives in countless ways, many that we don't even recognize. They join the great cloud of witnesses (Hebrews 12) who have lived for God and can testify to us that He is faithful.

Most of them would be surprised to find themselves in a book about heroes. Yet each of them chose to invest in the eternal. They had the vision to think ahead, to see the needs of those who would come after them. They may have founded or headed schools, publications, organizations and churches. They may have sacrificed a life of convenience to serve on the mission field. They may have taught children, or taken care of someone who was sick. But what makes them heroes is their commitment to truth and to the generations to follow them.

They made lasting contributions to the Fellowship of Grace Brethren Churches. As they now live on as witnesses in heaven, their investment in people and God's Word continues to live on here on earth, affecting us in many unseen ways: through people they influenced who then influenced others; through organizations that meet needs; through churches that have stood through time.

All of the heroes in this book are no longer with us here on earth, so we have no way of knowing the exact details of their lives, or what they were thinking at any given time. However, we have made every effort in our research to get a fair picture of what they were like. For most of the stories, we've taken incidents mentioned by friends or in writings and added dialogue and details to bring the characters to life and make the stories interesting for children. We trust that this literary license will not in any way misrepresent these individuals.

With each hero we have highlighted a characteristic that stands out and provided a definition to help children understand that characteristic as they read or hear the story.

Our prayer is that the spirit of each hero will shine through these stories, and that children will be inspired to imitate them by imitating Christ.

"We do not want you to become lazy, but to imitate those who through faith and patience inherit what has been promised."
Hebrews 6:12

Alexander Mack

Alexander Mack
(1679-1735)

Alexander Mack

Obedience

"We must obey God rather than men." Acts 5:29

Obedience: a willingness to obey

"Alexander, quick! Grab these blankets and get on the horse with Emmie! We're being invaded again!" Thirteen-year-old Alexander Mack ran as fast as he could to obey his mother. His three-year-old sister, Emmie, stood wide-eyed, watching all of the confusion as people rushed around her gathering a few belongings. Alexander clambered on the horse. Someone handed Emmie to him. He put his arms around her to calm her. "It's going to be all right, Em," he whispered. "I won't let anything happen to you. We're going for a little ride."

Later that day, with his family hiding safely in the forest, Alexander crept cautiously toward the light that showed where the trees ended. Just before he reached the beginning of sunlight, he jumped up and grabbed a branch. Silently he pulled himself up. Using the branches as a ladder, he was soon high enough to peer out from behind the leaves.

From his perch, he could see the invaders quite clearly. They had reached the ruins of the ancient castle that had been the home of the noblemen who had ruled Schriesheimer, Alexander's home town in Germany, for generations. But it wasn't the invaders that Alexander was interested in. He wanted to see whether his father was safe. Alexander's father was the village Burgomeister, or mayor. Mr. Mack had sent his family on ahead to hide while he found a safe place for the town's important papers and valuable treasures. He had promised to join them soon.

But Alexander was worried. The last time the town had been invaded by enemies, they had hanged the Burgomeister. Would his dad get away in time? As he watched the soldiers, he heard a shout. Another group of soldiers was arriving, surrounding a small group of prisoners with their hands tied behind their backs. Alexander almost lost his grip on the tree branch as he leaned forward. Was one of the figures his father?

Just then he heard a rustling on the ground below where he sat. He peered cautiously through the leaves. His heart leapt as he caught sight of a tall man in a black coat, standing at the edge of the forest. He, too, was watching the soldiers. Alexander scrambled down the tree as fast as he could go. "Father, you're safe!" he exclaimed as he ran into his surprised father's arms.

That night, huddled around their tiny campfires in the hills, the villagers tried to decide what to do. This was the third time their village had been invaded. Was there any point in even staying around with the hope that they would someday be able to return to their homes and lands? Would the invaders find the prized city hall steeple bells that the villagers had lowered into the well in the town square to keep them safe?

Suddenly they heard a shout from a lookout at the edge of the woods. The families rushed over, only to stop, stunned into silence, at the sight of the flames lighting up the night. Their village, their crops, everything they had left behind was on fire.

Five months later the invaders left. Wearily the townsmen returned to their devastated lands. Alexander and his family considered themselves very fortunate: their house and flour mill, although badly damaged, were still standing.

But as the townspeople tried to rebuild their lives, the army that the invaders had been escaping from arrived in town. They took over whatever was left of the buildings, wagons, livestock and roads. The invaders had forced the townspeople to pay taxes; now this army wanted them to pay taxes to them. The Macks, like the rest of the villagers, had nothing left to live on, much less to pay taxes. The village lived in fear of yet another attack.

Alexander was 18 years old before peace finally came to the region. But the childhood years spent in poverty, terror and chaos had left a deep impression on him. He had seen enough fighting. Surely it was wrong for Christians to kill fellow humans, even in war!

There were many other questions that filled Alexander's mind. Should babies, who could not understand enough to have a personal faith, be baptized? Why didn't many of the church members he knew follow the simple teachings of Christ? Why didn't the Christians he knew celebrate a special "Love Feast" as the Bible instructed? He looked forward anxiously to the time he would go to the university, where he could study and find answers to his questions.

Then another tragedy struck in his life. One of his two older brothers who were to take over the family's flour milling business died. Alexander was the son chosen to stay home from the university to help keep the business going.

But Alexander's interests were more along spiritual lines than on grinding flour. A new wave of interest for knowing God was sweeping over Northern Europe. People called Pietists were studying the Bible in small groups, and felt that they could worship God best by simply obeying the Bible. This approach seemed very practical and realistic to Alexander.

When he was 21 he married Anna Margaret Kling, and they began holding Bible studies in a large room in their mill. The meetings were considered illegal, since they were not being led by one of the three legal state religions. In 1706 the chief local law enforcement officer showed up at the meeting. He questioned the people who were there, and took back a police report that at least 50 Pietists were at the meeting. In his police report, he wrote that he had gone there personally to break up the meeting and scare them away. He stated that if he hadn't, the Pietists would have won hundreds of people over to their "false" beliefs.

That same night, Alexander, with his wife and two sons, packed a few belongings and escaped from Schriesheimer. They stopped in a number of towns before finally arriving in Schwarzenau. There they finally felt free to worship as they believed they should.

Alexander was becoming more and more convinced that the Bible was meant for everyone and that all Christians should obey it. He especially felt that only adults should be baptized. He was a very humble man. However, he was also stubbornly determined to obey everything the Bible said.

He was especially concerned that his baptism as a baby was worthless, since he hadn't been old enough to choose for himself to follow Christ. Alexander wanted to be baptized again, now that he was an adult, but that was against the law.

Alexander thought long and hard about the verse, "We ought to obey God rather than men." (Acts 5:29). After much prayer and Bible study, he met with four men and three ladies by the Eider River near Schwarzenau early one morning in August of 1708. The group wanted Alexander to baptize them. He refused, because he himself had not been baptized by trine immersion–dunking under the water three times. They finally agreed that the men should draw lots. Then whoever won would baptize Alexander, who would then baptize the others. The eight people who were baptized started the group that was later called the New Baptists of Schwarzenau.

As various groups of "New Baptists" developed, the rulers started to worry about losing their power and influence over the people. As more and more people turned against the New Baptists, Alexander saw his dream of living in Christian freedom and love being threatened. The situation was becoming more dangerous for Alexander Mack and his followers. Many people in the group had heard others talking about the freedom in the new continent of America. In 1719, after much prayer, a group of New Baptists boarded a ship for America. They eventually settled around Germantown, Pennsylvania, near Philadelphia.

Alexander stayed in Germany, but a year later the persecution became so bad that he had to escape to Holland. There Alexander developed more of his ideas of how a Biblical church should be run.

Finally, in 1729 he and the other New Baptists in Holland sailed to Pennsylvania. Alexander bought land in Germantown. Soon everyone was looking to him as the active leader of the Germantown Brethren group. He served faithfully for six more years, until he died in 1735.

Alexander Mack was committed to obeying what he felt the Lord had called him to do. He is one of the main reasons the Brethren have come to be known as "people of the Book." Even hard times could not change what he believed and stood for. Though Alexander Mack is credited for being the founder of the Brethren movement, he did not want to be known that way. He felt the huge responsibility to do whatever the Bible says that a person should do. His goal was not to start a new church. He was determined to "defend the truth of the Good News." (Jude 1:3, NLT).

Florence N. Gribble

Florence N. Gribble

(1879-1942)

Florence N. Gribble

Dependence on God

"Then I heard the voice of the Lord saying, 'Whom shall I send? And who will go for us?' And I said, 'Here am I. Send me.'"
Isaiah 6:8

Dependence on God: trust in God

A strange wave of shyness swept over Dr. Florence Gribble as she reached the door of the room where her daughter Marguerite was waiting for her. She hadn't seen Marguerite for five years. Would Marguerite even remember her? The last time Marguerite had seen her mother, she had only been six years old. How would she respond?

Florence opened the door. A tall girl flew into her arms. "Mother!" she cried. She hugged her mother joyfully. Florence pulled back for a moment to look at her, then hugged her to herself again. "Oh, Marguerite," she exclaimed. "I've missed you so much!"

Florence was a missionary to Africa. It had been hard to leave her daughter in the United States while she helped take care of sick Africans and told them about Jesus, her Savior. But Marguerite needed her education, and this was the only way she could go to school. There were no schools in Africa for her to attend.

Florence and her husband James had been the first missionaries who had tried to go into the deepest heart of Africa, to what is now called the Central African Republic. Her husband had died there of Black Water Fever, and now Florence was going back alone. But first she needed to go to France to study more about the diseases that were making the Africans sick. She had also decided that Marguerite could study in France, where she would be closer to her mother and maybe could visit her from time to time. During the lonely times of missing her daughter, she had often prayed that Marguerite would have many opportunities to see for herself how God could work.

Florence and Marguerite arrived in Montpellier, France, where both began to attend school. It soon became clear that it was going to be a challenge to adjust to this new culture.

As winter approached and the weather grew colder, Florence and Marguerite struggled to keep their hotel room warm enough. Though the room had a radiator, it very seldom worked. One day, Florence came up with an idea. "We have a fireplace in the main room. Why don't we try to build a fire?"

Florence took money from what little she had and bought fuel and built the fire. Florence and Marguerite were shocked when smoke began to fill the room. What had happened? Some of the other hotel guests came from their own rooms to see what was going on. Soon the hotel owner and the maid showed up. The maid exclaimed, "Don't you know any better than to build a fire in a fireplace?"

Florence had not known that in France, fireplaces are only for decoration, not for building fires. The fireplace did not have a chimney, and that was why the room had started to fill up with smoke.

While living in Montpellier, Florence decided that she needed to go to Paris to study so that she would be able to teach the children of missionaries who were going on furlough. (Furlough is when missionaries leave the country they are ministering in to go back home for rest and further ministries in their home country.) Florence and Marguerite soon began making preparations to leave.

They had one problem, though. They did not have enough money for the trip. Florence told Marguerite about the problem, and together they prayed for God to send them the money.

Every few days, Marguerite would ask her mother, "Has the money come yet?" And her mother would have to tell her that, no, they still had no money for the trip, and that they would just have to keep praying.

Marguerite did not understand that her mother had been in this situation many times. She wondered why her mother kept accepting invitations from people to a dinner to say goodbye. One day, while coming home from a "goodbye dinner," she asked her mother again, "Do we have money for the trip yet?"

"Not yet, dear," her mother replied.

Marguerite couldn't stand it any more. "Mother," she said, "aren't you afraid we won't be able to get enough money? Won't we be embarrassed when we have to tell everyone that we aren't going on the trip after all?"

Florence realized that this was a chance to share with Marguerite how important it was to have faith in God. She answered calmly, " He that believes shall not be ashamed."

Marguerite said nothing. She trusted her mother, but she also knew that you couldn't buy a ticket if you didn't have any money. And they only had a few days left before they had to leave.

As they reached the hotel where they were staying, the owner came out to meet them. "Here is a letter for you, Dr. Gribble. I did not allow anyone to take it to your room, because it came registered mail."

"A registered letter! What do you think it is, Mother?" Marguerite exclaimed excitedly. She knew that mail that was registered was very important.

"I don't know, dear, but let's hurry and open it," her mother replied.

Florence ripped the envelope open as fast as she could. "A special gift has come for you," it read, "and feeling that you might have some immediate need, I am forwarding it to you at once."

The letter was from Dr. Louis Bauman, the director of the Brethren Foreign Missions Board that sent missionaries to the different mission fields. Inside was enough money for the trip to Paris.

Marguerite sat down on the edge of her bed, trying to take in what had just happened. This was amazing! "God really does answer prayer!" she thought. She saw her mother bow her head, and she knew that Mother was lifting her heart in thankful prayer to the Savior who had once again shown His faithfulness.

Florence Gribble was a pioneer missionary, a medical doctor, a wife and a mother. But more than all of these, she was a dedicated servant of her Lord. Throughout her life, she had chosen again and again to follow God, no matter what. Even though her health was sometimes frail, which meant she was often sick, she was certain of her calling to the mission field. Marguerite knew that her mother had not always known about God. Florence's father had been a lawyer, and he taught Florence and his children that Jesus Christ was either a myth or a fairy tale. But he allowed Florence to go to Sunday School in a little church in their town in Nebraska. Florence was a very quick learner, and she graduated from high school at the age of 16. Shortly after that she felt the Holy Spirit telling her, "Give up the praise of men and follow me." She didn't really understand what it meant, and since she had no one to ask, she did nothing. She continued her studies and became a licensed teacher. Although she was very successful as a teacher, she struggled with an emptiness in her soul.

One day her sister invited her to a meeting of a Salvation Army group that had come to town. Here she heard the good news that Jesus could save her from her sins. The speaker invited those who wanted to know Jesus to come and talk with the group. Florence did not respond. Afterwards, however, she kept thinking about the message to receive Jesus as Savior. What did it mean?

Months passed. Then one day as she was alone, she remembered she had heard the words, "Believe on the Lord Jesus Christ and you shall be saved, and your house." Suddenly the words "Be saved" jumped out at her. It made sense! Getting rid of her sins was not up to her, but up to the Savior! She hugged that truth to her heart. Peace, joy, and love like she had never known before swept over her. She could not wait to share with her family and her friends what she had discovered. From that time on there was no looking back.

Some time later she attended a missionary conference. That day, she went forward to commit her life to being a medical missionary to Africa. As she heard about the many people dying in Africa with no one to tell them about Jesus, she understood what the Holy Spirit had meant about giving up the praise of men and following Him. It didn't matter that she had a successful job and that everyone praised her teaching skill. She would go back to school, learn to help sick people, then go to Africa to help heal their bodies and their hearts.

Florence immediately began studying for medical certification as a doctor. She had very little money, but a big heart and a willingness to work and study long hours. Early on in her time at medical school, she ran out of money. She would be unable to return to school the next term. As she packed her suitcase to go back home, tears filled her eyes. She started feeling sorry for herself, as if no one else had ever been in a situation as hard as hers. She had no money, no food – no way for her to pay for medical school. Then she thought of Abraham, who, even though he was unsure of his next step, trusted God. And just as God did not forget about Abraham, He certainly would not forget about her. Just as she was reflecting on God's promises, she heard voices downstairs. A minute later, her landlady appeared at her door.

"There's a gentleman waiting for you downstairs, Miss Newberry,"

As soon as Florence arrived downstairs, the man got right to the point, "My wife is very ill on Warren Avenue. Could you come and nurse her?"

This was truly an answer to prayer. Warren Avenue was just a block away, so she would not even have to pay a streetcar fare to get there. She became the woman's full-time nurse. When it came time for Florence to leave, the woman, who had been a very challenging patient at times, burst into tears and pleaded with Florence to stay with her: "I have had many nurses, some of who have professed as you do, to be Christians, but you are the only one in whom I have ever seen Christ." Though Florence could not stay, her time with this patient was truly the work of the Lord. Before Florence left, the woman told her that through her quiet testimony, she had led her to the Savior.

She soon earned her doctorate degree. She was now a doctor! She knew that she had received experience that would be extremely useful on the mission field.

Florence's first tour of mission service was in Kenya, East Africa. No sooner had she arrived on the field than she didn't know what to do about all of the sick people who were coming to her. Somehow the word had gotten out that a real doctor was coming. People from miles around showed up to receive treatment. Florence did what she could to help them. She enjoyed the demands of discipline and order that this life required. One of the other missionaries serving at that station was a man named James Gribble. After four years of working together on that field, they were married. The two seemed to have a special understanding of trusting God. Dr. Gribble soon realized she had married a man of great faith.

About the same time they both felt they should go to Africans who had never heard the Gospel message. James had made a trip to explore central Africa; there he had seen many, many people who had never heard the message of the Gospel. God gave him the assurance that He wanted him to go to these people. Florence felt the same assurance. Together they began making plans to go to what is now known as Central African Republic.

The Gribbles had been in Kenya for six years, so they said goodbye to their loved ones there and returned to the United States to find others who would share their calling to take the good news to the unreached people of central Africa. While they were in the States, little Marguerite was born. After many disappointments and hard times, they were ready to go to central Africa with Marguerite, who was then about two years old, and two other missionaries. It was wartime so they had to go a roundabout way to get there, traveling on a darkened ship at night for fear of the enemy.

They arrived at the border of Oubangui Chari, and they applied for permission to go to the interior to set up the first mission station. But because of the chaos left by World War II and ridiculous laws and procedures in the country, no missionaries were allowed to enter the country. They set up tents under a grass roof for shelter and found roots and jungle fruits for their food while they waited for permission. One day went by, then another, then weeks and months. Living under those primitive conditions, they ended up waiting almost three whole years. Their time was not wasted, though. They spent these "waiting years" telling and teaching the Gospel to anyone who would listen, studying native languages, preparing language dictionaries for new recruits that would come to help, translating the Bible, and praying regularly for the permission to enter into the heart of Africa.

Finally the permission was granted. James went on ahead to prepare a place to live. But Florence had become seriously ill. The missionaries decided that she and Marguerite should go to the States for a rest and for Marguerite to find a home where she could grow up "normally."

Shortly after Florence returned to Africa, the Lord called James home to heaven. But a firm, solid foundation of prayer and planning had been laid in Africa. Almost 80 years later there are more than

230,000 Africans who worship the Lord because of the faithful pioneer witness of the Gribbles.

Florence Gribble continued to serve on that field until the Lord came to take her to heaven on March 31, 1942—19 years after He had taken her husband.

Florence was talented in many ways, including the use of her pen. In God's grace she was allowed enough time to write in detail about her husband's pioneer life of love for the lost people of Africa in the book *Undaunted Hope*. Later, shortly before she died, she was encouraged by her friends to write her own biography, which she titled *Stranger than Fiction*.

James S. Gribble

James S. Gribble
(1883-1923)

James S. Gribble

Vision

"So that we can preach the gospel in the regions beyond you..."
II Cor. 10:16

Vision: the ability to look or plan ahead

The morning sun shone in James Gribble's eyes as he walked down the sidewalk, but he didn't seem to notice. He had one thing on his mind, and that was to set his life right with God.

He stopped at the steps of the First Brethren Church. He had been attending church there, but only because his mother kept after him to go to church. He did enjoy the lively, joyful singing, so he continued to show up every week.

But everything had changed since the accident. He couldn't get the scene out of his head. The woman, smiling and waving one minute as she climbed off his streetcar, lying on the street dying the next minute. It hadn't been his fault; even the police had agreed about that. But it had left him shaken and unsure of himself. He couldn't help but wonder, "If that had been me, where would I be right now? I need to give my heart to God." He cried out to Him, saying, "God, deliver me and I'll serve You." Many people make bold statements such as this when they're in a tight spot, but James really meant what he said. Now here he was, going to church with a new sense of purpose in his heart.

As James sat through the service that morning, he realized that he had found what he had been looking for all his life. Giving his heart to God was what he had been missing. As soon as the service was over, he went up to the pastor and asked him how he could become a Christian. After Dr. Louis S. Bauman explained to him the steps of salvation, James decided he wanted to publicly commit his life to God.

That night, James Gribble was baptized. Very soon after that, as he was reading the Great Commission in Matthew 28:19, he inserted his name into the verse: "Go, James Gribble, into all the world and preach the gospel to every creature." He was convinced that God was asking him to go to share the good news of salvation with people who had never heard it before. He decided that the dark continent of Africa was the place he needed to go.

When he went to talk to his pastor, however, he found out that the Brethren had no mission field in Africa. He didn't let that discourage him from what he believed God wanted him to do. He threw himself into studying God's word under the teaching and preaching of his pastor, Dr. Bauman.

God did not allow James Gribble to give up his hopes of going to Africa. While he was attending Eaglesmere Bible Conference, the call to Africa became even more real to him. His heart leaped when he heard that the central part of Africa was closed to the gospel. Those people had never heard of Jesus. That's the place he should go!

Soon afterwards, James learned that Africa Inland Mission had missionaries in Kenya. Even though this was about 800 miles east of where James really wanted to go, he decided to go there.

James had very little formal education, but he decided to teach himself as much as he could to prepare himself to teach people about Christ. Once he made that decision, friends noticed that they very seldom saw him without a book in his hand. When he went to be examined by the mission board, he passed the exam!

By faith he prepared to leave for Africa. When the time came to leave, he only had enough money to buy a ticket to England. He would need $250 to continue the trip from England to Kenya.

James got on the ship anyway, trusting that the Lord would provide. Just before the gangplank was lifted so that no one else could come on the boat, a man rushed up the gangplank. He asked, "Is there a man here named Gribble?" He handed James a small sack. It had just the amount of money James needed for his trip! The man had heard about James in a prayer meeting the night before. Convinced that God really wanted James to go to Africa, he went to the bank early the next morning. He took out all of his life savings and rushed to the boat, arriving just in time to give James the money.

This was just one of the many times God would work a miracle to provide the impossible. Throughout his life, James chose to trust God to provide everything he needed.

During the long boat ride, James met a missionary doctor who was also going to Kenya. Her name was Florence Newberry. Before long James realized that he was in love with her. He was too shy, though, to speak to her about it on the trip.

Once they got to the field, James waited and waited to talk to Florence. But he never seemed to have a chance. She was always busy with her patients. He became discouraged; she would never have time for him!

Finally he came up with a plan. He would pretend that he was sick and make an appointment with her! It didn't work out quite as he had planned. Florence quickly realized that James was not sick. He took advantage of the opportunity anyway, and admitted his love for her.

Florence was not interested in him. She told him firmly not to mention "love" again.

Though discouraged, James continued his work in Africa. He still had a deep desire to go to a place where the gospel had never been preached, and where no one else was even thinking of taking the gospel.

In 1910 he set out to find a place like this. Though he started out with another missionary, that missionary became sick and had to turn back. James kept going. Then James himself became sick with a disease called Black Water Fever. During his sickness and time alone, God gave him a vision. God told him that he had a lot more work to do, and that Florence would someday be his wife.

This encouraged James, so he approached Florence once again to confess his love for her. Again, she refused him. James did not give up, though. He waited for a while, then asked her again. Once again she rejected him. What should he do?

One day Florence was in a prayer meeting when suddenly she realized something. God wanted her to marry James! So finally, four years after they met, they were married. Together, they served in Kenya for two more years.

Meanwhile, James was becoming more and more convinced that God was calling them to reach the unreached tribes living in central Africa. He wrote to Dr. Bauman, who was also treasurer of the Foreign Missionary Society of the Brethren Church. Would it be possible for the Brethren to begin a new work in central Africa?

Dr. Bauman did not discourage him. Instead, he encouraged him to talk to the Lord about it. James began to think about the power of prayer. What if many, many people would commit to praying for central Africa? What if they recruited "bands" of praying people to back them up? As the idea developed in James' mind, he wrote home, "The prayer bands will be the strong right arm of the African work. We want a series of such bands stretching from the Atlantic to the Pacific."

As the Gribbles continued to pray, they felt that God was showing them that they should resign from missionary service with the Africa Inland Mission and return to the United States for a time. There they spent three years preparing and waiting to go to the mission field to which they were called. While they were in the U.S., their daughter Marguerite was born. The Gribbles faced many challenges during this time of preparation. They traveled to churches to share their vision, often struggling with financial needs and illness.

There were many reasons for not going to central Africa as missionaries, especially at this time. For one thing, the Karre tribe was very fierce and had killed many people. There was no one who would protect the Gribbles if any trouble developed. Secondly, James Gribble was not a trained pastor. Though very capable in many areas, including languages, he did not have the usual formal preparation for spiritual ministry. Both James and Florence had health problems and did not know if their health would hold out on the mission field. Also, their daughter Marguerite had recently been born, and it would not be wise to take a young child into the unknown. Because World War I was going on, it was dangerous to cross the Atlantic Ocean. Enemy submarines regularly hunted and sank ships that belonged to the U.S. or other countries that were on her side. On top of all this, the Gribbles had no money for preparation, supplies, the trip, or living expenses. Besides, there was no assurance that the French government at that time would give permission for them to enter central Africa once they arrived on the continent.

With so many problems, the Gribbles had reason to fear that the Mission Board would deny permission and advise them to wait for more favorable conditions before venturing into the jungles of Africa. But the leaders of the mission society recognized the Gribbles' dedication and wise trust in the Lord. They encouraged them to keep praying.

Their encouragement drove the Gribbles on to even more prayer and commitment. The more they prayed, the more they were assured that this was the right thing for them to do. They felt the time in Kenya had taught them much about depending on the Lord for everything.

They left in January of 1918 for the long voyage to Africa. Because it was during wartime, they had to travel without using any lights at night. When they finally arrived on the southwest coast of Africa, they began taking smaller boats for shorter distances to reach the mouth of the mighty Congo River. The journey took them almost two months.

Now the long "waiting game" began. It would be more than three and a half years of disappointments, physical suffering, illness, and hard manual work after leaving America before James Gribble would be able to enter Oubangui-Chari in the heart of Africa.

But James was a missionary with the heart of a pioneer, and he stayed true to his calling. He loved the Lord Jesus, and his dream was to tell the story of Jesus to the unreached tribes. He did not waste this time of waiting. Instead, he studied languages that he would use, wrote home, taught Bible classes with the Africans wherever he was, set up temporary living quarters, and continued to pray. Someone has commented that most of the mission work done by James was done on his knees, even while he was still trying to get permission to enter the Oubangui-Chari territory. The Africans began to call him "the man who has no evil spirit." He wrote at the time, "Whatever may be the duration (length) of our stay here, the Spirit has not given us the liberty to turn aside elsewhere; we must tarry (stay) until the door be opened."

Most of the delays were caused by the need for permission from the government authorities. Local officials claimed that they had to have direct permission from the government in Paris, France. Meanwhile, the Gribbles would have to live as best they could. This usually meant to set up their tents under whatever shelter they might find for protection from heavy winds and rains. They humorously named their two main camps "Camp Wait" and "Camp Wait-Some-More."

During this time of waiting Dr. Gribble became very seriously ill. She was the only doctor around; there was no doctor to take care of *her*. James prayed to God for her life, and others joined him. Florence recovered, but was very weakened. They finally decided that she and Marguerite should return to the United States. The other missionary with them, Estella Myers, went with Dr. Gribble part of the way, to the coast. James continued to wait alone, through very severe testing and several battles with the deadly Black Water Fever.

Finally, after three and one half years of waiting, the permission was given to enter the territory. James immediately packed up and moved the 100 miles to Bozoum, still 25 miles from the Karre tribe. There he set up camp and started dividing his time between surveying the territory, making contact with the people there, and preparing for constructing permanent buildings for the missionaries that he had prayed would come in answer to the call to help. The mission station was being officially opened.

Riding his bicycle on jungle paths a total of some 1500 miles, he scouted out the country. Finally he was able to report to the government in Bangui that he wanted to settle at Bassai, the heart of the Karre tribe for whom he had prayed so long. With great determination, James began setting up the mission station. He was not in good health, but he worked non-stop.

After receiving permission to enter the very center of dark Africa, James had only two and a half years to tell the Karre tribe, along with other tribes nearby, about Jesus. On June 4, 1923, as James fought another battle with the Black Water Fever, God called James Gribble to his heavenly home.

When news of his death reached the churches in the U.S., it was a great shock. Yet, because of his work, many other young people, and some older people, too, heard the call of God to go to the mission station he had established. There are now more than 900 Brethren churches established in central Africa. These churches serve over 230,000 baptized believers with an active hospital, and elementary and seminary level schools. African churches are sending out individuals and teams to continue to preach the Gospel message in that area. In fact, this part of Africa is considered to be one of the most - reached parts of the world. James Gribble's vision and prayers have truly brought the gospel to the darkest heart of Africa.

Estella C. Myers

Estella C. Myers
(1884-1956)

Estella C. Myers

Determination

"Never be lacking in zeal, but keep your spiritual fervor, serving the Lord." Romans 12:11

Determination: making up your mind and sticking to it

Estella stopped in her tracks, her hand still on the doorknob. Inside the room she could hear her grandmother's sharp voice. "I wonder who she's upset with now," Estella thought.

She pulled her hand away from the doorknob, afraid to open the door.

"I don't know what you're going to do about Estella. You know she'll always be the black sheep of the family."

What was Grandmother saying? Why was she upset with Estella this time? Estella backed away from the door. She could hear the soft murmur of her mother's voice and the harsh, angry response of her grandmother. Grandmother seemed to always be upset with her about something, but she had never realized before that her grandmother thought of her as a black sheep. Estella knew that being a black sheep was a very bad thing. That's what everyone called the son of their neighbors down the road, who was in jail for robbing a bank! Surely Grandmother didn't think that Estella would do something like that! Her family lived on a farm; she understood that a black sheep gave very poor quality wool and wasn't worth much. Was that really what her grandmother thought of her? What would it take to show her grandmother that she could do what was right?

Estella was afraid of her grandmother. Everyone in the family jumped to obey Grandmother. Even Estella's father, who ruled his home with a firm hand, gave in to his mother without an argument. But Estella determined that somehow she would show Grandmother that she was not a black sheep.

In school a few days later, Estella felt she had her chance. "Line up, class," she heard the teacher say. She looked up suspiciously from her work. Did this mean the class was to dance? Some of the older girls had told her that this teacher danced. Would she try to teach her students to dance, too? Estella was not going to dance. Her church taught that no one should dance, and Estella was determined to do what was right. When the rest of the class got in line by the door, Estella sat silently in her chair. The teacher was surprised by Estella's lack of obedience. "Estella, I asked the class to line up and get ready for the drill. Please do not keep us waiting," the teacher said firmly.

Estella was clearly embarrassed, but she refused to join the rest of the class.

"Estella, why won't you line up?" the teacher asked.

"It is wrong to dance; my father doesn't think a Christian should dance."

The teacher explained, "This is a simple drill, not a dance. We must have everyone participate. If you don't obey I shall have to give you a whipping after school."

Estella had never had a whipping. Frightened but determined, she asked her teacher, "Could you wait until tomorrow so I can ask my father what I should do?"

The teacher, not very happy, said sternly, "Estella Myers, you take your place in line right now or you shall receive the whipping. You know the results of disobedience."

Still Estella stayed in her seat. She was confident that she should not participate in a dance in any form. It would be better to be whipped than to disobey the command of the Lord. She finished the rest of the school day in fear and trembling.

After school the teacher patiently tried to explain that they were only lining up to practice a drill. Estella begged permission to talk with her father before making a decision. "I want to talk to

Papa. He will tell me the truth." The teacher, though not a Christian, recognized a sincere desire to do what was right. She allowed Estella to go on home without the whipping.

Papa Myers explained the difference between drill and dance to Estella. That ended the whipping episode. Though Estella was endlessly teased about her stand by both family and schoolmates, she felt the satisfaction of standing firmly for what she believed was right.

Many times in later life she would be challenged to "line up." When she was in high school she went through a time of mental depression, but she stubbornly held on to her commitment to be faithful to the Lord. The time of depression caused her to stammer and have poor use of the muscles in her face. When all looked hopeless for her return to good health, she prayed, "Oh God, take (what's left) of my life and use (it) for Thy glory. I can no longer use my brain. Lord, may I use my hands for Thee." Soon after that, she knew that God was telling her to go to Africa as a nurse. From that moment on, Estella set her face to take the Gospel where it had never been preached.

Becoming a nurse would take training and education. She did not have the money to pay for school. Estella did not let that stop her. She got a job selling cookbooks. Though still having difficulty talking with her face twisted by her illnesses, she memorized a sales speech. This effort paid off. Although few people had any hopes for her selling ability, she paid for her schooling and graduated. Estella knew that the Lord had called her, and that was enough to drive her to do her best.

Estella had been born and raised on the pioneer countryside of Iowa. Her father, a dedicated Christian who wanted to see Christians become what God wanted them to be, had taught Estella the importance of hard work, honesty, and holiness. She was her father's constant companion around the farm. Her mother had learned how to be careful with her money from years of living with very few extra things and she taught Estella how to use money wisely.

While preparing to go to the mission field, Estella experienced another of the many delays she would have before getting to the field. During that wait, she served as the county nurse of Lost Creek, Kentucky. She could have stayed to serve the Lord in that needy area; again, Estella gave up that opportunity in order to keep her commitment to preach Christ in Africa.

Another challenge came while she was on the ship on her way to Africa. World War II had brought danger to the seas. German submarines were stalking in the Atlantic Ocean, looking for allied ships to destroy. So the ships had to sail all night with no lights at all on board.

One night as Estella lay in her bed in the darkness, she began to have serious doubts about serving God in Africa. Getting there was hard enough. But once she was in Africa she would have to face cannibals and hostile natives. Did God really want her to go to Africa? There in the dark, fear began to take over. Maybe she should turn back.

As Estella struggled with her fears that night, God reminded her of a verse she had learned, "We wrestle not against flesh and blood but against…wickedness in high places." Strengthened by that verse, once again Estella determined that she would not give in or quit. She knew what was right and she stuck to it. She was glad for the Bible verse she had learned that had come to her in the dark, when she couldn't read her Bible for answers.

The place that had been chosen for a mission work was at the very center of Africa where the Gospel had never been preached. Estella's trip to that place was a long one, filled with opportunities to "line up" with the world and leave God out of the picture. Many delays, sicknesses that would take the lives of some of their companions, the inability to get travel permissions, lack of healthy living conditions, and personal illness would turn back someone who could not stand firm in their conviction to serve the Lord. Estella lived in a tent much of the three and a half years it took to get permission to go deep into the African bush to share the message of Jesus.

Finally they were settled on the new mission site in the Karre Mountains of Central African Republic. Soon Estella told Mr. Gribble, Missions Superintendent, that she wanted to go up into the mountains to tell the tribes there about Jesus. Mr. Gribble asked, "Do you really think that is a wise thing to do? Those people have never even seen a white person, let alone heard the story of salvation. They are hostile and we have no one who can accompany you for safety and support. You are doing so much here with your nursing, your translation work, and your study of the French and Sango languages. Your health has not been strong and you need all the rest you can get."

"But this is what I came to do," replied Estella. "It is the right thing to do and God will take care of me." Mr. Gribble knew Estella well enough to know that it was no use to argue. Estella planned her trip, contracted the necessary natives to carry the supplies needed, and started the journey.

On arrival at a village, she would tell the people that she had some good news for them. They were naturally interested, but of course were fearful. They had never seen a white person before. They weren't even familiar with clothing and baggage. At first they did not trust her, but she would walk away from her baggage to show she was not going to harm them. Little by little they would learn to know the Savior because of Estella's refusal to "line up" with what was considered sensible and proper. Years later she would become known all over that area of Africa as "Mama."

After 36 years of missionary service in Africa, much of that time doing vital translation work, Estella was found "asleep" with an unfinished letter. "I am just resting in the Lord. I know not the future, only hope that He will strengthen me enough to finish the translations. If it is His will to take me home, this will be O.K. I feel sorry for coming out to cause any trouble caring for me..."

The Lord had taken her during the day when she was all alone. Now she was ready to "line up" with the heavenly hosts welcoming her to a bright eternity.

With a simple funeral ceremony at Bassai (the first Brethren mission station in Africa), Estella was laid to rest with the Gribbles, who had taken the Gospel into a forbidden land with her. An African who had been with Estella the longest spoke of seeing the Light of the world introduced to the darkness of Africa. He summed up this dedicated life with, "Mademoiselle Myersie had the body of a white person, but she had the heart of a black person."

She was a true "pioneer missionary," completely dedicated to service for her Lord. She maintained a strong determination that brought her to the place of being willing to lay down her life to take the Gospel to the center of dark, unevangelized Africa. The Africans she taught have taught other Africans. Who knows how many people have come to Christ because of her determination to share the Light!

Alva J. McClain

Alva J. McClain
(1888-1968)

Alva J. McClain

Sound Doctrine

"Do your best to present yourself to God as one approved, a workman who does not need to be ashamed and who correctly handles the word of truth." I Tim. 2:15

Sound doctrine: sticking with the truth

"Hey, Mick, wait up!"

Alva J. McClain turned to wait for the friend who had called him. His parents walked on ahead through the doors of the church.

"Mick, I have an idea!" Joe panted. He lowered his voice. "What do you think would happen if the church bell started ringing in the middle of the service?"

Mick turned and looked up at the high steeple. He could see the bell inside. He thought about his friends trying to sit quietly through the long sermon. They could use some entertainment. Wouldn't it be great to see what people would do?

Joe was watching Mick's face for a trace of his mischievous grin. It wasn't long before that grin started spreading across Mick's face. The boys had been friends for a long time and could read each other's minds. They started walking slowly toward the door. If they could just wait until everyone was inside, they could sneak up to the stairs that led to the steeple.

It worked! Soon they were in the attic. They stepped carefully across the rafters. Between the strong wooden boards there was no floor, just a thin layer of plaster. They moved slowly, hoping the boards wouldn't creak. They were right above the sanctuary, and they could hear everything that was being said.

"Wait until the sermon has started," Mick whispered to his friend.

They sat on a rafter and leaned against the wall to wait. It was hard to sit quietly. Mick didn't dare look at Joe—the suspense and anticipation were sure to make them laugh. All he could see of Joe was his shiny shoes.

"Nice shoes, Joe," Mick commented.

"Yeah, my dad bought them for me yesterday," Joe answered.

Mick fought against his jealous feelings. His shoes were old and scuffed. It took a lot of polish every Saturday night to make them presentable for church on Sunday. He sighed and shifted his position slightly. He concentrated on imagining the reactions of the people sitting below them when they heard the bell.

Finally, Mick couldn't stand it any longer. He stood up and started for the bell rope. He felt Joe grab his shirt.

"It was my idea! I get to ring it!" Joe hissed.

"Oh, no you don't!" Mick hissed back. He was not going to be cheated out of the fun of ringing the bell. He yanked away and saw Joe coming after him again. Mick took a step just as Joe lunged. Joe missed the rafter and stepped on the thin plaster. As his weight came down on his foot, the plaster broke and his foot went through the ceiling.

In the sanctuary, all eyes had turned upward to see what was causing the commotion. Joe's dad stood up. He recognized that shoe!

Mick's dad saw the look on Joe's dad's face and looked around the room for his son. Then, his face bright red, he started up the steps for the steeple. Mick heard his father's voice, "Alva J. McClain, come here at once!" Once again his love for pranks had gotten him into trouble.

Many years later when Dr. McClain would refer to this story in his Theology classes, he would remind the students that it's best to stick to what is right to do. "Be sure your sin will find you out." (Numbers 32:23)

Alva J. McClain grew up in the state of Washington, where he learned that to get somewhere in life a person had to dedicate his interests and efforts into it. As a young boy he was slightly small for his age, but he made friends easily. Two of his favorite things to do were teasing his sisters and participating in athletics. His enthusiasm for life got him into all kinds of scrapes. He loved doing things that others might only think about.

While still young, Mick learned to train horses. He had a number of "cayuses" (racehorses or ponies) that he trained and entered in horse shows. Mick never let his small size slow him down in anything. He became quarterback for his high school football team and led them to several valley championships. The rules for football were different back then. One time, for example, his team only needed a few more yards to score. They huddled, then took their places. As soon as Mick got the snap, his teammates literally picked him up and threw him over the defending team. They got the touchdown!

After graduating, Mick went to the University of Washington. There he quarterbacked the Washington Huskies. He also played on the university's baseball team. One day while running to base after hitting a fly ball, he collided with another player. Back then baseball players wore metal cleats on their shoes. The other player's cleat punctured Mick's leg. Soon he developed blood poisoning. Although doctors were able to save his life, his leg was weakened. The incident ended both his education at the University of Washington and his active participation in sports.

So Mick stayed home to recuperate and help in his father's nursery business, raising pedigree fruit trees, which grew well in that fertile valley. He learned a lot as he worked with the growing plants, and later would use his experiences as illustrations for his sermons and class lectures.

About that time Mick decided he no longer needed to go to church. He took up smoking and got mixed up in the wrong crowd. He wasn't living his life for the Lord; he was following the ways of the world. He continued to watch life around him with curiosity, though. One time he watched as the line men installed the new telephone line that was going through their town. One of the newer workers was sent up the pole to connect the lines. The worker put on his spikes and safety belt for climbing the pole. Then he carefully climbed up as you would if you were rock climbing and began to make the hook-up. But it took two hands to do that, and the young man needed one hand to hang on. Finally the foreman called, "Lean back in the safety!" McClain would later use this illustration as he taught from the book of Romans about putting all your faith in God's safety.

In spite of his love for sports, Mick always found time to read and acquire more knowledge. He spent much of his spare time in the town's library. This intense love for knowledge was a passion that lasted his entire lifetime.

Mick was 22 when he met Josephine Gingrich. The two soon became attracted to each other. Family members predicted that when Jo found out about his rowdy past, she would lose interest. But evidently Jo saw something worthwhile in this young man, and on June 7, 1911, they were married. The marriage lasted for 57 years, until Mick's death.

Mick and Jo had been married for 15 months when his father encouraged him to attend the church service where Dr. Louis Bauman was speaking. It had been at least five years since Mick had been in church, but he mentioned to Jo that maybe it would be interesting. Mick did not expect to hear anything new, but when Dr. Bauman told how the Bible predicted historical events and had foretold details of the coming of Jesus, the promised Messiah, Mick listened intently. Mick's desire for truth and knowledge gave him a thirst for more. He and his wife returned that evening. At the end of the meeting, when Dr. Bauman asked those who would like to take Christ as personal Savior and Lord to come forward, both Mick and Jo stepped out and became true believers by faith. Mick threw away his cigarettes that same night and began reading the Bible. The more he read, the more sense it made.

Now Mick wanted to know more about what the Bible said. He moved to Los Angeles, where he studied at the Bible Institute of Los Angeles (BIOLA). From there he went on to various Christian schools of higher learning, serving as pastor of various churches while studying. He eventually earned his B.A. degree, Th.M. degree, and Doctorate of Divinity – all in the same year! He was in constant demand as a speaker in churches, schools, and conferences across the country, and was invited to teach at a number of Christian colleges.

Ever since his decision to follow Christ, Dr. McClain was always interested in training men to preach the Word of God. He knew the

Bible well, and was very concerned that Christians were starting to have false views about right and wrong. Because of his interest in training pastors, he was hired by Brethren College in Ashland, Ohio, to develop the seminary training there. But most of the college students and faculty were not ready to give up the errors that had crept into their thinking and behavior. Dr. McClain held to his convictions just as firmly. Conflict developed, and in the end Dr. McClain was fired. In response, Dr. McClain, Dr. Herman Hoyt, and a number of concerned pastors and students called a prayer meeting. As a result of this prayer meeting, the group decided to establish a new Seminary. Grace Theological Seminary was founded in 1937. Dr. McClain served as its President for 25 years. During this time, Dr. McClain also directed the founding of Grace College. His unusual understanding of the Bible and his ability to express himself from the pulpit or by writing made him a trusted leader and teacher in the Fellowship of Grace Brethren Churches.

Although he wrote many books, one of Dr. McClain's crowning achievements was the book *The Greatness of the Kingdom.* This large book explains what the Bible teaches about the history and the future of both the church and the nation of Israel.

Though often plagued with poor health, Dr. McClain lived to be 80 years old before the Lord took him home to the joys of heaven. Throughout his lifetime, Dr. McClain trained many young people for ministry, giving them a deeper understanding of the Word of Truth.

Russell I. Humberd

Russell I. Humberd
(1893-1965)

Russell I. Humberd

Witnessing

"Go out to the roads and country lanes and make them come in."
Luke 14:23

Witnessing: telling others what you've learned about Christ

Twelve-year-old Russell Humberd was listening carefully as the pastor closed his sermon. "God loves you and wants you to be a part of his family. He sent His son Jesus to die for you. Won't you accept His invitation today?" Russell knew he wanted to accept the invitation, but he was scared. Still, he slowly walked down the aisle to the front of the church. The pastor prayed with him. Russell had become one of God's children. As soon as he got out of church, his buddy Sam punched him in the shoulder. "You don't really believe all of that stuff, do you, Russ?" Sam asked him. "Why shouldn't I?" Russell replied. "Aw, what do all of those old people know? Church and God stuff is for old people, you know. They're almost ready to die and probably don't have much chance of sinning a lot and losing their salvation. We don't need that. I just go to church because my folks make me." "What's all this about losing your salvation? How do you do that?" Russell questioned. "Don't you know? If you sin enough or do something really, really bad, God may decide not to love you anymore, and He may not let you into Heaven." "How do you know that?" Russell asked in shock. "Who told you?" "I'm telling you, it's true. It's like this: you know how my dad always gets real mad at me and kicks me when he's drunk? Well, God's kind of like that. If you cross Him the wrong way, He might decide to get rid of you." "Wow, I never knew that. Is there anything I can do to make sure He doesn't get too mad at me?" Russell asked. "Well, I heard once that being baptized is pretty good luck. Maybe if you get baptized and then don't sin much after that, you'll be okay." Sam said.

This really concerned Russell. How could he not sin? It seemed that every day his mom got upset with him over something or other. And he did pick fights with his brother an awful lot. What could he do to make sure he got into Heaven? A thought hit him. "That's it! I'll get baptized and then kill myself. That way, I won't have the chance to sin and lose my salvation. I'll get into Heaven for sure then," Russell told himself. "But how will I kill myself? I'm kind of scared to do that. Well, I'll get baptized first," he thought. Shortly afterward, his pastor baptized him in a nearby creek. He never did commit suicide, but he did not have peace that he was truly saved.

Russell became interested in Anna Marie Black, who lived on a farm. Anna Marie was a spunky girl who helped her father a lot around the farm, especially by driving the horse and buggy. Russell must have visited her often. One day, after they started dating, Russell had to drive past the Black home on an errand. As they reached the Blacks' driveway, Russell's horse just naturally turned down the drive. Russell and Anna Marie were married in 1915.

Russell got a job at the Christian School in Lost Creek, Kentucky. One day he was sitting in the office of G.E. Druschel, the school director. Some visitors from Moody Bible Institute were also in the office. Tilting his chair back against the wall, Russell was explaining to them about his dilemma of losing his salvation and then dying before he could get it straightened out with the Lord. One of the visitors asked, "Don't you know about the assurance of salvation?" He went on to quote Ephesians 2:8-9, "For by grace are you saved through faith; and that not of yourselves, it is the gift of God, not of works, lest any man should boast." When Russell heard these words, his chair came down with a bang. For the first time, he realized that salvation was not up to him, but up to God. This was a true turning point in his life.

After two years of study at Moody Bible Institute, he was officially recognized as a pastor by his home church in Flora, Indiana, in January of 1921. After more study, he became a pastor in Lake Odessa,

Michigan.

Rev. Humberd's great desire was to make God's teachings simple so everyone could understand them. He began to make charts and pictures that would help people understand God's truths. He also wrote 44 booklets explaining God's truths and had them translated into Spanish, Portuguese, Bulgarian, and two languages of India. He carried his Bible charts all over America as he traveled to preach and teach. He also sponsored signs along the highways giving Bible verses and Gospel messages.

Surprisingly, Rev. Humberd was called by some "the shyest man in the world." He was more of a "doer" than a talker. But this did not stop him from serving his God and trying his hardest to spread the Gospel. Wherever he went, he handed out little booklets that explained the Bible and salvation. He was not embarrassed to give anyone a booklet and encourage them to read it.

At home, he used every opportunity to teach his own children about God's truths. One day he and his small sons were clearing some land. They had a fire going in a large hollow stump, which made an ideal furnace. One of the boys found a branch with dead leaves and threw it in the fire. Whoosh! The fire shot out flames and heat that knocked the boy to the ground. Immediately, Rev. Humberd made sure the boys were all right. Then he told them about Shadrach, Meshach, and Abednego in the fiery furnace. He explained that through God's special protection, they were not harmed, though they had to stay right in the hot flames.

Another day, he and his children were digging potatoes. One of the children called his attention to an old potato he had found buried. It was dirty, wet, and rotten – a pretty sorry sight. Again, Rev. Humberd brought out a spiritual truth, "Unless a kernel of wheat falls to the ground and dies, it remains only a single seed. But if it dies, it produces many seeds." (John 12:24)

R. I. Humberd never wanted to forget how important it was to give up his own life in order to produce fruit in the lives of others. Those he trained and led to Christ stand as witness that he did, indeed, produce many seeds.

Homer A. Kent, Sr.

Homer A. Kent, Sr.

(1898-1981)

Homer A. Kent, Sr.

Deliberate

"...swift to hear, slow to speak, slow to wrath." James 1:19

Deliberate: careful; considering all the facts before making decisions

"Hold on, Ernie. I have to look at one more thing." Homer Kent slid off his donkey and leaned over to look carefully at the tracks in the desert dust.

Ernie flicked his ears to ward off a fly and brayed softly. He was used to Homer's frequent stops. He was used to waiting as thirteen-year-old Homer examined every inch of the ground.

Homer knew that donkeys don't talk, but he still talked to Ernie all the time. There weren't many other children near their New Mexico home. Homer's parents had given Ernie to him as a gift when they moved to this area from Ohio, and the two went everywhere together. Television hadn't been invented yet, or even ball-point pens. The Wright brothers were preparing to fly their first airplane at Kitty Hawk, but, of course, Homer and Ernie didn't know that. Nor would they have cared.

They had plenty to do. One day they might investigate one of the old abandoned mine towns nearby. The next they might spend exploring the open spaces of the desert. They could build a fort with tumbleweeds (although it might not be there when they came back the next day); they could meet up at any time with a horned toad, a gila monster, or a jackrabbit.

Homer took in every detail of this desert land. He had a lively interest in the world, and he wanted to know everything there was to know. With his donkey and plenty of opportunities to explore, he had everything a boy could need.

When they finally got home, Homer made sure Ernie was settled for the night. He washed up quickly at the pump before going into the dining room. He could hear the voices of the rest of the family as they got ready to sit down for dinner.

Homer slid into his seat at the table. The food smelled good after his long hike. He began to eat quickly. He was halfway through his food when he noticed that his mother was not joining in the conversation. She sat quietly, staring at her still-full plate. "Is she sick?" Homer wondered. He didn't have much time to think about it, because just then he heard his father clear his throat.

"Homer, Eleanor, your mom and I have some news for you."

Homer's fork stopped in mid-air. He felt like he was going to choke. What if they said they were expecting another baby? He looked across the table at Eleanor. Her look told him that she was thinking the same thing.

"We're going to move to California in a few weeks," Mr. Kent continued. "We think it will be a better place for the whole family."

Homer's heart sank. "Aw, Dad, why do we have to move?" he asked. "We like it here."

Then a thought struck him. His eyes widened and he drew in his breath sharply. "How are we going to move Ernie? He can't walk all that way."

"Now, Homer," his mother said firmly, "you need to realize that your dad and I have discussed this for quite some time, and the job opportunities are much better out there. And the neighborhood we're moving to is no place for a donkey." Mother sighed. "We'll have to sell Ernie."

A few weeks later, the family moved to the lovely port city of Long Beach in California. Homer soon found that this, too, was a place for adventure. Giant breakers crashed against the shore. Monster-sized oil derricks on nearby Signal Hill announced the fact that Long Beach was a place of underground riches. No longer did the wind roar like a freight train across the empty mesas and valleys; now it whispered a soft caress under the gently swaying palm trees. The family decided that this was the place for them to make a permanent home. Though he missed his pet donkey, Homer soon agreed that it was a neat place to live. So whether in the desert or by the sea, Homer was developing a keen sense of details and an interest in exploring.

One evening the Kents were invited to attend a meeting in a tent where a young evangelist was speaking. What they heard about God and His offer of salvation made them want to know more. Soon the First Brethren Church at Fifth and Cherry in Long Beach, became the central focus of their lives. "Fifth and Cherry," as it was affectionately called, quickly grew into a great church under the leadership of its pioneer pastor, Louis S. Bauman. The godly people of the church encouraged the young men and women to serve God with their lives. Homer was one of the ones who answered that call.

As World War I was winding down in Europe, Homer graduated from Long Beach Poly High, and went on to the Bible Institute of Los Angeles (Biola). In no time, it seemed, he was finishing his studies there and looking forward to graduation. "So, Homer, you reached the end of Hope Street, huh?" his friend Jack teased him. Students called it the "end of Hope Street" if they graduated without finding someone to marry. Homer wasn't bothered in the least. "Aw, Jack, you know there's no end of Hope Street," he laughed. "I'm waiting for someone really special, and if it's God's plan, I'll find her."

But Homer had many other things he wanted to do. He attended seminaries in Ohio and Missouri, then went to Ashland College. His interest in history grew, and in 1924 Homer was accepted for an expedition by the famous archaeologists Melvin Kyle and William Albright. He developed his skills of determining history by spending six months digging through ruins of ancient times in Palestine and Egypt.

But something else had happened while he was at Ashland College. He met that "special someone" God had for him. Alice Wogaman, an education major, captured his heart. He married her the summer he graduated from the school. Alice was an outgoing, friendly, and talented helpmate; she helped balance Homer's sometimes cautious nature.

Soon after, Homer was called to serve as pastor at the First Brethren Church of Washington, D.C. It was 1925, and the news of the day was the famous Scopes trial in Tennessee, where William Jennings Bryan defended the Christian view of human origin. Flapper dresses were in fashion that year, and the Charleston had everybody dancing.

The people at the church welcomed the newlyweds warmly. When the Great Depression hit, there were many people needing assurance and hope. Homer's strong, consistent messages from the pulpit were a welcome relief from the discouraging situation in the country.

Living in the nation's capital during those years was an adventure. One source of escape from the harsh realities of low pay, bread lines, and widespread unemployment was baseball. Homer sometimes went to see the Senators play at Griffith Stadium. The owner of the Senators would send a season ticket to each pastor in Washington, D.C. When Homer received his pass, he immediately thought of his oldest son, eleven-year-old Homer, Jr., and wanted him to enjoy baseball also. Then he found out that he could take his son free if his son could fit in the turnstile with him. This seemed to work for them. Soon his other son, Wendell, was joining them. Homer took his two sons to numerous games, giving them opportunity to see some of baseball's greats such as Walter "Big Train" Johnson, the Senator's blazing right-handed pitcher, and the great King of Swat himself, Babe Ruth.

Homer continued to explore and learn. He was recognized as a careful person who could be trusted to pay attention to details. In 1940, he was called to teach full-time at Grace Theological Seminary in Winona Lake, Indiana. The school was only three years old. Homer had been a visiting professor from the beginning, but now he was to devote his life to the school. The move from Washington, D.C. was something of a culture shock for the family, but they soon adjusted.

Not only was the school new, but so was the Grace Brethren Church. A year earlier, in 1939, two groups of different ideas had decided to separate from each other. Pastors as well as church members had to decide which side they were on. Many people were struggling with hurt feelings. Yet, as people worked together, they developed a new spirit of optimism. Dr. Homer Kent's quiet, effective leadership helped smooth the way for healing and a positive attitude.

In addition to teaching, he served as Registrar of the school and later as Vice-president. He wrote two books, *250 Years...Conquering Frontiers* (a history of the Brethren church which carefully deals with the big church split) and *The Pastor and His Work* (a handbook for pastors which is still a strong help to pastors on practical matters). He served as pastor of the Winona Lake Grace Brethren Church, and in 1968 he served as moderator of the Grace Brethren Fellowship.

For 48 years, Dr. Kent served on the Board of Trustees of the Foreign Missionary Society of the Grace Brethren Church. Though he attempted to retire a number of times to give younger men a chance for service and experience, he was encouraged to stay. During those years the Mission Board faced some very difficult situations. Other Board members remember that many times it was Dr. Kent's careful analysis and humble opinion that helped people think wisely. Various projects and ministries were strengthened and allowed to continue because of his counsel. Missionaries seemed quick to point out how much they appreciated knowing that Dr. Kent was on the job.

Homer Kent is best remembered as a quiet, gracious, careful man whom someone called *the grace of Grace Seminary*. He was a good listener, approachable, even-tempered, and kind to everyone. "That a man be found faithful" was his greatest desire, and perhaps his greatest legacy.

Russell D. Barnard

Russell D. Barnard
(1898-1986)

Russell D. Barnard

Consistency

"I am compelled to preach. Woe to me if I do not preach the gospel!" I Cor. 9:16

Consistency: keeping to the same way of thinking and behaving

"Russell, can you come here a minute and help me?" Grandma called from the back door. Six-year-old Russell lived with his grandparents in Delphi, Indiana. Money was scarce and the entire family was expected to help with the work.

Grandma got no response from Russell, but remembered she had asked him to see if the chickens had laid any eggs that day. She called again. There was no response. She set out for the chicken yard. When she was nearly there, she heard Russell saying in a commanding voice, "Yes, don't you know that God loves you? Don't you know that He died on the cross for you? Don't you want to believe on Him now?"

Stepping around the corner, she peeked to see what was going on. The chickens, used to Russell's visits, were standing with heads cocked to one side. Russell had one hand in the air to emphasize his point.

Not wanting to embarrass him, Grandma stepped back behind the coop and called, "Russell, are you there?" Russell called back, "I'm here with the chickens."

"Are you all right?" asked Grandma.

"Yes, I'm fine. I was just practicing my preaching. I want to be a preacher when I grow up."

But the path to becoming a preacher was not easy for Russell. He had no money to go to school to learn to be a preacher. His family was, as he described it later, "the poorest of the poor." Before Russell was even grown, his grandfather became very ill. Russell had to take over the responsibility for the family farm. For years he worked hard to make a living for his family. But he never lost his deep desire to preach the truths of God.

One day he attended Sunday services at the Brethren church in Flora, Indiana, about 9 miles from his home. He was fascinated by what the Brethren church taught. When he was 14 he accepted the Lord as his Savior. He began helping in the Sunday School and in the Christian Endeavor youth ministries. Then one day he got his first chance to speak in public. He was asked to make an appeal for help for the Armenian-Syrian people. He did a presentation showing pictures using glass slides in a projector. His practice as a boy paid off – Russell found that people were interested in what he had to say.

After high school Russell studied at seminaries in Ashland, Ohio, and Winona Lake, Indiana. In 1922 he was ordained as a minister in the Brethren church. Later he would be recognized with a Doctorate of Divinity degree from Grace Theological Seminary.

God honored the faith and the heartfelt desire of that little country boy. Russell D. Barnard grew up to be one of the leaders of the Grace Brethren Church. While he was pastor of the Brethren Church in Dayton, Ohio, he had to take a courageous stand for the doctrinal position of the Brethren church. A small group that had control of the Delegation Committee, with the power to "seat delegates," refused to allow the Dayton church to be represented at the national conference. They thought this would cause the church to back down. Russell Barnard firmly but lovingly refused to change his stand. At the same time he was very careful not to act in an unchristian way toward anyone.

This soul-searching experience provided a solid background that prepared him to face the many challenges that came a few years later. In 1946, he became the first full-time General Director of the Brethren Foreign Missionary Society. This responsibility for heading up a growing missionary effort became his life's work. While Dr. Barnard was director the number of missionaries grew from about 40 to more than 100, with missionaries in seven foreign countries.

Hard work in his youth, fierce love for the truth, and having to deal with delicate problems gave him a sincerity and tenderness that ministered to many people. He was a gentle man with time for anyone who needed it. For example, a college student contacted the Foreign Missionary Society about going to a certain mission field. After graduating from college, the student became an interim pastor instead of starting seminary right away, and because he was no longer in school, he was drafted into the army. Two different times Dr. Barnard contacted the young man to ask if he was still interested in missions. Dr. Barnard's quiet, sincere way of showing concern helped the young man keep his eyes on the commitment he had made to the Lord. When the young man was discharged from the army, he enrolled as a student at Grace Seminary. While he was there, he got a job to help support his family. Soon he found that he enjoyed his job very much, and he began to think that maybe he should stay in that line of work instead of going to the mission field. Before making a decision, however, he went to talk with Dr. Barnard.

Dr. Barnard listened intently as the young man explained what he was thinking. Then he leaned forward. "Once having given out the Word, it is not so satisfying to wait tables." The young man thought about what Dr. Barnard had said, and it helped him to renew his commitment to the mission field with joy and peace in his heart.

Dr. Barnard served as General Director of the Brethren Foreign Missionary Society for 20 years. He was largely responsible for developing many more effective ways of organizing missions. He helped set up a "Total Support" program to help missionaries get the money they needed to go to the mission field. He wrote many letters to missionaries and candidates around the world. He seemed to know when they needed a little encouragement to strengthen them. Because he was still very interested in Brethren ordinances such as baptism and communion, he wrote a very complete booklet explaining their meaning and practice.

In 1966 he retired from his position as General Director of the Foreign Missionary Society. However, this did not stop his active involvement in missions. For eight more years he continued to organize and direct missionary conferences in Brethren churches across America. In 1974 he and his wife Ferne finally retired and moved to

Grace Village in Winona Lake, Indiana, where their lives continued to be a positive influence for the great cause of Christ.

On March 10, 1986, Dr. Barnard passed away into the loving arms of his Savior whose Gospel he faithfully preached and taught through a long lifetime. He had been consistent in serving the Savior he loved.

Leo Polman

Leo Polman
(1901-1979)

Leo Polman

Availability

"Whatever your hand finds to do, do it with all your might."
Ecclesiastes 9:10

Availability: ready to be used

Eight-year-old Bob was excited! The "Musical Polmans" were coming to his church that evening. His older sister had told him all about them. "They're wonderful singers – you'll love their songs," she said. "And you should see Mr. Polman lead singing – he gets so excited!" That evening, Bob enjoyed the first part of the service very much. Leo Polman was the song leader and soloist. His wife, Leila, played the piano, chimes, piano-accordion, and sleigh bells. She even had an invisible trumpet that she "held" in her cupped hands. It sounded just like the real thing. Bob, who loved music and singing, sat on the edge of his seat, taking it all in.

Then Mr. Polman announced they would sing the "Grumble Song." Although the Polmans were well known for this song, Bob had never heard it. The name sounded a bit strange to him. For some reason, when they announced the song, he thought of the way he had complained to his mother that afternoon about a chore he had to do.

The song introduced some well-known Bible stories where people grumbled to God. Bob laughed at the way the Polmans acted out parts of the song. Then the song got a little personal with the phrase, *"You'd* better stop *your* grumbling…" Bob thought back to all of the complaining he had done that afternoon. He had whined when his mom would not let him wear his favorite shirt because it was dirty. He had grumbled about what his mom had fixed for lunch. And he had made a fuss about taking out the trash.

Bob didn't remember anything about the regular sermon that evening. He had already heard the sermon that spoke to his heart. He decided right then to ask the Lord to help him the next time he felt like complaining about something.

The Lord used the Polmans' ministry to reach many people. Their ministry began when Leo and Leila Polman married in 1921 and started traveling with a popular evangelist, Dr. Britton Ross. Leo led the music and taught children; Leila played the piano. Leo loved to use his interests to illustrate spiritual truths. For example, Ruth Tietje described how he took advantage of his stamp collecting:

"Mr. Polman bought a high-powered magnifying glass to determine any flaws or unusual markings on stamps. From it and his stamps he developed an interesting object lesson for young people.

"First of all," he says, "sinners are always under God's eye: He can see all sin more clearly than I can see the flaws in my stamps through the magnifying glass. Now I wonder if you could tell me what a missionary is. Do I hear someone saying that a missionary is someone sent with a message to others? That's a good definition.

Here I have a missionary in my pocket. Why, here it is on this envelope. Look. It's a stamp. Now how can it be a missionary? Well, this little stamp can go anywhere to tell good news. It's just like a missionary.

Here are some other reasons why it's like a missionary. First of all, it has a picture and image on it. These pictures represent the country they are sent from. Well, a Christian must have Christ in his heart. Then he carries the image wherever he goes.

Another thing—this stamp bears a message. Probably mostly good news, although not always. The missionary carries good news about the love of God for the world and the coming of Jesus to die for the world. But he also has to tell of Satan and hell and the awful judgment that awaits those who will not yield their hearts to the Lord Jesus.

Another thing about a stamp: it sticks to its job. A missionary will stick to his job no matter how hard the going.

Well, say, this little stamp isn't very big, is it? But look at the work it does. If you are a Christian, what are you doing to be a missionary?"

Leo firmly believed that every Christian should be a missionary. He wanted to help people understand that they could be a missionary, a witness for Christ, anywhere they might be. Whether giving an object lesson or selling literature door to door, Leo wanted people to know God as he did.

Leo had been born in Joliet, Illinois, in 1901 to Polish Catholic parents. His mother had hoped he would become a priest. However, after the family moved to Los Angeles, Leo attended an evangelistic meeting where he heard Billy Sunday. There he committed his life to the Lord. Shortly after, he studied at the Bible Institute of Los Angeles. There he met Leila Neher, his future wife.

Leo was a gifted singer and a very good salesman. Leila was also very musical. Together, Leo and Leila formed an evangelistic team that preached Christ all over America. In time they had three children, who also became part of the team.

This was only the beginning of a lifetime of ministry preaching God's Word, singing and playing music, selling and handing out Christian literature and books, and editing and publishing Christian publications.

The influence of these servants of God was not limited to music. Shortly after graduating from BIOLA, Leo started a new church in South Gate, California. Later, he moved to Fort Wayne, Indiana, to pastor a church there.

Each year the Polmans would go to National Conference in Winona Lake, Indiana, to represent their church. Important decisions were made in the business meetings, and there were always interesting speakers to challenge the people who came to represent their churches.

But Leo kept seeing young people whose parents had brought them to the conference. They were wandering around Winona Lake all day with nothing to do. "What a waste," Leo thought. "These young people could be singing together and learning the Bible, instead of getting themselves into mischief." The more he thought about it, the more convinced he was that something special needed to be done for the young people.

Finally he talked it over with Leila. "Bethany Camp, at the edge of the lake, is the perfect place to have a conference for the young people," he told her. "We have to do something for them. But if we want to reserve the campground for that week, we need to pay $200 down payment." Two hundred dollars was a lot of money back in 1938. The Polmans just looked at each other. What could they do? They barely made enough to get by as it was. And what if they reserved the camp and no young people came? That money would just be wasted.

But they were convinced that a youth conference was needed, so they went to their knees in prayer. When they were done, Leila looked at Leo with a gleam in her eye. "Leo, you know that money we got from selling the living room furniture when we moved. We have exactly enough!" Leo put his arm around her. "But Leila, you're supposed to use that money to get new living room furniture."

"Leo, these young people are more important than living room furniture. We'll get along until we can save up more money." Leo smiled. He was proud of his wise, caring wife. She was right. The young people were more important than furniture.

Excitedly, they began to plan for the first camp. "How many people do you think might come?" Leila asked.

"Let's see," Leo calculated in his head. "I think we might be able to get twenty-five."

"Then let's plan for thirty," suggested Leila. So, with the help of their three children, they planned classes and meals for thirty people. And they didn't forget to pray.

When the week of youth conference arrived, the Polmans were ready. They had bought food, and Leila was to do the cooking. The young people began to arrive. By the time they were able to get a count, the Polmans had 106 young people at their first youth conference! Now they weren't worried about losing their down payment; now their worry was how they would get enough food for all those young people. But the whole family pitched in. That week, Brethren National Youth Conference (BNYC) was born. Today, over 2500 people go to the youth conference each year, thanks to the sacrifice and vision of the Polmans.

While serving the church in Fort Wayne, Leo saw the need for the Brethren Fellowship to have a national magazine and a center for publishing and selling good Christian books and magazines. The family again worked together to edit and publish a small magazine, the Brethren Missionary Herald. Everyone helped with addressing, folding, and mailing this new publication. The magazine grew as more and more people subscribed. Eventually Leo became full-time editor and publisher of the Brethren Missionary Herald magazine, as well as many books.

The Polmans helped many people, from bank presidents to poor country farmers. Leo and Leila loved people. Whether discussing stamp collecting at the town square or chatting with children wherever they found them, their interest was to serve the Lord. It didn't matter whether they were in front of a thousand people or sitting next to someone. They continued their ministry of "preaching Christ" and trying to help others come to know the Savior.

Leo developed cancer in 1977. A week before he died, he had a telephone conversation with Dr. Charles Mayes, who was also battling cancer. The two men talked about their families and their health, and then Dr. Mayes said, "Leo, I guess the Lord is going to take us home," to which Leo replied, "I'll see you there."

They met shortly after that in their eternal home, probably singing as they had never sung before.

Harold H.
and
Ada M. Etling

Harold H. and Ada M. Etling
(1905-1977)   (1907 - 1989)

Harold H. and Ada M. Etling

Training

"They never stopped teaching and proclaiming the good news."
Acts 5:42

Training: guiding someone's actions or ideas

It was crowded in the car. Lois grumbled and her sister, Janie, who was six years older, frowned back at her. *It's not fair,* Lois thought. *Why do we have to take all these neighbor kids to church every week? I just want to have one week where it's just our family. I can't believe we have to take nasty old Billy with us. All he does is pick on me. And look at his shoes! Who would dare go to church in muddy, worn-out tennis shoes?* Suddenly, they rounded a curve and the beautiful leather-bound Bible she had received for Christmas flew to the floor. She was just about to bend over to pick it up when Billy stomped on it. She sighed as the car came to a quick halt. "Everyone be patient," Pop said. "This is the last stop we have to make. Katie and Michael have never been to church before, and I want all of you to be nice to them. I just met their parents this week and they said that we could stop and pick up their two children for Sunday School." Lois wondered where any more children would ride, but when Katie and Michael got in, one of them wiggled in between her parents and the other sat right on the edge of the seat next to the back door. The ride to church was not a long one, but it seemed very long that day because the children were so crowded.

Katie and Michael were soon coming every Sunday. Then came a day when Lois's family no longer needed to give Katie and Michael a ride. Their parents started bringing them to church. But there would be others to take their place in the car, and Lois and her sister wondered if there would ever be a "normal" ride to church.

"Mom and Pop" Etling were always excited about their ministry to children. "Mom" Etling was especially interested in the junior high age children and "Pop" was just concerned for all children. Sometime later Pop Etling would be known as "Mr. Sunday School" as he served as National Director of Sunday Schools for the Fellowship of Grace Brethren Churches. Mom and Pop believed that Sunday Schools would help build healthy churches. Pop had the heart of a pastor, and he had a deep desire for everyone to be saved, but especially for children.

You couldn't be around him very long before you were hearing about Sunday School. Pop Etling was a soft-spoken, patient man— the kind of man that you just had to like. He was very concerned about helping teachers to do a good job when they taught the Bible.

Harold Etling had been born on Valentine's Day in 1905 and grew up in Akron, Ohio. In 1930 he married Ada M. Marquis. She shared his desire to train young people. Ada, or "Mom," was especially fond of children; she would often be found serving the church nursery. Mom Etling continued this ministry in her local church until her death in 1989. She also wanted to help girls, so she taught SMM (Sisterhood of Mary and Martha, now known as Serving My Master) and was in charge of the groups for the entire country.

Though he had not been raised in a Grace Brethren Church, Pop joined it in 1947. He became pastor of Ellet Grace Brethren Church in Akron, Ohio. He also served as church pastor in a number of other churches over a period of 20 years.

When you ask people what they thought of "Pop" Etling, many respond with the word "enthusiastic." He always seemed to throw himself enthusiastically into doing something that he believed really mattered. The Etlings were known for their hospitality – they were always inviting people to their house to enjoy some of Mom Etling's good cooking. Both Mom and Pop played the piano well, and Pop often served as choir director.

While he was the pastor of a church in Greensburg, Ohio, Pop Etling produced a 20-minute radio broadcast – live from their own living room! The theme song for the show was, "If you want joy, real joy, wonderful joy, let Jesus come into your heart." The Etlings would not miss an opportunity to share the Gospel message. Pop sang with a quartet that visited quite a number of churches in the Akron area; Mom played the piano for the group. Pop was often called upon to lead singing for special meetings, including Christian radio programs. He also taught at the Akron Bible Institute.

In Greensburg, Pop Etling served as captain of the local fire department. The Etlings lived about 3 minutes from the station. The entire family would help Pop get to the fire when the alarm sounded. Janie would make sure his trousers were tucked into the big fire boots. Lois was to hand Pop his fire helmet. Mom Etling would hold open the big heavy fire-proof coat for Pop to put his arms through.

One day Janie's school caught fire. Pop went up on the roof with four other firemen. Suddenly the roof began to sway; they felt it begin to crumble. Pop knew they were in danger. Since prayer was a normal thing for Pop, he simply lifted his heart in faith to ask his Lord to protect them. God did. Though there was a lot of damage to the building, the men on the roof were not hurt. Mom Etling was at home with little Lois. When she found out it was Janie's school that was on fire, she picked Lois up and ran all the way to the school in a panic. She went quickly through the crowd until she found Janie and Pop, safe and sound. Whenever the family would remember that terrible day, they would comment, "The Lord was good!"

In 1954, Harold Etling was asked to become the first Sunday School Director of the Fellowship of Grace Brethren Churches. He served in that position for 18 years. Pop Etling took this responsibility very seriously. He felt that a Sunday School teacher should have every advantage possible to be able to explain the great eternal and loving truths of God. He believed that "the Sunday School fed the church," and that without the training that children and adults received in Sunday School, there would not be enough good leaders for the churches. Pop Etling lived by the motto, "Only one life, it will soon be past. Only what's done for Christ will last." As director of Sunday

Schools, he was determined to live in a way that would bring lasting results. His goal was to visit each of the Grace Brethren churches during the year. He traveled constantly, mostly by train, since he did not like to fly. But he also claimed that he could get more work done on the train. Even while traveling he thought of his family. Lois remembers that Pop would often bring home a "Story Book Doll" for her and her sister.

Because of his untiring efforts and cheerful attitude, Pop soon became known as "Mr. Sunday School." Both Pop and Mom would hold Sunday School workshops and conferences. Mom, as always, had a special love for the very youngest children who came to Sunday School. She would tell teachers, "You tell them to sit down and be quiet, but God put something in them that says, 'Wiggle!' Who do you think they should listen to, you or God?"

Pop Etling continued his work by writing books that would help teachers do a better job of teaching in their classes. Mom Etling enjoyed working with him, often checking and proofing his work. He wrote two books, *Brethren Beliefs and Practices* and *Commentary on Matthew*, which were published by the Brethren Missionary Herald.

Pop developed the Christian Education Department of the Grace Brethren Church. While serving as Director of the Sunday School Board, this ministry grew to be a strong force in training children and youth across America and around the world. It is now called CE National (Christian Education National) and provides practical training, help, and encouragement to thousands of young people, as well as adults. One of the buildings at CE National is used for retreats and as a place of refreshment for pastors, missionaries and other church leaders. It is called the Philemon Center, after the man in the Bible who served God by "refreshing the brethren." It is dedicated to the memory and inspiration of Pop and Mom Etling because of their gift of hospitality.

Pop Etling passed away January 3, 1977; Mom died in 1989. Those who knew them thank God for their faithfulness and encouragement. Later generations are blessed by the continuing work which they began.

Herman A. Hoyt

Herman A. Hoyt
(1909-2000)

Herman A. Hoyt

Uncompromising

"But as for you, be strong and do not give up, for your work will be rewarded." II Chronicles 15:7

Uncompromising: not weakening or giving up one's beliefs

It was two o'clock in the morning. Herman stretched and tried to shake off the sleepy feeling that was settling upon him. He had been studying all night for tomorrow's exams. He was an excellent student and did not need to worry about his grades. But he was never satisfied until he had felt he had learned his lessons well. He must stay awake! If he could get in just two more hours of study, he felt he would be ready.

Suddenly a thought struck him. Somewhere he had heard that cold feet would keep a person awake. Careful not to wake his wife Harriet, he picked up his book and tiptoed down the stairs to the kitchen. Slowly he opened the cabinet under the sink. *Screeecchh!* That cabinet could definitely use some oil! He made a mental note to fix it soon.

Herman dug around in the darkness until he found the tub his wife used to wash their clothes. He filled it with cold water and took off his shoes and socks. He set the tub beneath a chair, sat down, and stuck both feet in the water. "Ack!" Herman shrieked, nearly falling out of his chair. Well, he was finally wide awake. Relieved at being able to concentrate, he went back to his book.

A little while later Harriet came downstairs looking for him. By then he was thoroughly involved in his studies. "Herman," she exclaimed.

"Do you want to catch your death of cold? You'd better come to bed right away!"

"I'll be all right. I've just got a little more studying to do," replied Herman.

His determination to do a good job paid off for Herman. He graduated at the top of his class. It wasn't just his studies, though, that Herman tried to do well. When Herman felt something was right, he was willing to go to any lengths to do it—no matter what personal sacrifice might be involved. God was preparing him to do a great work for the sake of the Gospel and the spreading of God's truths.

Herman Hoyt had been born in Greenfield, Iowa, on March 12, 1909. He was about four when his family moved to Dallas Center, Iowa. Here they attended the First Brethren Church. When Herman was nine years old, he asked Jesus into his heart and began a determined, faithful path of following the Lord.

He graduated with honors from elementary school and as valedictorian of his high school class. After teaching public school for a year, he enrolled at Ashland College, where he again graduated at the top of his class. During his senior year he taught Greek at the college. Then he attended Ashland Seminary and graduated in 1935 with highest honors. His New Testament professor there said he was "the ablest Greek student he had ever had."

Herman Hoyt had many interests and abilities. He loved sports. While in school he played both football and basketball. His high school football team even had a perfect season – they went an entire season without any team scoring against them.

Herman also loved the outdoors. He was a successful gardener and raised much of the food his family ate.

Herman's main concern in life was to know and teach the great truths of God. So upon graduation from Ashland he immediately accepted the offer to teach full time in the seminary. But the seminary where Dr. Hoyt was teaching had been struggling with the influence of the world. Dr. Hoyt was concerned that the seminary students were not being taught to live Godly lives. Because Herman and fellow professor Dr. Alva J. McClain took a stand for what they believed, they were dismissed from the seminary. This uncompromising stand for the truth is one of the main characteristics of Herman Hoyt's life.

After Dr. Hoyt and Dr. McClain were dismissed, a number of people who were concerned about the direction the college was headed held a prayer meeting. In that prayer meeting the first plans to start Grace Theological Seminary were discussed.

The new seminary was started in the First Brethren Church in Akron, Ohio. Soon after, it moved to Winona Lake, Indiana, and it wasn't long before students eager to learn the truths of God were filling the halls of the new school. Dr. Herman A. Hoyt taught at the seminary, as well as serving in many other ways. When Dr. McClain died, Herman became the seminary's president, a position he held for the last 15 years of his teaching career. He retired in 1976 and moved to Pennsylvania to be near family members. He continued his ministry of Bible conferences and writing. He loved to speak about prophecy, the Second Coming of the Lord, and Brethren distinctives. Many of his writings were on these subjects.

Though he was completely uncompromising when it came to Bible truths, Dr. Hoyt was a very caring and sensitive Christian. He proved this in his devotion to his younger brother, Rex. This brother suffered from Bright's Disease and had gotten behind a couple of years in school. This made Rex feel like he wasn't as smart as the other kids in his class. However, Herman noticed that when Rex played music, he was very good at it and was able to enjoy it. Rex learned to play clarinet, flute, bassoon, and piano. In order to encourage him, Herman would ask Rex to play music at a nearby church where Herman was the student pastor.

Another of Herman's brothers, Solon, tells of how Herman took him under his wing. When Solon started seminary, Herman would often stop by his brother's home to check up on him and give him any encouragement he could. He also made sure Solon was studying properly, especially at examination time. Herman suggested to a group of believers in Huntington, Indiana, that they ask Solon to become their pastor. They did, and Solon was able to get valuable experience that would help him serve God the rest of his life.

Sometime later, while Solon was helping Herman pick beans, Herman abruptly stood up and looked at him seriously. "Solon, wouldn't you like to go to Argentina as a missionary and help start a Bible institute?" he asked. At the time, Solon wasn't too sure about that abrupt introduction to the idea. Eventually Solon did apply for missionary service. He ended up spending 43 years as a missionary in Argentina.

Herman was always concerned about helping young people in ministry. While Herman was president of the seminary, a young married student came to him needing to drop a class after the registration deadline, which was against the rules. Dr. Hoyt quietly listened to the student's story. Then he said, "Well, Brother, since we made the rules and not God, we can break the rules according to the need. We'll have that fixed up for you. Keep preaching. Keep studying, and may the Lord bless you."

In 1985 Dr. Hoyt was called back to Grace Theological Seminary to be presented the "Grace Seminary Alumnus of the Year" Award. His books and other writings still proclaim and explain the great truths of God throughout the world.

Dr. Hoyt died peacefully in 2000 with members of his family present. His influence continues in the lives of his students and those who heard him preach, or who read his writings. He was "uncompromising" to the very end.

Clyde K. Landrum

Clyde K. Landrum
(1909-1998)

Clyde K. Landrum

Encouragement

"Therefore encourage one another and build each other up, just as in fact you are doing." I Thessalonians 5:11

Encouragement: to cause another to be hopeful, brave or confident

"Come indoors right now!" Mrs. Landrum called from the back door of the cabin. The children scrambled to obey. When Mother spoke in such a stern voice, it was foolish to disobey her.

Just before he slipped through the door, Clyde poked his sister. Their eyes met, and they read each other's minds. "Keep quiet. She'll never find out."

Inside, their eyes fastened on the long, thin branch their mother had cut from the peach tree. If Mother had a switch, she must consider the crime to be very serious. Clyde gulped, then concentrated on acting unconcerned. Never, never would he allow his face to give him away.

His mother waited until all 12 children were lined up. She began to walk along the row, looking in each child's face. When she reached the end of the line, she finally began to speak.

"Has anyone seen the special jar of peaches I was saving for the pastor's visit?" she asked.

The children all looked at each other. Pastor's peaches? All the Landrum children knew that Mother saved her best peaches to serve to the pastor. Who could have done something so unthinkable?

Clyde acted surprised along with all the rest. Out of the corner of his eye he could see his sister Fern's version of a surprised look. "She's doing a good job," he thought proudly. "Mother will never guess it was us."

Mother was speaking again. "Well, I know that someone has seen it, because I found the empty jar behind the woodshed."

Clyde stopped himself from glaring at his sister. "Do I have to teach her everything?" he thought. "I would have found a better place to hide it. I should never have left it up to her."

Mother continued, "You know the rules. Whoever ate the peaches will be punished. If you 'fess up now, though, I'll go easier on you."

No one moved. Mother began to walk along the row again, looking carefully at each of her children. Did anyone's face have peach juice on it? Clyde was glad he had thought ahead and washed his face in the creek. Did anyone look guilty? He was certain he wouldn't. His sister, on the other hand, wasn't as experienced as he was. He didn't dare turn his eyes toward her, and he held his breath as Mother approached Fern. Finally he felt, rather than saw, his mother move on, and he let out a silent sigh of relief. Then he found himself catching his breath again as she came before him.

"Breathe normally," he told his body. "Tilt your head and look her in the eye—show her how hurt you are that she would even suspect you." For a moment Mother stared at him. Did she know? Was she suspicious? He forced himself to keep looking her in the eye, and finally she turned and went on down the line. Whew! What a relief!

He turned his eyes slightly to look down the row at Fern. "She'd better not crack," he thought anxiously.

Mother reached the end of the row and turned back to face her children. "I'll give you one more chance," she said, slapping the switch against her palm. "Who ate pastor's peaches?"

The children shrugged and looked at each other, but no one spoke. Mother waited.

Clyde forced himself to stand still. His neck itched. His hand desperately wanted to reach up and scratch it, to adjust his uncomfortable shirt. But Mother was watching, and she just might interpret such a movement as a sign that he was guilty. No, he must stand still.

"I'm giving you one more chance," she said calmly. "You might as well confess, because there is a feather on the nose of whoever did it."

94

Clyde reached up quickly and brushed his nose. He didn't feel a feather. Then he heard his mother say, "Clyde, Fern, you stay here. The rest of you may go outside."

Years later, Clyde would chuckle proudly as he told the story of his mother's clever trick. He was very proud of his parents. They loved God, and even though the family didn't have much money, they were determined to see that their children were taught about God in school.

"We need to pack up all of our belongings and get ready to move," Dad told the children one day. Clyde stared at his parents. Move? How could they leave this farm? The other children must have been thinking the same thing, because his brother Sewell spoke up. "Do you mean we will leave the farm?" His dad nodded. "I know you all love the farm that we have all worked so hard to keep, but this is more important."

"What could be more important than our home and farm?" thought Clyde. Before he could ask the question, his father explained. "There is one thing I want more than anything else for my children," he said in a determined voice. "I want them to be prepared to serve God in whatever way they can. We are moving close to a school that will teach you about God along with your other subjects."

Clyde was a little scared, but he was also excited about the move. Soon the family was ready to leave their home in Clayhole, Kentucky, to move to a place called Lost Creek. There they found a cabin right across a ravine from the Christian school.

Every morning Clyde would get dressed, take his lunch, and walk across a log that had fallen over the ravine. He would line up with the other students and say the pledge to the American flag. Then they would all say the pledge to the Christian flag, and to the Bible.

The schoolmaster, Dr. G.E. Druschel, was strict but fair. He taught his students to love God and to always want to know the truth. Dr. Druschel reminded his students often that God had made them for a special reason—to serve God. Clyde often wondered how God would use him.

When Clyde finished school, a man everyone called "Daddy Hills" asked to talk with him. "Clyde," he said, "I've had my eye on you, and I believe God wants to use you to tell others about Him. I would like to help pay your way to Bible college." Clyde was excited. What did God have for him next? With the money that "Daddy Hills" provided, as well as his own hard work, Clyde was able to go to California to study at the Bible Institute of Los Angeles (BIOLA).

But God had another surprise for Clyde. Clyde met Ruby Larson, a lovely young woman who was studying to be a nurse. Soon they were married. As the years passed, Clyde often thanked God for the strong supporter that Ruby was for his work for God.

After he graduated, Clyde went back to Kentucky and finished his studies. Finally he was ready to be a teacher.

But what he really wanted to do was become a pastor. One day he got a letter from the Brethren Church in Uniontown, Pennsylvania. They were looking for a pastor, and someone had told them that Clyde Landrum would be just the person to ask. Clyde and Ruby packed up and moved to Pennsylvania. That was just the first of many churches that God called him to pastor. God even allowed them to start several new churches. God also gave them two sons, Phil and Jerry.

Clyde was a man of vision, always full of ideas about how to help people know and serve God better. He didn't just have ideas, though. He was also determined to work hard to make sure those ideas came true. He helped to develop a club for children called Missionary Helpers Club. This club helped children learn about and pray for Brethren missionaries. Clyde also worked with the Foreign Missionary Society, helping to send out missionaries. He was very interested in the work of Brethren chaplains in the Army, Navy, Marines and Air Force, and traveled around the world to visit them and encourage their work. In fact, his goal was to encourage any young person who wanted to serve God. One young pastor remembers when Clyde brought him a very expensive Bible as a special gift of love and encouragement.

Clyde loved to read, and wanted people to have good books to read. One day he got a phone call asking him to be the editor of a magazine, the Brethren Missionary Herald. As he worked with the magazine, he saw the need for good Christian literature. Clyde started a publishing company for books called the Brethren Missionary Herald Publishing Company (BMH Books). His work with the magazine and publishing company was one of his favorite jobs.

One of the things that mattered most to him, though, was helping provide children with opportunities to attend Christian schools. As pastor of Community Grace Brethren Church in Warsaw, Indiana, he became very concerned about whether schools were teaching students to love and serve God. Finally, he went to the church board and told them, "We need to start a school here that will teach children about God. We can use this building." Soon they had found several teachers and Brethren Elementary School was started. The school was later named Warsaw Christian School. It would be many years before other churches realized how important Christian schools could be and started offering Christian schools for their families.

Clyde's friends and family remember especially how he loved jokes and good-natured humor. He always had a funny story to tell. He stayed active, too—even after he was grown up, you never knew   when he would bend over and start walking on his hands. As a grandfather he loved to take long walks with his grandchildren. He never lost his love for taking a challenge: A picture taken of him in his seventies shows him standing on his hands on the rafters of a church that was being built.

More than anything else, Clyde is remembered for loving God and loving people. He always wanted to make sure that people knew Jesus. Before he died, he was very ill with a brain tumor, and wasn't able to recognize much of what was going on around him. One day he saw his niece sitting in another room and asked his wife, "Who's that?" His wife told him the niece's name. It was obvious, though, that he didn't realize who it really was. His face grew serious and he asked, "Does she know Jesus?" Even when his mind was failing, Clyde knew what really mattered in life.

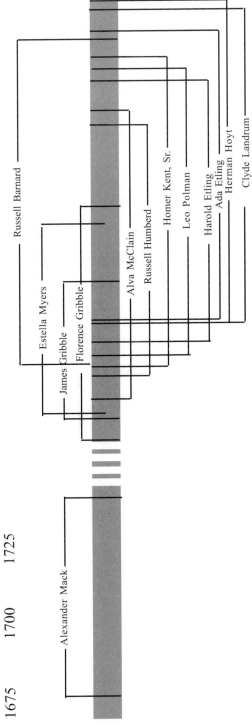

1675   1700   1725   1875   1900   1925   1950   1975   2000

Alexander Mack

Russell Barnard

Estella Myers

James Gribble

Florence Gribble

Alva McClain

Russell Humberd

Homer Kent, Sr.

Leo Polman

Harold Etling

Ada Etling

Herman Hoyt

Clyde Landrum

99

Bibliography

Durnbaugh, Donald F., ed. *Meet the Brethren*. Philadelphia: Brethren Encyclopedia, Inc, 1995. 123 pages.
(Brief history and present condition of the five largest Brethren groups.)

Eberly, William R. *The Complete Writings of Alexander Mack*. Winona Lake: BMH Books, 1991. 120 pages.

Gribble, Florence Newberry. *Stranger Than Fiction*. Winona Lake: The Brethren Missionary Herald Company, 1949. 249 pages.
(The life of Dr. Florence Gribble)

Gribble, Florence Newberry, M.D. *Undaunted Hope*. Winona Lake: BMH Books, 1984. 438 pages.
(The life of James Gribble)

Guiles, David. "The Dream of James Gribble." Rodeheaver Auditorium, Grace College. Winona Lake, IN 26 Feb. 2002.

Hamilton, Benjamin A. *Gribble's Dream . . . God's Design*. Winona Lake: BMH Books, 1987. 300 pages.
(Story of the founding of the Brethren Missionary work in Central African Republic)

Jobson, Orrville D. *Conquering Oubangui-Chari For Christ*. Winona Lake: Brethren Missionary Herald Company, 1957. 160 pages.
(History of the Early Years of the Brethren Missionary Work in Central African Republic)

Kent, Sr., Homer A. *Conquering Frontiers: A History of the Brethren Church*. Revised ed. Winona Lake: Brethren Missionary Herald, 1972. 245 pages.

Kinsley, Bob. *His Greatest Legacy*. Nappanee: Evangel Press, 1996. 95 pages.
(The history of the Brethren Movement and the "dilemma of the 19th Century Brethren.")

Rohrer, Norman, B. *A Saint in Glory Stands*. Winona Lake: BMH Books, 1986. 137 pages.
(The story of Alva J. McClain)

Ronk, Albert T. *History of the Brethren Church.* Ashland: Brethren Publishing Company, 1968. 524 pages.

Snyder, Ruth. *Estella Myers: Pioneer Missionary in Central Africa.* Winona Lake: BMH Books, 1984. 167 pages.
(The life of Estella Myers)

Willoughby, William G. *Counting the Cost: The Life of Alexander Mack.* Elgin: The Brethren Press, 1979. 176 pages.

About the Authors

Viki Rife heads up the Publications Department of CE National. Having been raised by missionaries in Argentina, she has command of both Spanish and English. While in Argentina she also studied French in the secondary schools. She has had an intense interest in journalism and served as editor of the Grace College newspaper while studying journalism there. She and her husband John have three grown children and attend the Leesburg Grace Brethren Church, where she is active in the youth and children's work, especially among needy girls.

Bob Cover, Sr., is retired and lives in Warsaw, Indiana, with his wife Joene. They have been married for 49 years. Bob and his family served for 10 years on the Argentine mission field, where he served as pastor of various churches, managed a bookstore, and published the national church magazine *El Heraldo*. After returning to the U.S. he became involved in Christian schools, serving as assistant director of the Midwest Association of Christian Schools International, and principal and administrator of two Christian schools. He was also chaplain for a community hospital as well as for a large nursing home.

Mallory Nixon, the sketch artist and graphic designer of this book, holds a Bachelor of Arts Degree in Art Education from Bluffton College. He is also a 2002 graduate of Grace Theological Seminary, where he obtained a Master's Degree in Youth and Family Ministries. Along with his wife Chris, Mallory lives in Brunswick, Ohio, and is actively involved in leading the youth ministry of Southern Hills Community Church.

Holly Jones is looking forward to a career in journalism as she finishes her last year at Grace College. Her command of spelling and grammar was helpful in the final writing and editing of manuscripts. Holly distinguished herself as a fifth grader when she won the ACSI National Spelling Bee held in Washington, D.C. for grades 5-8. She attends Church of the Open Door in Elyria, Ohio, where she has been involved in children's ministries. She lives in Vermilion, Ohio, where she grew up.

there anything you need that hasn't been provided?" Bringle was cutting him off at every place Stidham had attempted to meet him.

Stidham knew that no one had called Bringle from DC since he had arrived back at the unit area. Given the early hour of that arrival, he sincerely doubted that the call had come that morning. Something was wrong, but he had no resources to determine the nature of the problem nor could he fix it. The one thing he was certain of was that he had more other problems that he could do something about than he had time to worry about, so this was one that would have to wait for another day to receive his attention.

"So you are leaving immediately?" he asked the agency man even as Bringle began to close the suitcase he had been packing on the bed while they talked.

"Yeah, I've got a flight out of Nashville in about two hours. I should just make my flight. I'll see you in a few days." Bringle was picking up the case and starting for the door.

"Okay, have a safe flight. Let me hear from you." That was about all that Stidham could muster.

Bringle was out the door and headed for the elevator. Stidham stood for a few minutes in the hall and thought, *What a strange bird.* He thought he would never understand what the man was thinking. He told himself that there may have been other problems on Bringle's mind. They may not even have concerned Stidham. That may have been why he had acted so strangely. Regardless, Stidham had to focus on his team and their mission. He could afford no distractions at this point.

That evening, the team assembled for the trip to the post theater, where the entertainment was thoroughly enjoyed. The Man in Black as Johnny Cash was known and his associates put on quite a performance. The theater was packed with soldiers and spouses who had been given the extra passes that weren't needed by the team. A special guest appearance was made by Little Jimmy Dickens from the Grand OL' Opry. There was no mention made by the entertainers as to who had made the arrangements for them to be there. The folks from the Army's Morale, Welfare, and Recreation Division were there to administer the event, but they never took credit for staging the occasion. It was a strange occurrence. When it concluded, the team from the Campbell Army Airfield compound went about their business, and no one questioned them as to why they had received the special treatment at the concert.

Week 7

Dallas 21–Philadelphia 17
Baltimore 35–Miami 0

The next morning, they received some more special treatment. They were ordered to pack up their belongings that would not be accompanying them to Ft. Pickett. These were placed into storage in the facility designated for deploying soldiers. No explanations were given; but the pervasive feeling throughout the team was that they must be deploying soon. Perhaps it was rumored that they might not even go to Ft. Pickett but rather straight to Guam.

While this did not prove to be an accurate reading of the tea leaves, it did emphasize to the men that they were in a very short window of opportunity for the deployment that they knew was coming. What this actually accomplished was to remove any need for the team to return to Ft. Campbell from any of the sites they would be conducting training prior to their deployment. That evening, they were ready for the C-141 that took them to Ft. Pickett when it pulled to the Green Ramp at 1900. They had assembled, drawn all their cold weather gear, and moved with their special parachutes from the pack shed to the ramp. They took notice that no hangers on were standing by to get a jump in with them on this day. This flight would be for them only. By 1930, they were on their way.

As they took off from the Airfield, they knew they had closed a chapter in their military careers. None of them realized just how momentous a turn they were taking as the pace of the mission increased. The flight to Ft. Pickett was just over an hour and a half. At 2115, the light came on for jump status. They had been on the oxygen enhancement for an hour, so they quickly switched from the plane's source to the cylinders they carried as part of their equipment.

Having donned all the cold weather gear, they moved in their shuffling manner to the rear ramp of the plane. As they were given the thumbs-up by the jumpmaster, they watched as the ¼ tons were positioned out onto the ramp. At the time indicated by the load master they went into the night sky. Shortly after, the men began to join them.

As they came down through the sky of Virginia, the thought occurred to Foster that Virginia is for lovers. Well, tonight he loved what he was doing; and with a scream, he experienced the rush of reaching terminal velocity. In only a few moments, he had dropped from thirty-one thousand feet altitude to six thousand feet and felt the yank of the parachute opening, letting him know that the technology of the day had persevered again, and he would soon be on the ground.

He began to try to pick out landmarks but soon realized the futility of this as the area had been blacked out especially for this exercise. He did indeed recognize the airfield about a minute before landing in the grass just off the runway. The next soldier in the stick, Nuckles was not so lucky. He came down square on the runway with his ninety-two pounds of gear and the momentum of the jump. He hit with a thump and a thud as he rolled into the landing. He was dazed for a few seconds and then quickly gathered himself and his gear and was moving to his assigned duties when Sergeant Patterson got to him.

"Are you okay?" Patterson came on the run. His concern was real. He knew the force of the impact that had just occurred. He had read about men who had experienced similar landings and later developed severe medical conditions. He was not going to let this happen to this young man.

"I'm all right," Nuckles informed him as they joined up with the balance of their stick. "I just took a pretty solid landing on the pavement. I thought I was clear of it but caught just the last couple of feet. When I rolled, I was in the grass. I guess that saved me from any real harm."

What Nuckles did not realize was that he had sustained compressions of three vertebrae in the lumbar area of his back. What Patterson knew from his reading on the matter was that Nuckles was in such good physical condition that his musculature faculties would take over, and he would not know for years that he had done the damage to his back.

Patterson grabbed the younger man and almost forcibly held him for a moment. "I know that right now you think you are okay. But humor me on this, we are going to do a line of duty statement and place it in your medical file to protect you in the future when someone in diapers now tries to tell you that you never did this." The LOD form was quickly filled out and witnessed by both Patterson and Foster. The men then proceeded to pursue the duties of their mission.

The exercise had taken a different form on this day as their stated mission had morphed into securing of the airfield. As they moved around the confines, they discovered that there were OPFOR placed in strategic positions that they had to neutralize. It made for an interesting twist to the mission they had been primed for since the first day they had been organized. Stidham had thought that they had to be ready for the unexpected objectives that they might be given or that opportunity might offer.

Ft. Pickett also offered the hilly terrain of the foothills of Virginia, more closely resembling the terrain of the expected objective in that faraway land they would soon encounter. Stidham was attempting to give them familiarity with every aspect of the environment they would be encountering. He had chosen carefully. His training resources had been exploited using the knowledge of the country they would be operating in when the time came.

After securing the airfield at Ft. Pickett, the leaders were called to a meeting where they were given a mission of moving across post to a mock-up village simulating a Southeast Asian hamlet. There they would find the layout very similar to the small facility they had practiced on at Ft. Campbell. They were about twelve miles removed from the objective. They would move under cover of darkness and on foot to the vicinity and take the village before dawn. This mission was exactly the training they were proficient at performing and represented what they would need to execute flawlessly in country if they were to be successful.

The men, after receiving their briefings from the element leaders, began to realize that Stidham had once again been far ahead of them in planning the events they had encountered to this point in this little backwoods outpost tucked away in the hills of Virginia. Their confidence in their leader was as high as it had ever been. They were gaining that swagger of men who knew they were good at what they did and believed that no others could do it better.

The movement to the objective was executed according to the plan laid out by Stidham with tweaks from his element leaders. They were in position and moved in synchronized movements along the trail. Stidham had arranged for light OPFOR presence along the way, just enough to keep the men alert but not enough to really delay the operation. The presence of these foes had been noted, and each occurrence dealt with in an expedient manner. Any referee would have judged the threat to the mission to be eliminated. None had avoided detection and had the subsequent opportunity to slip ahead of the unit and report its movements to HQs.

Arriving at the SP, the practiced routine was followed, and the village was soon in the hands of the team. They were becoming a well-oiled machine, performing the individual tasks required to result in execution of the team mission so routinely that they now anticipated the movements not only of their element members but of the other elements as well.

Following the after-action review that was now standard following any combined training event for the team, the men were happily surprised to find that they had been scheduled for marksmanship training on one of the new computer scored ranges that had been installed at the post. Ft. Pickett, during World War II, had been home to as many as seven divisions but since had become a sub-installation of nearby Ft. Lee. If not for the training provided for the Virginia National Guard and Army Reserve units, much of the post would have fallen into disuse. Still, there were worse things than being near the home of the quartermaster corps.

While the men were honing their skills on the ranges and, of course, griping about the accuracy of the scoring, Stidham took the opportunity to visit a friend at Ft. Lee. The result was that there were new cold weather gloves and face scarves forthcoming from the visit. Since we were involved in a jungle war at the time, cold weather technology had been pushed to the back burner for the time being.

While the men were checking out the new range scoring system, VunCanon had made friends with the first shirt of a VNG (Virginia National Guard) company that was preparing to fire. When he found out that he was dealing with a ranger team, he was only too happy to allow them to fire as a couple of extra orders in the rotation. He did request that the team members provide tips for any of his soldiers who were struggling. By the end of the day, quite a few guardsmen had improved their efforts from the tips they had received.

The men were glad to get the new issue even in the small amounts that were available. The gloves allowed for more intricate finger and hand maneuvers, while the scarves were infinitely more comfortable, particularly with the oxygen masks that the men were wearing during the jumps. With creature comforts on the increase, how could morale help but follow? No one even pretended to hate to see the old items leave the inventory.

Stidham paused as he was completing the briefing for the move to their next objective. "Anyone have questions or information to put out?"

Patterson, who never made any comments unless called upon, raised his hand. "Sir, may Nuckles and I see you when we finish here?" was all he said.

This caught Nuckles completely off-guard. He looked at Patterson in a questioning manner, but the medic was looking elsewhere.

When the meeting broke up, Stidham nodded to Patterson and looked for Nuckles, who had headed for the latrine. When he was called to by Patterson, he replied, "I'll be right there."

Returning, he hoped to find that whatever the meeting was about had already been disposed of, but there was to be no such luck. The two veteran soldiers waited for him where he could not possibly miss them.

Stidham nodded to Patterson. "You called this meeting, Sergeant. What's it about?"

"Sir, you need to know that Nuckles hit the runway pretty hard when we jumped in here. I would feel better if he were evaluated by someone with more medical knowledge than I have. I weighed his gear after we were on the ground. It came out at 87 pounds. That's quite a jolt on a fellow." Patterson was not being unprofessional, and he clearly cared about the young soldier.

Nuckles spoke up. "Sir, it was just a little bounce when I hit. There hasn't been any pain or soreness or stiffness. I had forgotten about it until now. Sergeant Patterson did a line of duty and put it in my file. I see no reason to waste some doctor's time with this." He clearly did not want to miss out on the mission that was coming at them at breakneck speed. Additionally, he was not fond of spending time in any medical clinic.

Stidham pondered the situation for a moment. He appreciated the gung-ho attitude of his young soldier and did not want to do anything to diminish his enthusiasm. Yet he could not risk taking him with them if he was less than 100 percent in his ability to perform. Also, he had been approached by one of the men who seriously considered themselves responsible for the welfare of the team.

"Why don't we do this? You go on sick call right now." He pointed to Nuckles, who started to protest. "You go with him and tell the doctor what you have told me. Do not tell him about the mission but explain the nature of our work. If he clears him after examining him, then he stays on the mission. If not, he gets better. If he's better by the time we leave, he goes. If not, he stays. Is this agreeable to everyone?"

Both men nodded their assent. Nuckles was certain that Patterson was trying to get him thrown off the mission. When the major was out of hearing, he said to the medic, "Why do you want me off the project. I thought we were friends."

Patterson grimly shook his head. "I don't want you off the mission. But if you go and you have physical problems, it could impact the success of the mission and getting those guys out, or it could even result in some of our team getting hurt or killed. I can't let anyone put us in that position, friend or not."

Nuckles thought about it and relaxed a little. "I see your point. I guess it's up to me to convince the doctor that I'm good to go."

With that, they swung into the quarter-ton vehicle they had been preparing for flight. Nuckles looked at Patterson and laughed. "Where is sick call around here anyway?"

"I'm sure it's on main post. Head that way," Patterson retorted.

Arriving on main post, they spotted a sign for the medical clinic. Walking in, they noticed they were the only customers at the facility at the time. "Shouldn't have long to wait." Nuckles mused as he handed his medical file to the young PFC working at the front desk. "I need to see the doctor. It seems I may have landed on the wrong spot when we jumped in the other day." This was the only explanation Nuckles was inclined to give him.

They had a seat and, after fifteen minutes, were called back to the examination room. A young captain greeted them shortly. When he looked at the sergeant, he explained, "We need to be sure you get all the facts. Brevity is an art with Private First Class Nuckles."

"I see." The young captain had already begun to tell Nuckles to strip off his blouse and T-shirt. He prodded the area of the lower back as he listened to the account of the landing. It was clearly evident that he was not impressed by people who jumped out of perfectly good airplanes, but he was professional enough to keep that opinion to himself.

After several pokes and prods produced no response from Nuckles, the young captain stated, "At this time, I see no sign of any damages caused by this landing. Sometimes they don't show up for an extended time. I recommend that we take an X-ray and see if there's damage there that's not showing up yet."

In a few moments, Nuckles was whisked away by an X-ray technician, told to remove his upper garments, and pull his trousers down so there would be no interference with the powerful machine. In another five minutes, he was back in the examination room. The young captain returned. "Well, I see no permanent damage from the pictures. I will send them over to Ft. Lee to the hospital and have an expert review them. Come see me in three days."

"All right, sir." Nuckles reply was enthusiastic. He knew he was not going to be here in three days. He had heard "no damage." He took this to mean all clear.

Patterson, on the other hand, was less enthused. As they headed back to the field, he asked Nuckles, "Why don't you sit this one out?"

Nuckles looked at him with pain in his eyes. "Sarge, you said I need to get checked. I did. The doc says no damage. Please don't tell me that this isn't good enough. If I have to walk over to Ft. Lee to that hospital, I will, but I belong on this mission. Maybe if I were one of you older guys, I could see sitting it out. You fellows have done your thing for the country already, and I appreciate your being willing to go again, but this is my first time. Please don't make me miss this."

They rode the rest of the way to the airfield in silence. Nuckles was apprehensive as they drove into the compound. When they parked the quarter ton back on line with the others, they looked for Stidham. Finding him talking to a group of soldiers, Nuckles politely waited on the periphery of the group. Patterson waited to judge the gist of the conversation and determined that he could interrupt.

"Sir, we are back from sick call. Reporting for duty, all issues have been cleared." That was all. Nuckles felt like a part of the group again. He knew he would be going along now.

When he and Patterson were away from the others, he grabbed his hand and thanked him profusely.

Patterson looked at him solemnly and said, "When this is over, I hope you are still thanking me."

Shortly, the whine of the engines told the team that they were soon to embark for the move to Ft. Indiantown Gap (FIG). A special iteration of the exercise was planned for them at this picturesque little post near Allentown, Pennsylvania. As they boarded the plane, Stidham breathed a sigh of relief. He had lived in fear that the state of mind that Bringle had exhibited on his last visit might indicate the planning dates being moved around. There had been no hint of an adjustment to the schedule. Every day that they accomplished their training goals made the success of the mission more possible in Stidham's mind. This was becoming more and more doable.

As the men boarded the plane, the C-141 that they were now assigned, this bird and this crew was at their disposal as they moved around the country. Stidham thought about the training restrictions that had been placed on the force, but how easy it had been for him to get every item he had requested so far. He hoped he was on a roll that would eventually see some American servicemen coming home by a route no one was expecting.

As they went through the masking for the enriched oxygen treatment from the plane's resources, Stidham had the leadership elements of the team gathered about

147

the area near the front of the passenger compartment. Even with the four quarter-ton vehicles aboard, the team did not take up nearly the entire compartment. They had a large open area to use as they needed while in flight. After going over the postflight specifics, Stidham told them all to relax for a few minutes before the jump indicator light went on in the passenger compartment.

Stidham was concerned about the rugged terrain they would encounter in the area around Ft. Indiantown Gap. He had chosen the area for an iteration because he thought it closely resembled the topography they would likely encounter in the Duc Lo region when they jumped there for real. Still, any airborne veteran would prefer a level landing zone to a hilly, rocky, uneven one any day. He could not afford to get any of his troops injured at this late stage in the operation. He needed them all at the top of their game. Making matters worse was the fact that they were jumping at night as all their practices from this time forward would be.

Soon the jump indicator lights went on, and the cargo was placed in the delivery mode and was soon clear of the aircraft. After that, the men were soon going off the rear ramp into the darkness of the Pennsylvania night. Hurdling down from thirty-one thousand feet as they approached terminal velocity, it seemed only seconds before the tug of the parachute harness deploying told them that they had reached six thousand feet, and it was time to concentrate on getting to the ground.

Sure enough, Wiznewski, who had gone out first, landed on a side hill lie. He quickly tucked and rolled and started to gather his equipment for storage. Even though his landing wasn't in the optimal area, he would be able to function. Soon he was joined by the remainder of the first stick of jumpers. They had secured their chutes and stored them and then began to look about for the four vehicles. They quickly located them three in really optimal locations, one sitting on the edge of a ravine with a tire hanging out in space. Another six inches and it would have been destroyed going into the ravine.

This was a sobering thought for the team. They could have key parts of the operation removed from the equation by pure luck of where the equipment happened to land. They had known this all along, but this event reinforced the idea deeply into their brains. Surveying the area, it was decided that they would leave the vehicle where it was but scotch the wheels that were on the ground to prevent the vehicle from rolling off into the blue. When the time came for the vehicles to start, they would crank it and attempt to back it onto firm footing. If this was not successful, they would attach a rope and pull it back from the precipice.

Foster, after assessing the situation and making a plan, went to inform VunCanon of the situation and the proposed resolution. After hearing him out, VunCanon told him he had done the right thing but thought this needed to be bumped to Stidham's level. Soon they were telling Stidham of the situation. He asked if they had thought about the center of gravity of the vehicle shifting when they put the operator into it to start the engine. This could possibly tip the vehicle off the edge it occupied.

After considering this, Foster came up with the solution. They would secure the vehicle by rope to a tree in place until they could determine if the vehicle could self-recover or if they would have to use another vehicle. This would preserve the application of the noise discipline they had been focusing on since the beginning of the training for the operation.

Soon the quarter ton in question was trussed and bound to the closest substantial tree, and operations proceeded to the point that they were ready to fire the vehicles in unison. They all started smoothly, and the questionable placement of the one vehicle led Ash to back it away from the ravine it had threatened to inhabit. They were all four at their designated RP in a few minutes. The quiet of the morning returned to the woods of the Pennsylvania hillsides that were close by.

Stidham had come to the area to check on the progress of the vehicle recovery. He was pleased that there was no further need for his involvement but, before continuing to his other duties, gathered the four operators around him and reiterated his instructions to them. "You do not bring these vehicles forward until I give you the word. If I am unable to give the word, we probably have run into a buzz saw and won't need them anyway. Do each of you understand?" He looked around the circle at each of the young men and acknowledged their nodding that they understood. Then he looked at VunCanon and asked, "Top, did you hear what I said?" VunCanon too nodded his assent.

The simulated Vietnamese facility on this post had been altered in several key ways as Stidham had requested from the range operations team. The similarity to the pictures the team had seen so many times now was eerie. That this had been accomplished through verbal and written instructions was amazing as the pictures had been classified and therefore not sent along with the range orders. Stidham studied the layout from the SP as the morning lightened slightly and the teams began their movements to each of the objectives by individual elements. He made a mental note to thank and congratulate the postoperations personnel for their attention to the details he knew to be so important in allowing his team realistic training opportunities in preparation for this mission. Hopefully, they would have a group of freed ex-POWs to show the nation how much they had contributed.

The movements were ascertained by the elements to be more difficult than any they had so far encountered due to the terrain features they were facing as they obtained their marks. They were slightly off schedule as they began the final movement to contact. The OPFOR personnel that had been obtained for the exercise were actually Montagnard people who had been allowed to immigrate into the United States due to the persecution they had faced in their own country and the loyalty they had shown to the forces of the United States. They did an excellent job of presenting the defense of the facility. One problem with using them was that the veteran members of the team would be tempted to sharpen the Hmong they had learned in the Highlands.

Scandretti's team was the first to note the craftiness and dedication they were facing as compared to some of the forces they had dealt with in previous exercises. They soon knew that these folks were good and motivated. Very soon, all the elements were fully engaged. Stidham was keeping a close eye to make sure that any physical contact did not get out of hand. After a hard night of jumping and moving in the dark, he knew that there might be some frustration building on his team.

As the team elements realized that the opposition was the mountain people that most had worked with in South Vietnam, they became more engaged but retained their respect for these dogged people who had been such staunch allies for years. There were actually a couple of recognized sightings. Both parties were professional enough to ensure that the Old Home Week observances were saved for the postexercise period.

Slowly, steadily, and craftily, the rangers made their moves and executed the individual portions of the planned operation. Before the sun was giving the warming effect of its rays, they had subdued the inhabitants of the facility and found five POWs in the confines, and they were being treated by the medics for a variety of injuries, none of which would prevent their movement in the quarter tons. The only flaw to the plan was the continuing lack of a large body of water and a submersible vessel to link up with once the quarter tons had delivered the POWs to the transfer point.

Stidham knew his guys were frustrated over the lack of development of that part of the plan. But he also knew that each iteration of the operation had allowed for the building blocks to be placed in their respective order as they were required. The water part was coming as they moved further into the execution phase.

Stidham was somewhat surprised when he found that Bringle had not made an appearance on post at Ft. Indiantown Gap. He was not registered with the BOQ, range control had not heard from him, and he was nowhere to be seen as the team repacked their gear in the itinerate space he had secured for them. They were not openly griping about the accommodations, but it was obvious they had come to expect better than they had here. Stidham pointed out to them that they had as good an area as the units that were permanent party on that post. He told them that there was an alternative; the old fort stockade was available. Taylor had seen this dilapidated structure, and he assured the team they were in the Ritz compared to that choice. There was no serious griping after that.

There were some serious reunions taking place that evening with the former OPFOR combatants. It was indeed a small world as the rangers made renewed contacts with individuals they had left half a world away, and most thought they would never see one another again. The mutual respect shown by both parties told the young members of the team how high regard each had for the other.

Abramson approached Stidham during the celebration, which had broken out. "Sir, can we take these guys with us? They are far and away the best OPFOR we have faced, and they are thoroughly versed in operating in the NVA style and doctrine. What an improvement to that part of program. Sir, you asked me to function as the S-1. That is my recommendation from the personnel side."

Stidham grinned and replied, "Lieutenant, you know that these guys can't go with us, and secondly, we do not have permission to relocate them from PA. They have official sponsors here who are working with them to settle them in the area. I'm afraid we would be impeding their progress by doing what you are suggesting. Other than that, yes, they are great, and it is fantastic to see so many of the leaders of their community who have made it here."

Abramson knew the major was right. He decided to give up the pursuit of that rabbit and to hunt another field. He was soon engrossed in trying to remember the vocabulary he had built up while serving in these people's native part of the world. He certainly, like so many others, had fond memories of his time there even though they had been engaged in the grim business of survival.

Stidham hung around for a short while and then made his disappearance. He was not keen on celebrating extensively with his troops. Normally, he would make a perfunctory appearance and then pick a moment and inconspicuously make his exit. That strategy was in full effect today. With a nod to Mizell and VunCanon, he was off and soon had found a phone that he could conduct official business upon. He had work to do to get ready for the mission.

The timing of the next phase of the operation was of great concern. He had discussed with the medics the physical condition of the team members. He was greatly concerned that so many of them were not only north of thirty, but several were pushing forty. While he didn't think of that as ancient, he did know that the strenuous demands put upon men who were making frequent jumps was extremely stressful for their bodies. He had to be careful that he gave the men enough downtime to recover from the jumps. He knew that he had never made so many jumps as they had made since the beginning of the school portion of this operation. He was thankful that he had insisted that the veteran members of the team accompany the young guys only when they were the primary instructors. This had saved them some wear and tear.

He had decided that they were going to take ten days. He knew this might bite him as there was a vital link in the operation that had not been performed to this point. But he knew his team could not function with broken limbs and sprained joints that were liable to be building up if he kept pushing them at the pace they had been going.

Even though he had scheduled the downtime for the team, he had a special mission in mind for his young four. They had been functioning as radio telephone operators (RTOs), but the skills were self and friend taught. They had picked up the observed skills of the older men and adapted them to their use. They had not had any formal training. He had an idea that he might get them into a special weeklong crash course at the schoolhouse at Ft. Monmouth, while the other guys were recuperating. He didn't think there would be any complaints from those guys who would be renewing acquaintances from the other world. He believed that both parts of the team would come away better for the break.

He soon had made the arrangements to send his four star students up to Monmouth. He had finagled a training flight opportunity for them on a Huey that was getting its official exercise. They would get a return ride in a week. He also had adjusted the estimated time of arrival (ETA) with his contacts at Ft. Devens. They would be pushed back ten days from the expected time originally planned. This was on time for so many in the execution of their duties, but it was not typical of how his outfit was run.

He soon had to retrieve VunCanon and the senior leaders from the celebration they were enjoying to bring them up to date on the developments he had put together. After he had briefed them and been rewarded by the unanimous approval of the downtime decision, he told them of the training opportunity for Foster and his minions. He noticed that his junior officers had not been enthusiastic about this, but they had not vocally expressed their thoughts on the matter. But he knew body language and theirs was expressing opinions that needed to be voiced.

He asked VunCanon to brief Foster on the upcoming class and dismissed the team NCOICs. Then he turned to the junior commissioned officers. "I don't need you to tell me you have reservations about the class. Let's hear what they are."

Abramson stood up and said, "Sir, these guys have busted their butts just like everyone on the team. If there is a time-out, why not let it be for everybody?"

"Good point, Lieutenant, but have you thought about this? These guys are the primary operators of the radios we will be using to contact the navy when it is time to get out of Dodge. They have never had a minute of schoolhouse training. I recently talked to friend in the signal corps and found out they have some really nice stuff coming on line that we can get our hands on, but we have no one who is qualified to use the stuff we can get. Not only are we getting training, but we are also getting state-of-the-art equipment, which has not been available to us up to now."

Captain Scandretti took advantage of the pause in the conversation. "Sir, I felt exactly like Lieutenant Abramson until you told us this news. I guess that's why they pay you the big bucks. You have your finger on the pulse of the army, it seems to me." Mizell and Jamison nodded their assent.

"I was concerned about everyone being treated equally, but I see now why it has to be this way. We all have to be the guy sometimes who has to give a little extra. I can live with that." Jamison had said his piece.

Stidham looked around the circle. "We all know there was a time when your leader would have told you "this is what we are going to do." I didn't like being told things like that and, if possible, won't do business that way, but I believe this is the best solution for all. Are there other reservations I haven't heard yet?"

"No, sir, you gave us a chance to be heard. We are with you all the way." Scandretti spoke for the entire group. Stidham had scored big in the eyes of the junior officers. He had listened to their concerns, addressed them, and built a consensus for the actions they would be taking. What more could a company grade officer expect?

Stidham looked around again and slowly said, "I was thinking that you guys would fall into the classification of old farts that would need time off, but maybe not. Would any of you care to accompany our four young friends to Monmouth? I am sure I can get a few extra seats in the classroom."

You could have heard a pin drop. Stidham had just declared checkmate. Finally, Mizell raised his hand. "Sir, I would be honored to accompany these young men. From the things you were saying, we all need to know this stuff." Having volunteered himself for the extra duty, he quickly put one foot of each of his fellow officers into the ring. Slowly, they all nodded their willingness to give up their time off for the good of the team.

Stidham knew this was the endearing quality they shared that made his team so special. They truly had one another's back and were not about to give up on one another. Seeing a task that needed to be completed, they had all volunteered to get it done. Not willingly and not lightly, but they had all offered.

He made contact with his source at the school. They were able to accept two of the officers into the class space for the week. Now he had to decide which two. He had the four pull straws to determine who went. Mizell and Jamison were the winners. They were very happy to plan to attend the class. Their anticipation was tempered when they discovered they were flying from FIG to Ft. Monmouth on a Huey helicopter. The workhorse of the Vietnam War from the American perspective, the Huey was not known for its creature comforts.

Bringle had come into the picture with no announced arrival. He had asked Stidham for time to meet with the team. He had met with the veteran members first and, knowing their feelings for him ranged from ambivalent to hostile, had met the younger guys separately. He still had visions of great things for these young men. After meeting with him for a half hour, they all had developed their own set of suspicions about him. Bringle exited from the meeting with the new trainees. In his mind, the meeting had gone extremely well. He was impressed with the newest members of the ranger team. They were still in the dark about the details of the mission. But only slightly more so than the more experienced leaders of the team. They didn't have the need to know everything. This thought made him feel better about the plan that was beginning to come together.

His contact with the leaders, while not acrimonious, had not been thoroughly enjoyable. These men had all had some contact with him in the field except for the one young lieutenant whose single tour had brought him into Nam after Bringle's departure. Still, he felt there was a working relationship there that could be developed over time.

Speaking of time, he had to prepare to brief Barstow on his latest two trips. He was fast coming to the end of his burn. The pressure of the jet lag was really slowing him down. Pulling a legal pad from his briefcase, he began to list the important action items from both visits. He had placed a great heading at the top of the first page when he felt the stewardess awaken him to tell him to buckle up. They were beginning their descent into Dulles' traffic pattern. He had drifted off and slept throughout the entire flight. His trip through the baggage area and the retrieval of his car from long-term parking was uneventful, as was his trip home.

The next morning, he was beginning to shake the cobwebs from his brain, when he thought, *I never prepared my notes for Barstow.* Well, he had time when he arrived at Foggy Bottom for that. During his drive, he began to put together the elements of his report.

When he walked into the office reserved for him on the seventh floor, he was somewhat surprised at the note on the door. The ADO wanted to see him immediately. He was soon on the elevator going to the eleventh floor. He got off and went directly to Barstow's office where he was waved in at once.

"Well, how did the meeting go in Paris?" Barstow was not inquiring about the agricultural involvement of the North Vietnamese, but rather about the elements of the trip that had led him to initially send Bringle over there. He had not foreseen the possibility of involvement at the depth it had apparently sunk. He was quite honestly tempted to pull the plug but dad-blamed if he could see walking away from the chance to get a group of POWs out of there. The only thing better would be if he could get them out of the Hanoi Hilton. He didn't think that was likely, so he decided to play the hand he had been dealt.

Bringle quickly brought him up to date on the status of Dinh's providing the routing information for any payments to a Swiss bank account, the fact that no money had changed hands, and the request for more schedule information. Bringle went on to tell his boss of his recommendation that one more iteration of exchanges of prisoners go through Duc Lo before the rescue team be sent in.

With that out of the way, he switched gears to Stidham and his project. He filled in the gaps that were apparent from his knowledge of how the mission was taking place. He covered the planning of operations and hit on the preciseness of the preparations for the execution of the plan, the commander's concept of the operation, and the need that he foresaw of an extensive travel agenda for the team. As he saw it, there would be a requirement for several takeoffs aboard air force transports, but few if any landings. He believed the flight crews would be free to return to their home base before they had completed any flight.

Barstow had begun to think that Stidham was probably the man for this task. He was overcoming every obstacle that was encumbering his team and amazingly enough not getting his feathers ruffled by Bringle, which Barstow realized was no small feat in and of itself. He knew from experience in his own bureaucratic world that oftentimes, those attempting to help are the biggest hindrances. His esteem for Stidham was steadily growing. While he had never doubted the intentions of Bringle, he had often found his capabilities to be exceeded by the task he was asked to execute. He had to watch this operation closely. He couldn't let it blow up on this team or for that matter, on the prisoners who might be affected by any misstep in this mission.

Bringle settled into a routine. Daily, he was checking the flyover pictures first thing each morning, he was monitoring reports from Stidham, and he was maintaining his contacts at the Department of Agriculture while he waited for the next round of bilateral talks to be scheduled. He suspected that he would not have long to wait. He felt the crescendo of excitement building as more and more parts of the plan he had put into motion were made into reality.

Peter Carter came to his office on one morning during this time. He handed Brindle a file folder, which had been logged into the NSA system back in May. Bringle was soon looking at a picture of an open area that seemed vaguely familiar, but he couldn't place where he had seen this area or the context in which he knew of it. Carter expectantly bided his time. Finally, Bringle looked over the folder at the analyst and said, "I'm drawing a blank here. Help me out."

Carter produced a second folder whose heading identified it as having been created in early July. Opening the folder, Bringle noted the now-familiar compound they had come to refer to as Duc Lo. It slowly began to dawn on Bringle what the other folder had been. "We were watching some nearby activity when we happened to pick up these coordinates. Six weeks later, when we were to shoot the same area, our pilot lost his aiming point again and shot this same area. Since this was not an area of interest, we just filed these photos away. One of our interns was tasked with cross-referencing these coordinates and came up with the match. We have conclusive proof that this way station has not been active more than three months. I thought you would be interested in these shots."

Carter answered some questions about the possibility of previous shots of the area. There was no record in the files of any development in that area before the past three months. There was no evidence that this could have been an active point, which had fallen into disuse and then been resurrected, even for different purposes.

Barstow, on the other hand, had observed Bringle at work for most of the thirty years. He had always felt a bit of reticence toward the field operative, but there had never been enough mud to stick to him over the years to get him into a pot of sufficiently hot water to burn him thoroughly. Therefore, he had been allowed to operate. There was a tenet in the shady agency world that what didn't kill you made you stronger. Bringle had certainly been involved in enough shady deals to have been thoroughly brought to a boil, but it had never happened due to the combination of good fortune and the throwing of others to the wolves, which had been done without regard for those. After all, they were all expendable commodities of the United States government.

Bringle left immediately for his meeting with Stidham and was soon driving into Ft. Indiantown Gap in a rental car he had picked up at the Harrisburg Airport. Driving across post, he was soon in the temporary quarters that had been arranged for Stidham's team and had parked in front of the old wooden buildings that housed the fledgling faculty of the team. Walking into the orderly room, he was impressed that Cansler remembered his name and welcomed him to a fresh pot of coffee that had not been brewed more than a few minutes. Cansler had arrived from Ft. Campbell to bring everyone up to speed on developments and update any paperwork needed by team members.

It didn't occur to Bringle that the team had been alerted to his arrival since he was accustomed to his place of anonymity in the world. As a part of agency operations, he had been trained from day 1 to affect every unassuming option in his appearance and never to attract attention to himself. This attention he was receiving, while flattering, was also working to make him ill at ease.

Stidham was counting on this reaction from the agency man. He had learned early in his career that it was a tactical advantage to keep the person one was dealing with off guard as much as possible. For that reason, he was always tossing monkey wrenches at the plans developed by those he regarded as possible adversaries. His relationship with Bringle had never been comfortable. He had seen him in country doing things that were questionable at best, but there had never been enough evidence found to cause the loss of his position. But enough of these incidents had made Stidham very wary of any involvement with him. He felt that there were elements to the mission that Bringle had not gotten around to informing him about. He hoped that having him here would lead to a clearing of the air, resulting in better planning information for his team.

Taking the proffered cup from Cansler, Bringle was about to inquire of Stidham's availability when, as if on cue, in walked First Sergeant VunCanon. Greeting Bringle as if he had made an appointment, the first sergeant graciously extended every courtesy imaginable to the civilian. Stidham was not physically watching all this, but with the paper thin walls of the old building's construction, he had kept abreast of the developments. Giving the top sergeant a few minutes, he indicated to Captain Mizell, who had been in his office during the initial entry by Bringle, that it was time for him to come into the scenario.

Knocking on the first sergeant's door, Captain Mizell was soon engaged in conversation with Bringle. While Bringle was not likely to be put off his guard by casual conversation, he was somewhat taken aback when the captain started off with "I haven't really had a chance to chat with you since that that thing at Bien Hoa." While this sounded innocuous enough, it was a startling opener for Bringle. He had not thought about the incident referred to by the captain in years.

Basically, Bringle had been running one of his operations in the area when the young lieutenant at that time had become aware of some of the fringes of what had been occurring. Bringle had to get out of the area quickly but had managed to do so with his pride mostly intact and with the money he had been siphoning off the top wholly preserved. In his book, this had made it a successful operation; and if the lieutenant had been left to absorb the damage, well, that was the price of being expendable.

Stidham did not know the full story, but it was the frequency with which such incidents seemed to follow Bringle that he was concerned. He allowed Bringle to stew while pondering the intentions of this young captain until he felt the proper moment had come for him to discover his visitor. He walked across the hallway to the first sergeant's office, threw open the door, and feigned surprise at seeing Bringle. Of course, he had received Bringle's message about the mission and was fully expecting him either that day or the next. He was trying to gain the advantage of momentum by throwing unexpected concerns Bringle's way rather than allow the agency man to come in and dictate the flow of information. In this way, Stidham hoped to shake loose any juicy morsels that had been forgotten to be passed to the team.

Stidham had carefully rehearsed with the participants in the slowdown, their roles that very morning. He had been careful to accuse Bringle of nothing, but he did want a reminder that he knew of the reputation that Bringle had as a fast player who sometimes had a stronger self-interest than his nation interest. Stidham hoped to ensure that they were all playing with the same deck of cards even if not quite on the same team.

As Bringle came into Stidham's office, it was his turn to throw the haymaker first punch. "We have confirmation from our source that the facility at Duc Lo will be operational from 9 to 13 November. We need your team on the ground at that point." He delivered the news matter-of-factly to the major.

Week 8

Dallas 20–New York Giants 23
Baltimore 13–Green Bay 10

Arriving at Ft. Monmouth, the six men reported to the school and were in class that afternoon. The new radio equipment was very similar to the ones they had used for years except for the transmission capabilities that had been enhanced. The twist was in the peripheral equipment. The microphones were much more sensitive, giving better quality to the voice transmissions. The antennae had been upgraded to expand the range of transmissions from the base station. The new boxes were capable of being linked to give even more powerful volume to distant messaging. The automatic encrypting feature made the message content more secure, but it did not give additional time to any transmission. It was still possible for the enemy to triangulate on extensive messages that exceeded the threshold of length.

Probably none of the six fully understood the full implications of the receipt of the new system. They would not until they field tested the system later. For now they spent the week learning to set up and operate the new gear. The four young men knew they were destined to be the primary operators. Indeed, when VunCanon had told Foster of the class they would be attending, he had indicated that they would be the only team representatives in the class. Mizell and Johnson had not yet volunteered their time. The younger team members quickly picked up the techniques required to utilize the new system effectively and were of great assistance to the more senior officers.

Mizell was struggling with the setup for the antennae during the third day of the class. Jamison observed his struggles, and his sympathy was overwhelming as he needled his cohort about his understanding of the new technology. Later, as they headed to the mess hall for the evening meal, Jamison asked him, "Did you ever get that antennae deal worked out?"

Mizell grinned and said, "Yeah, I found an expert who explained it to me."

Jamison replied, "They do have quality instructors here, don't they?"

"Sure do, but my expert was Nuckles. My dad used to say if he didn't understand some new-fangled thing that had come out, he would just ask a young person. That young man is scary good at using this stuff. I would say that our communications mission is in excellent hands. All those guys are better at this stuff than either you or me, but he is the best of the group."

They entered the mess hall where they found the balance of their team. Joining them at the table they had secured, the six were soon engaged in a discussion of the use of the new technology as it applied to the team mission. This was where the two officers' knowledge of what lay ahead put them at the advantage. However, this was neither the time nor the place to fully develop the topic. That had to wait for a more secure location. They were able to let the younger team members know that there were still items for discussion upon the subject.

As day 5 wound down, the men were finishing the last of the hands on portion of the instruction. As they were checked off, they were taken to the central issue facility where they were issued a complete set of the new equipment. They were then delivered to the helipad for the post. Soon the sound of the eggbeater rotors of the Huey was heard, and they saw their approaching chariot. As soon as the refueling was completed, they were quickly loaded onto the chopper. With the four sets of new equipment, which the officer's had been kind enough to sign for, the baggage area of the chopper was quite impressively filled as they took off to rejoin the team back at FIG.

Arriving at FIG, they were taken directly to Stidham, who asked them to set up a demonstration of the equipment for the team the next day and to be prepared to answer questions. Mizell and Jamison would be in charge of the expose, but they knew they would be deferring to the younger men to effectively explain the workings of the new system. Stidham knew the important feature was that they be able to establish a communications link with the navy who would be some distance removed from their location. This was the bottom line they had to achieve. Everything else was window dressing in his estimation.

The new equipment did call for new load plans for the quarter-ton vehicles as they were prepared for loading for the next drop. There was more cubic footage required with the encryption devices, and there was also the spare sections of antennae, which would be needed to achieve the maximum range of the system. These issues were not showstoppers, but they did have to be addressed. The new plans were made, equipment was shifted, and two additional bundles were required to be added to the equipment drop list.

Stidham was pleased by what he observed as the six team members went through the demonstration. The officers had obviously spent the week learning the new system, but as he suspected, the younger members of the team were much more confident in the utilization and developing the boundaries of the systemic advantages inherent to the new stuff. They just got it. But they didn't flaunt that knowledge, yet the pride they demonstrated in being subject matter experts (SME) about something brought out something in them that Stidham had not seen previously.

Calling VunCanon over, he asked the first sergeant, "Do these guys seem different to you than when we sent them off to school?"

The first shirt considered the query and then responded, "I guess they do. For the first time, this is an area they know more about than any of us. They have the most current schoolhouse knowledge. That is what I think has changed them. They get to be the pros on anything regarding this system. I think it is also apparent that this system is not just an add-on for our team but also a mission multiplier. It truly expands the horizons of what we can accomplish. Not only do they see it, but the older guys are also recognizing it and acknowledging that they now have a unique niche in the team operation. This was a stroke of genius, sir."

Stidham certainly was glad to see the developing acceptance of the newer team members. In the back of his mind, he had struggled with the consequences of this acceptance not developing from the day they had been identified as the candidates. He knew that such acceptance was essential to making the team function. He had always been concerned with Bringle's theory that the country needed new heroes, and they were producing them here. He was more worried about surviving this mission and getting those men out of the POW camp than making heroes of anyone. He knew the heroes were the men who were stuck inside that POW camp in a faraway country where they were not being treated very nicely.

Arriving at home, Bringle found that things had come unglued. First, the banker from the Cayman Islands had been trying to reach him to confirm the arrival of an unexpected deposit of $100 into his account there. Then he found that his Swiss banker was calling to frantically try to arrange the reversal of that deposit. Additionally, this man was concerned about the state of mind of his unnamed client whom Bringle knew to be Cho Dinh, who was extremely agitated over the porous membrane of the accounts in the Swiss bank. His money had passed right through. As of this moment, he was not aware of Bringle's involvement in any dealings with the account. The banker assured Bringle that he could keep his involvement in the dealings with Dinh's account quiet.

Bringle did know, however, that his involvement could not be kept quiet for long. It had to dawn on Dinh to whom he had given his account information, and then it would simply require connecting the dots to arrive at whom had cleaned out his money. Bringle was desperately trying to come up with a plan that would allow him to keep this windfall. As was his custom, he rationalized that once the money was in his account, it did in fact belong to him. He contacted the banker in Geneva.

Getting him on the phone, he demanded to know how such a thing could have happened. The banker who was, of course, highly embarrassed insisted that the fault had been with the failure of an underling to deactivate the transfer instructions. This was precisely the reaction Bringle had hoped to achieve. "Well, then your bank is going to have to clear the money." Bombastically, Bringle was soon bullying the Swiss man into admitting that the fault lay entirely in his operation. Bringle felt no remorse for making the man account for money that was indeed resting very comfortably in his own account. Concluding the phone call to Switzerland, Bringle wished the banker good luck in getting the money accounted for within the mistake proof system of the Swiss bank.

As soon as he hung up the phone, he was making another overseas call to a contact in Hong Kong. He had an account that he had used there for many years. He was greeted warmly by his contact there, especially when he heard the details of the transaction that would be coming his way. He would soon be in charge of managing over $3.6 million that Bringle had been stashing away for years in the Cayman Island accounts that were about to be deactivated.

Then he made another phone call to his Cayman Islands connection. Letting the banker there know that the instructions would be coming shortly, he now knew that he had sequestered all his holdings into a single bank in Hong Kong. Pausing to take a sip of the Jack Daniels drinking whiskey he appreciated, he mused that even though he had been upset at first with this turn of events, it had all worked out to his good; so therefore, it must be good for his country as well.

With this transaction complete, Bringle was confident that Dinh would never be able to trace his money that had surreptitiously disappeared from his Geneva account. Bringle did find it unusual that no other transactions had gone through the Swiss account. He assumed that if the Vietnamese was willing to play this game, it wasn't the first time he had played. He would bet he was a regular player. Maybe he had the good sense to isolate his accounts, so if something akin to what had transpired happened the damage would be limited to that affair. *Good on him*, thought Bringle.

Now he had to devise a strategy to minimize the damage to Operation Duc Lo. He had decided that the Vietnamese was in an untenable spot with his people. If he reported the duplicity, he would be admitting that he had committed treason to start the ball rolling. His life expectancy would be measured in seconds if he pursued that line of reasoning. Bringle was willing to bet that the facility would be operational just as promised.

As Bringle pondered the situation, it dawned on him that if the POWs were rescued on the 10 or 11 of November, there was a very good chance they could make their first public appearance at Subic Bay on Thanksgiving Day or thereabouts. What a story. He had friends in the media who would pay big money for a heads up of such a headline. Making a quick phone call to his friend at UPI (United Press International), he soon had the attention of the huge news organization. They would have an A-team reporter in the Subic Bay area for the week of Thanksgiving. He would officially be doing background work for an unnamed story he was developing.

Before going up to the seventh floor to brief Barstow, he checked his notes. He still had some things to accomplish, but first, he had to make sure that the brass here at Foggy Bottom still considered him just above the imbecile level. He was counting on their amazing capacity to underestimate the abilities of those who were working for them. This strategy had never failed him in almost thirty years, and he wanted to ensure that it was in play now.

As he went into the briefing, he noted a couple of obvious details he had omitted from his brief. He believed that if you give management the opportunity to micromanage the minutiae, they would be too lazy to really look at the significant details. After all, they had done their due diligence to find the minor flaws in the plan. Almost as if on cue, Barstow spotted the omissions from the detailed brief. He instructed Bringle at once to make the corrections, which were exactly what Bringle had already done. He managed to keep the smile off his face as he acted contrite. "Thanks for your input, boss." He stammered as he picked up his notes and headed for the door. "I'll get these changes made and send you confirmation through interoffice mail." With that, he was gone.

The confirmations of the corrections were lying upon his desk when he returned to his office. He waited about three hours and dropped them into the interoffice mail receptacle in his area. *That was easy enough*, he thought. *I sure am going to miss this place when I retire.*

Over the next few days, he stayed busy confirming with his contacts at Pacific Fleet Command that the submarine would be loitering about the area he needed it to be in for the extraction. He also confirmed the CEOI codes and date requirements for communications with the ground troops currently training for the mission. A few bottles of fine Tennessee drinking whiskey were discreetly dispatched to the appropriate addresses in the Pearl Harbor area, and he was confident that the submarine would be standing by when called.

He passed on in message traffic to Stidham as confirmation of the contacts that Stidham had already made with the naval office at Pearl Harbor. He was not running over Stidham nor did his actions signal a lack of confidence in the man. He had to lay these issues to rest for his personal satisfaction.

He was soon confirming the logistics of the plan with the air force, reserving a C-141 for the use of his team from 9 to 11 November. He knew that it wouldn't be needed the entire period, but better to not cut it too close. Besides, he was simply moving the public's money from one pocket to another in the same suit, and he had not even taken any of it for his services to them. Once again, some roses and chocolates were soon being delivered to an address in Guam.

Bringle still believed that he could pull off this daring rescue, even though he was aware of the major mistake he had made. He had made mistakes before, and they had always made the winning that much sweeter when he pulled out the unforeseen outcome. This had enhanced his reputation as a bumbling, incompetent operative who had somehow gotten the results that were required of him. In his mind, another chapter of this narrative was about to be written.

He intended to play out the part, right up to taking the money out of the bank. He was growing surer of the success of his mission every day. He felt the old sense of timing coming back to him as he met the milestones of operational planning; he was actually looking forward to the day when Stidham and his guys would be ready to fly.

Bringle had called Stidham that morning. He had been somewhat put out with Cansler when the young man had told him that the major was not available to take his phone call. After a few minutes, he had agreed that the major would return his call when he was able. Cansler was not about to give up the major's whereabouts to someone on an unsecure telephone connection.

Cansler had then made arrangements to get a post messenger out to the DZ he knew they were using, waited for the major to arrive, been released, and returned to his duties in the orderly room. He had done his part.

Stidham had detached himself from the team as soon as possible and gotten to a phone post haste. He had a feeling that time was indeed growing short for the training and preparation of his team.

Upon hearing Bringle on the other end of the line, he had gotten a jolt. The mission really was on the fast track now. Up to this point, Bringle had always talked nebulously about a mission timeline, which fluctuated from sometime in November to the Chinese New Year in late January or early February. Now he was talking about sometime sooner than this, although still not allowing himself to be pinned down to a specific date-time group. Stidham had the idea that early November was now in play as a possible go date.

Indeed, Bringle listened to the plans for the jump, which Stidham did not mention being a HALO effort. Bringle assumed it would be night operations for the team and mentally prepared himself for up to 50 percent casualties expected from such an operation. He didn't mention how expendable each of Sridham's team was in his mind. So they were both holding some of their cards but sharing enough information that the mission could go forward.

Bringle had not found it necessary to indicate that he had a rock-solid reason to believe that the time frame around November 11 was probably the next hot date for Duc Lo. Neither did he see any point in relating the trials of dealing with Cho Dinh, who Stidham did not know was the prime contact for the conduit of information which had so far proven so reliable for this mission. Bringle also did not know that Stidham and Cho Dinh had had contacts before when the latter had been serving in South Vietnam with the NVA. If he had known of this involvement, there is a great chance he would have walked away from the mission.

However, he was preparing a special use of the facility for the times he had given Bringle due to the fact that Cho Dinh was feeling that he had been cheated out of his $100,000. Indeed, the facility would be very active during that time slot.

Bringle was somewhat appeased by the inaccessibility of Stidham when he learned that it had been caused by his taking part in an actual jump, preparing for the taking of Duc Lo. He was also encouraged to hear of the progress and great success of the training program of the four young rangers. He had nothing but compliments for the completion of that phase of the training, but he also had to impress on Stidham the shortness of the time remaining to accomplish all the things necessary to pull off this mission and, of course, to rescue these American heroes.

Bringle was requiring flyovers from the U-2 pilots on a daily basis. There had been no visible activity at the facility known to him as Duc Lo, but there did seem to be a fair amount of military activity taking place in the immediate vicinity. Units were staging through the area as they prepared to deploy south into their sister country.

Keeping Barstow and his boss happy had begun to take a significant portion of Bringle's time. He could see that the time was coming for him to be needed in the field. It was better to distance himself from any fallout if the problem with Cho Dinh was ever discovered. But he was relatively certain that his banker friends in other countries would not give up the details of those transactions that had resulted in a traitor's funds being deposited in his accounts. He felt that was simply poetic justice, with all the sacrifices he had made for his country over the years.

Still, just to cover his bases, he prepared a request from the pension agency of the US government. He was surprised to discover that, with his accumulated annual leave and credit for his sick leave, he had enough time to retire with credit for thirty years' service. He prepared a request for retirement effective December 1 just in case things went south on him again. He was covering all of his bases.

He decided to take a trip up to Ft. Indiantown Gap to assure himself of the readiness of his (Stidham's) team. Making those reservations took him about half a day. He was on a flight the next morning. He had once again flown into the civilian airport, this time at Harrisburg, Pennsylvania, rented a car, and driven to the Gap, as it was known in the military jargon of the day. Making his way to the nondescript headquarters that Stidham had established, he was surprised to see a face from his early days in Vietnam departing the area. It was the man known to Stidham as the NCOIC of the HALO team of experts. Bringle had known him when he was paratrooper in Vietnam during the buildup following the Gulf of Tonkin incident. Stidham had asked him to up one last time to go over the use of the HALO technique. Stidham was still searching for any small advantage to use to his purpose.

The man hardly paused as he was leaving the area; Bringle was relatively certain he had seen no hint of recognition in his reaction. Reflecting on the situation, Bringle decided to let it pass. They had crossed paths over there; there had been some conflict but no charges brought against either party. As far as he was concerned, case closed. He wrote it off to just passing luck.

Still, as he walked into Stidham's operational area, he was wondering what the man had been up to in this place. Walking into Stidham's office, he inquired, "Was that Bill Marlow I passed in the parking area?"

Stidham looked up from the paperwork he was fighting with today and grunted. "Good to see you too. And yes, that was Marlow. I didn't know you two were long lost friends." It was obvious they were not friends from the tone Bringle used when saying the name.

"How is the preparation coming?" inquired Bringle, deciding to let go of his unease at seeing a face long ago erased from his memory.

"We will be jumping tomorrow. Care to join us?" Stidham extended the invitation only because he knew that Bringle had never voluntarily left the inside of a plane before it was on the ground.

"I would love to, but I am just here for the day. Have a big meeting in DC tomorrow." Bringle pulled some recent photos from his briefcase and pushed them over to Stidham. "Our facility is sitting empty now, but I have pretty reliable information that it may go hot again in early November."

Stidham began to study the photos, looking for any signs of occupation and, as he considered this, almost automatically responded, "Not our facility. I don't want my name associated with this trap." Finishing his inspection of the photos, he asked, "Are these my copies?"

When Bringle nodded, he gathered them up and slipped them into a folder already marked with the security panels required. "You know we should have the room set up for top secret before these things come out." His reprimand was not offensive but let the agency man know that his screwup had been noted.

"Do you have any needs for me to grease the skids at any of your practice sites?" Bringle decided to change course. "I haven't received any requests. Just want you to know I can help if needed." He wanted to make sure that Stidham remembered he had been making things go better for his team since day 1. Stidham thought to himself, *Not only for my team but also him primarily.* He almost verbalized the thought and then decided better of it.

"Well, if you won't accept our hospitality and accompany us in the morning, what else can we do for you?" Stidham was running short on time and patience for a man who continually dropped in on him with no warning. He thought about bringing him current on the HALO operation and, after considering it, thought, *I'm not even 100 percent certain this is our best course of action, but if I let him in on it, he has a way of blowing things into something I wasn't planning. I will leave it alone for now at least.*

Stidham quickly pulled out the team statistics for the required dog and pony show he had learned was necessary to bring visiting dignitaries up to speed on the operation of his team and often brought justification for the expenditure of funds that they needed. It had yet to fail him, so he kept it current.

Week 9

Dallas 0–St. Louis Cardinals 38
Baltimore 17–Buffalo 17

The team had two days to assimilate the new commo gear into their operation. The independent elements who relied upon the old PRC 77s would never admit it, but they were jealous of the new machines. They were all lined up to try anything that made the job easier. Stidham wasn't buying into retraining his entire team at this stage in the operation. He had used this gear for years and was comfortable with it now. They would stick with it.

After two days of dry runs, the team was ready for the real thing. They would leave that evening for Ft. Devens and their last rehearsal mission in the United States. The time was drawing close. The pre-operation brief went very smoothly. The men had heard it so many times; they were mouthing the words before they were out of the speaker's mouth. They were primed and ready. Stidham knew the signs, and he was apprehensive of this exercise. Over-preparation was as much a danger for an operation as lack of preparation. He did not want his team developing an attitude of "this is old hat stuff we do in our sleep."

He called VunCanon and Mizell into conference, and they heard his plan. The three men were confident that this would get the attention of every one of the team members. As they boarded the C-141 for the flight after loading and securing the equipment with the blessing of the loadmaster, they had no way of knowing the shake-up that was about to occur. The men were soon strapped into their rear-facing seats, with the oxygen masks in place over their faces. Each man had his cold weather gear laid out beside him. They had so far experienced no problems with the extreme cold air at thirty-thousand-plus feet; they wanted no new ones tonight.

The flight seemed unusually long to the men as they waited for the clearance to jump. They were hardly aware that the most direct flight path took them through the most congested airspace for civilian air traffic in the United States. Therefore, the pilot had laid out his route in a more circuitous pattern that avoided the major population centers of the northeast as they came closer to Ft. Devens. It really had taken longer than it normally would have, but who was in a hurry anyway?

As the C-141 entered the restricted air space over the Ft. Devens cone, the men prepared for their exit from the plane. The indicator light soon showed them it was time for the equipment to head south, and it was promptly on its way to the ground. Then it was time for the personnel. As they had practiced so many times, they were leaving the plane, experiencing the bubble, and then heading for the ground. It was amazing to Foster that he could spot the lights of Boston even from this distance, given the altitude of their start. As he approached terminal velocity, the lights slipped over the horizon, and he was jumping into darkness.

It took a while for his night vision to acquire its acuity, but he soon had the level of vision to which he was accustomed. As he neared the ground, he was able to pick out the outlines of the equipment that had already reached the ground. He had developed the habit of spotting the grounded equipment from the air. He quickly noted the location and the apparent status of accessibility. This time, the gear had landed on even ground within five yards of the points that had been drawn on the topographical map they were using for orientation. From the air, he noticed no visible damage, but this was just a cursory look. They would check closely once they were on site.

As he hit the ground, he was already securing his individual equipment from the jump and was disposing of the extreme cold weather gear he was wearing. Stowing all this in his pack, he was at the same time mentally checking off the arrival of the balance of his element and noting the landing of the other elements as he heard the soft thuds of men loaded with equipment striking the ground. Moving quickly and efficiently, he checked with Ash, Nuckles, and Wiznewski to be sure they had no significant injuries or deviations from the plan.

Having ascertained their status, he proceeded to move to the designated rally point where he expected to find VunCanon, Stidham, and Gibson preparing for the operation. When he arrived there, he was surprised to see VunCanon and Gibson, but Stidham was not in sight. VunCanon looked worried. He told the younger man, "Stidham was killed in the jump. I have sent for Captain (P) Mizell. He will be taking command of the operation."

Foster was taken aback. While they all knew the dangers of jumping from airplanes and particularly from the heights they had been jumping, it had never occurred to him that an experienced man like Stidham would have a failure of equipment. He had sometimes wondered how the four of them had managed to never resort to even a backup chute, except, of course, for the one time in jump school when they had been required to employ the reserve chute. This was, of course, just to assure the jumper of the efficacy of the reserve.

Mizell got to the RP at that moment. VunCanon took him to the side and related the news. The medics, except for Patterson, had gone to look for Stidham's remains. Mizell meanwhile assembled the leadership of the team, including Foster and Patterson. Mizell quickly redrew the operational plan, moving only himself to the command slot and putting Goldman into the element leader slot of team 1. When they had verbally walked through the plan, he turned to Foster. "When they find Stidham, we want to secure his body in one of the quarter tons until we finish the mission."

Foster protested, "Sir, with all due respect, we should get medical assistance here at once. We have to report all that has happened here."

Suddenly Mizell broke into a laugh. "You have never played the game before, have you? He's not really dead. He has simply been taken out of the play. This is a test to see how the team reacts to the loss of a key leader."

Foster nodded slowly, feeling very foolish for his misguided assumption about the men of the team. "I'm sorry, sir. I didn't know this was a part of the exercise," he finished lamely.

Mizell slapped him on the back. "We'll just let him ride around in style with you guys while we move on with the plan. He'll enjoy getting to see things as you guys see them."

Foster saw Patterson coming back to the rally point. "We found him. He was off target slightly from the jump and landed in a tree." He reported somberly. Foster thought, *He acts as if he really found a dead man out there. I can't believe that we are supposed to take these events so casually.* That was all he had time to run through his mind.

Mizell was asking, "Which vehicle do you want him in?"

"We'll use Nuckles vehicle." Foster made the decision quickly. He was going to be down at least part of a vehicle for this iteration of the exercise. *Well, that's why we practice*, he told himself. "If there is nothing else, sir, I need to inform my team of the changes."

"Dismissed." Mizell had also moved on to other important items he would need to address with the team as the exercise proceeded. He considered the portion of the plan affecting the vehicles as taken care of. He had assigned Foster the task, and he knew that the young man would do as he was tasked. There were other facets to be considered.

The movement of the elements to contact was a pivotal point. While Sergeant First Class Goldman was thoroughly familiar with the concept of the operation, his exposure had been as NCOIC, and now he would have to function as the OIC. Not only had his responsibilities expanded, but his team was also no longer balanced into three two-man teams. He had to adjust the movements of the team for fire and cover considerations as well.

Functioning without Stidham as the head of the operation threw the team into an unfamiliar pace of the operation. It was obvious from the start that the timing was off on the synchronized portions of the plan. Not off greatly, but ever so slightly. Each time there was a slight pause or something occurred shortly before the team was accustomed to its occurrence, the men would pause to regroup, throwing the timing off even more on the next segment.

Still, as the events wound down at the mock-up facility, the task of liberating the four POWs found in the confines that day had been accomplished. Mizell called forward the quarter tons. The POWs were evaluated and loaded into the transports. They were taken to Mirror Lake, where they were loaded onto the rubber rafts that had not been used in any exercise up to this time. Today they were utilized, and the POWs were soon at the simulated linkup point with the navy.

The navy had actually brought a submarine from the Atlantic fleet to an offshore position to play the communications piece of the operation. The new radios worked terrifically, and the linkage was superb. It remained to be seen how the linkup itself would go with the Pacific fleet underwater craft that would be used in the actual operation. There would be time for a practice exercise when the team reached Guam.

Stidham had been placed in the quarter ton that Nuckles was operating, so there were only three vehicles available for transporting released POWs. With only four in the play, that created no problems logistically in removing them from the area. Stidham, however, was close to going crazy as he observed from the vehicle the progress of the exercise. He was unaccustomed to being out of the action. He had, of course, made the decision to remove himself from the play to give the team the confidence that they had a good plan and to experience what it would be like to lose a key member of the team's leadership.

The minor snafus (situation normal; all fouled up) they had encountered were to be expected as they adjusted to his loss. It would have been a similar outcome if another leader had been removed from the play. The results would probably have not been so pervasive, but the problems would have arisen, regardless which key member was removed. The team had realized that with a good plan in place, no team member was irreplaceable. Upon further reflection, Foster decided it was a good thing that he nor any of his guys were important enough to have been removed from the play for that iteration.

When the team and all of its equipment were secure, they assembled for the after-action review. Waiting for them was Bringle. Stidham was not surprised by the appearance of the agency man at the post. He had known there would be an exercise at this post, and due to the time-sensitive nature of the information he had been providing for the team, Stidham had to be updated. Still, he couldn't help a slight bit of frustration with the attitude of the spook.

The condescending atmosphere that Bringle managed to bring with him every time they met was really working on Stidham as he struggled to deal with the man, so he could get the intelligence reports he needed to make his final adjustments to his plan. It would have been so much easier to work together. He somehow had to make it work for a few more days. Then he would have it out with his associate.

Bringle was there to share his most recently acquired photographs of the facility, which was presently sitting empty, but Bringle had solid information about the timing of the next usage of the camp. Naturally, upon hearing of the problems encountered with the loss of the key personnel, he, who had never been on any of the missions with the team, was all about straightening out the issues.

The team listened for about ten seconds and tuned him out. If he had good ideas, they were of no value because no one was hearing them.

The team seemed to react to his presence with a distrust that none of the men could explain, but they all shared the feeling. Some were more adamant than others, but without fail, they did not trust this man who seemed to come and go as he pleased. They were appreciative of the things he brought, but things brought to them did not buy him their trust.

Stidham soon noticed that the AAR session had dried up. His team was not opening up with the outsider present in the room. They had been quick to point out the positive contributions of the men who had stepped up in his absence. When Bringle had interjected himself into the discussion of the first issue that had arisen, it had been like turning off the water tap. The information stopped flowing. Stidham soon saw that it would not come back on until the outsider was out of the picture.

Calling a halt to the proceedings and sending the men off to complete the preparations for their next move, Stidham brought Bringle up to date on the things he needed to know. He got the information from Bringle that he needed. He then explained that they would be moving out to Guam shortly. The trip was being broken down into manageable legs. This would avoid the team arriving with an advanced case of jet lag when they got to Guam, resulting in a better state of readiness for his team.

Bringle assured him that he would see them there; he would be bringing them up-to-date intelligence reports that would be essential to the team preparing and kicking off its operation. They would indeed see each other there.

With this, Bringle excused himself and was soon on his way to do whatever the agency required of him. The team was relieved to see him go. While Stidham sensed their reticence toward Bringle, he would never allow them to voice it to him. The team had to understand that Bringle had a role to play in the operation. He would be on guard to ensure that the role did not expand beyond the necessary mark, but the team had to acknowledge the part he played in their mission.

Stidham had VunCanon reassemble the team, and the aborted briefing resumed. This time, the criticism of the play was open and honest. Suggestions about improving/changing the scenario were given honestly; there were no egos on display. Mizell took many of the suggestions; he was professional in his approach. He was open to adjustments he had not considered initially. Smiling, Stidham realized that one day this man would be ready to assume the leadership of such an operation.

Soon the topic had moved to the next iteration of the exercise. This was when it was explained that they would be in Guam when that occurred. The gravity of the situation was not lost on any team member. They knew the days were growing short, and they would be performing with their fellow servicemen's lives on the line soon. They had no time to even grouse about the role Bringle would or had played in their lives to this point. The intensity of the team had moved up a notch; Stidham knew it and appreciated the professionalism that made it happen. He had not told them anything that had caused the change; they simply recognized the signs. Even the new members of the team were buying into the more intense preparations.

They were soon making plans for the operation to be conducted in Guam. They had the OPORDER out and were taking it apart as they identified the tasks spelled out for them and sought out the implied taskings that were hiding inside the orders. Their experience as soldiers led them to the understanding of these implied tasks without anyone having to point the details out to them.

Stidham had laid out their itinerary so that they would never travel more than two time zones between stops. They would have a layover of at least four hours when they stopped. There would be a meal taken at every planned stop. He wanted to outlaw jet lag. He intended to have fresh troops when he arrived in Guam. He had no intention of having his men not operationally ready when they arrived.

Gibson soon informed him that all the oxygen canisters had been refilled by the staff at the hospital, and they were fully functional from that standpoint. He had the crew of the C-141 in their BOQ quarters resting and prepping for the long trip they would be executing for the team. He had confirmation from COMPACFLT that the navy indeed had the submarine standing by in the vicinity they needed to be for the exercise to proceed. All systems were on go.

He had the men quartered for the evening; he told them they would be departing the next day. They would not be returning to the mainland until the operation had been completed. The men were not allowed to tell anyone of the pending deployment; most of them had no one to tell anyway. There was not a married man among them, and few had any living relatives with whom they regularly communicated. There would be no noticeable void when they deployed.

Still he had to allow them to unwind; the NCO Club was there if they wanted to have an adult beverage or two that evening. There were few takers; the older men knew they had better rest while they could. The younger men went to the club, quickly realized that they were rubbing elbows with an older crowd, and were soon back in their quarters, ready for an evening of restful slumber.

Bringle spent a few minutes looking at the records he had been presented and commented about the individual weapons qualifications results. They were outstanding, but Stidham knew that if they became the focal point of any aspect of his mission, the team was indeed in trouble. He felt like he had just dragged the proverbial red herring across the trail. Amazingly, Bringle, who, in his own way, played Barstow with his bag of tricks, did not recognize the tactic when it was used on him. Bringle seemed somewhat distracted but not inclined to share the source of his angst, so Stidham was attempting to rid himself of the man from the agency. He could see no benefit to having this guy or any other waste his time at this incredibly important point in the mission planning he was carrying out.

Stidham nodded at the papers carrying the vital statistics of the team. "Oh yeah, forgot to tell you. This morning's jump is not reflected on these numbers." Again, he could not bring himself to mention that this jump had been a special event, the first of the HALO jumps had been made. He would leave it alone unless the agency man was here to question what the issue of the cold weather gear had to do with jumping into a tropical jungle. His anxiety was soon relieved as he realized that those procurements had been made through front-door channels, and the agency would not be routinely looking at those expenditures. He would, however, keep that in mind in the future.

Unknown to Stidham, Bringle had indeed been at Ft. Pickett, arriving shortly after the team had landed. He had checked with the operations section at post headquarters and found the team had occupied their assigned areas from range control. Due to the lack of BOQ space on post and his disdain for sleeping in the field, he did not find it necessary to go to the field to visit the troops. While he saw himself as a hero maker for these guys, he did not wish to share any of their discomforts since Stidham had made it plain that he would not be welcome on the mission.

He wanted to be certain that the mission was progressing according to plan and that everything was on track. Finding it so, he checked out of post headquarters and returned to his office in DC. Had he remained another three days, he might have found out about Nuckles near escape from a debilitating injury that would have prevented his accompaniment on the mission. Oh well, it all worked out even without Bringle to pull the strings of the puppets. He was living a charmed life. Now the team had moved on to other areas, and Bringle was finding it easier to withdraw from contact with them. This enhanced his ability to see them as expendable items rather than as individual people.

These guys were getting good at these night jumps. Bringle had not observed one of the jumps and was not aware that the HALO technique was being utilized for them. He had chosen to not be at the LZ for any of the jumps, and the altitudes of the jump reports had not gotten his attention. If he noticed the jump altitudes at all, he wrote them off as a simple error. No one jumped from those places. Stidham had never specifically mentioned altitude to him. Further, Stidham had not needed his assistance with procuring the needed equipment to make the jumps possible, having procured everything through the normal military channels.

He was beginning to get some questions from Barstow about the expenditure of funds and the lack of visible progress. He had been able to slough it off to this point as he had repeatedly narrowed the dates to the early November time frame. He was concerned with Cho Dinh. He had every reason for concern.

Dinh knew by now that he had been duped out of the money that was supposed to have been paid. Bringle never had been able to keep his hands off those funds. It was well known in the field that if you were dealing with Bringle, he was skimming funds from your pot. While Dinh knew the man he had selected to make the advance to, he had not expected such blatant thievery from someone who professed to care about his countrymen. Dinh doubted if the treatment being received by the men being held had improved very much.

Bringle was preparing for the October round of peace talks. He had hoped to not be required to attend, but it was necessary for him to be there. Therefore, he had cut short his trip to Ft. Pickett and come back to Washington. Catching the diplomatic flight from Dulles, he knew that he would not be taking too many more of these jaunts.

During the sessions of the peace talks, he had hardly kept his eyes open. He was surprised when Dinh approached him with papers to be exchanged. There in the stack was the information he needed. He quickly noted to Dinh that the money would be replaced in his account and hurriedly wrapped up his end of the peace talks. Dinh had assured him that the facility would be active from 9 November to 13 November. They had to be ready to go.

Bringle could not bring himself to part with the money he had purloined from Dinh's account earlier, so he prepared justification through Barstow for an additional payment due to additional information being acquired. This $50,000 was indeed transferred to the North Vietnamese's account. Bringle was still short by that amount from what had been sought by the would-be traitor. He never paid full price for his information.

He did not realize the gravity of the situation he was playing himself into. He had an entire thirty-two-man team of US Army Rangers who were putting their lives on the line based solely on his word. The man giving him information felt like he had been swindled. This was not lining up to present a pretty picture when the exposure came. Yet he still believed he was in the hero-making business.

Bringle resolved in his mind that Cho Dinh had placed himself in a traitorous position in his own country. Therefore, he reasoned that the turncoat had few or no options in dealing with him. From his perspective, Dinh was out of options. He simply had to accept whatever scraps of change Bringle was willing to slip him. As was so often the case in dealing with foreign agents, however, not all the cards were on the table.

Minh Tran, who was the minister of defense in North Vietnam, was also known to have an undercover group of operatives who were active in undermining any stabilization efforts that the South Vietnamese government or its allies might undertake. They had operated much as any bureaucracy with some high water marks and some disappointments. Bringle had no way of knowing that Cho Dinh had been placed on the peace negotiations team by Tran in hopes that he might spot any US counter-operatives. He had been ecstatic when he saw Bringle on the American team.

Dinh and Bringle had had dealings in the South for many years. Never as a consistent source, but they had crossed paths enough to recognize each other. When he had reported this twist to Tran, there had been a polite nod, but surely the American who had a reputation among the clandestine services of not being the best around would be under the auspices of a more senior operative. The two Vietnamese had decided to try to smoke out Bringle and see if they could expose his handler.

Therefore, they had made the approaches, offering information about the facility nearby to Hanoi. They had even managed to make sure that a certain group of American POWs were actually there on the days they felt certain that American U-2 spy planes would be overflying the area. The rest had taken care of itself. Now they had presented a schedule of use for the facility. They were not sure that the American, dumb as he was, would have the authority to attempt a rescue, but they would play out the charade just in case they could make it work. They had seen no evidence of a senior handler. If the Americans were trusting this goofball, all the better for them.

When Cho Dinh had come in with the story about the money transfer going through his account, it had caused some consternation for Tran, who didn't know that Dinh had any Swiss accounts. He probably thought he was the only servant of the people who was entitled to such a luxury and a private retirement plan. He had eyed the transactions in the account suspiciously, still not absolutely convinced that Dinh was not himself maneuvering the contents of the account in some fashion. He knew if he caught him at it, he would take the money, and Dinh would very quickly disappear, never to be heard from again by Americans or Vietnamese.

With these deep-rooted distrust issues simmering between the two men, it was no wonder that they kept such close watch on each other. Of course, Tran had the advantage of being the superior in terms of rank, power, and prestige within the government. Still, he knew that he could not afford for Dinh to know too much of his business. He was carefully considering exactly what Dinh's next assignment would be and where it might take him. Tran felt it likely that it would not be a safe assignment sitting in restaurants and hotels in Paris, France. More than likely, it would involve travel via the trail through the Southeast Asia area known as the Ho Chi Minh Trail. If it turned out to be a terminal assignment, well, he had been a useful ally for a while.

Tran would make certain that he had the access codes and passwords for the accounts that the junior man had shown him. The activities that had engaged Bringle so thoroughly would soon be in need of a new manager. No use letting any funds lay there after the current possessor was out of the picture. He was pretty sure that Dinh was approaching the limits of his usefulness, and besides, he had demonstrated an interest in self-employment, which could not be tolerated by any government official in any underling. It jeopardized his ability to conduct his own skimming operation. There was only room for so much graft in the people's government, and he was intending to occupy all of that space.

With this backdrop behind them, the two men began to plan for the occupation of the area that the Americans had told them they called Duc Lo. They had arranged for a combat regiment moving into the rotation to go to the south to bivouac in the area and conduct limited operations. Tran had even insisted to one of his cronies that four US POWs be placed in the facility on the ninth of November. They would be moved safely to Hanoi by the end of the tenth. He had a strong suspicion that the United States would attempt any action to rescue them on the eleventh since that was a conspicuous holiday in the states.

Unknown to Dinh, Tran had also arranged that Dinh would be accompanying the regiment as it made its way down the trail. No particular care was to be taken to assure his safe arrival in the south.

Dinh, for his part, was feeling that he had passed the test of loyalty by bringing the matter to the attention of his superior. He was not experiencing any doubts that he would be enjoying the fruits of his labor shortly. He had even gotten some hints from Tran that he might be allowed to keep a portion of the proceeds that Bringle had so generously sprinkled into his account. It had not yet occurred to him that Tran's motivation for such a move was to find any other accounts he might have and clean them out for him as well as the one he had led him to. This game was being played at a relatively high level of duplicity by players not normally accustomed to dealing with these exact stakes. They were, however, warming to the tasks.

Tran had insisted that Dinh personally be on hand to assess the actions that Bringle might bring into play during the early November time frame. He had assured his junior partner that he needed a man on the ground whose trust was beyond question. Dinh thought he had progressed to the point that he would not be doing field duty in the South again unless there was to be a major promotion in it for him. He was disappointed, but how do you argue with your boss in such an autocratic system. He decided to salute and plan to be there when the time came. After all, he had a declaration of trust and appreciation from his superior.

He involved himself in the details of the plan, making sure that every sign was laid out to the Americans that the time was right for the actions they so desperately wanted to take. He made sure that every indication was of a lightly guarded facility, which was simply a way station for a layover of a few days on the line to Hanoi. No disturbance of the façade that had been established at the facility was allowed. The military commander was complaining that he could not adequately employ the forces he had to bring into the area without major changes to the layout.

Dinh made certain that he was available to go over the details of why no changes that were apparent from the air could be allowed. He then oversaw the maintenance of the facility's image as presented to the air and from nearby ground surveillance positions. The military commander responded that if we are seriously expecting an invasion by the US forces, they should be reacting with much more force than this. Dinh could not give him every detail, but he did remind him that Tran would be looking on from afar and that he had been sent to represent the senior man. This seemed to appease the military man who was able to find some unobtrusive alternative employment for some of his force. They would have a significant reserve if needed.

During the time leading up to the ninth of November, Tran had hit on the idea of using mannequins to approximate US soldiers. They knew that the United States was using U-2 planes for surveillance and assumed they would use it for this purpose. They knew that the flights always came from the same direction. It had been a simple matter to pose a half-dozen dressed-up mannequins for prisoners in the facility. Tran had sent Dinh to oversee the operation. At first, the mannequins had been placed outside and left in the same position.

Dinh had to have a heart-to-heart talk with the commander. This was unacceptable because the Americans would make multiple passes. People who didn't move after being let out of cages would be suspicious even to the American he had been dealing with. Secondly, there was the possibility that the Americans were engaging in personal surveillance. There might be someone with a pair of glasses out there in the woods observing the station more frequently than they had assumed. Therefore, the activity around the facility had increased in volume and frequency.

Dinh was not overly happy that he had been ordered to remain at the facility until the American move was made. He felt reasonably certain that this would occur by the eleventh of November, but he had become accustomed to the power center that he perceived Hanoi to be. He needed to be there to defend his turf— there were always up and coming young people looking to supplant the mid-level manager types that he had fought so hard to become. He was not willing to give up his seat near the throne, especially if it involved sleeping in bug-infested quarters out in the boondocks. After all, he had spent the majority of his zeal for the revolution just getting to the place he now occupied.

He had fought with the military man at the facility over the positioning of the troops. Now he needed him to have them available to respond when the Americans came. On the tenth of November in the evening, he had them move in reinforcements and increase the weaponry supporting the facility. Just over the ridge to the west on a very fast avenue of access, he had suggested the military man place the reactionary force. While he suspected it would be needed shortly, he avoided tipping off the other man as to the coming events. This nervous Nellie might have a heart attack. If he thought he was about to be attacked, he might retreat.

This had to be a neat operation. At least there was no confrontation over issuing ammunition to the primary guard force. They might even be able to kill some local wildlife to supplement the meager rations they received daily. They were in position to be seen and to lay down some serious resistance if the damned Yankees came to their neck of the woods.

Week 10

Dallas 45–Washington 34
Baltimore 17–Miami 34

The next morning, they all arose early. VunCanon never woke the first soldier. They were working their way through the personal hygiene tasks that each day brought them before the assigned wake-up time had arrived. Stidham looked around the bay and realized this level of maturity was why he loved working with these men. He didn't have to run a babysitting service. They knew what to do and did it.

Stidham looked at each man and knew he must now really get their attention. He had Cansler pass each man two blank envelopes and a clean sheet of paper. Groans went round the room from the men who had done this before. Turning the operation over to VunCanon, the men were soon addressing the first envelope to whomever they chose, with the understanding that they would never be mailed as long as they came home. The paper contained a note that they had accepted assignment to this mission, understanding the dangers inherent and willing to undergo whatever came to accomplish that mission.

Team element leaders were soon looking over letters to assure that no breach of security was contained in the letters of each man. When they were declared clean, the men were instructed to place the paper into the addressed envelope. They then placed that envelope inside the second envelope and sealed it. Then they wrote their name across the seal of the outside envelope. When all were completed, VunCanon collected them and handed them to Cansler, who was entrusted with their keeping until the team returned from Vietnam and the letters would be given back to the individual. None liked to think about what would happen if they didn't return, but they knew the purpose of the envelopes.

This brought Stidham to the point of sending Cansler back to Ft. Campbell. He had become an intricate part of the team but by his own account had not wanted to be part of the tactical mission. Therefore, he would be sent back to Campbell to work with Ms. Cross and await the return of the team. They quickly said their good-byes, and he was dispatched to do his magic from that location.

While the four-man cell augmented by the two officers had been attending school at Ft. Monmouth, Nuckles had purchased a 1966 Chevy Nova that they had used to ride around in the area. When the time had come to leave, Nuckles had intended to sell the car; however, the leaving had been orchestrated by Stidham, and Nuckles had not completed the transaction. He had left the car on post at Ft. Monmouth and figured he would work out something about it later.

It seemed that now was as good a time as any. He approached Cansler, and they made a deal. Cansler would take a bus to Ft. Monmouth, pick up the car, and drive it to Ft. Campbell. In exchange, he would have the use of the car until the team returned from their mission. He would be able to pocket the money he received for the bus fare in excess of the ticket taking him to Ft. Monmouth. It looked like a win-win situation for both him and Nuckles.

The mess hall had been instructed to prepare a sumptuous meal for them, and they had not failed. The send-off from the mess staff was first rate. They had not cut any corners. Stidham noted that each of the element leaders and NCOICs made a point out of going to the staff of the dining facility to thank them for the attention they had received. He made a note to thank them for the appearance of grits on the breakfast menu, which he figured correctly was a first at that installation.

Soon they were back at their quarters. Each man picked up his ALCE (army load carrying equipment) pack known as Alice and their spare duffel bag crammed with extreme cold weather gear, which would be crucial for their arrival on the ground from the enormous height they would be exiting the plane over Guam. They shuffled onto the bus transporting them to the airfield at Pease AFB. They were just a memory to the few people who ever knew they had been on the grounds of Ft. Devens. They had a nice bus ride to the AFB and relaxed as they began their journey. They had no idea when they would return.

The plane ride to Scott AFB in Illinois was eventful only in the fact that the team landed in the plane. This was the first plane ride they had taken and landed rather than jumping. After refueling and the mandatory meal and a leisurely walk through the Base Exchange, they were back on the plane and soon en route Hunter-Liggett Army Airfield in California. Once again, a quick stop, a meal, refueling of the aircraft, and a refreshing walk around the area. Almost before they knew the stop was over, they were taking off for Hawaii. They landed at the Marine Corps Air Station there. Stidham had arranged for them to RON (remain overnight) there, and they found the BOQ to be most satisfactory.

Rising early the next morning, they enjoyed the officer's mess at the BOQ and were soon on their way to the ramp where their chariot awaited them. As they proceeded to go through the preflight ritual, they were made aware that this would be the last time they would be landing with the aircraft, at least for the foreseeable future. This flight would end with a jump over the island of Guam. Extra care was taken as the extreme cold weather gear and the oxygen canisters were checked for serviceability. No one wanted to experience an emergency at this late stage of the execution of the preparation for the exercise.

The tension among the team was growing as each man dealt with the coming operation in his own individual manner. They were purposely avoiding small conversations because some of the team did not wish to engage in small talk at this point. Any conversations were kept short and involved the business of the operation or its equipment.

Throughout the flight, Nuckles and Foster had sat side-by-side in the strapped rear-facing seats of the aircraft. Nuckles had nervously checked the lashings on the quarter ton he was responsible for operating when they were on the ground. He had checked those lashings at least five times, each time taking every precaution to ensure that he had missed nothing the last time. Finally, after a bout with turbulence over the Pacific, he had gotten up to check again. Foster slipped alongside him as he made his inspection.

"This thing hasn't moved since we took off." Foster was grinning when he said it. "I keep thinking that I forgot something too." He added this lamely as Nuckles ruefully grinned back at him.

"Do you reckon these guys are even aware that we can't be still?" Nuckles indicated the passenger compartment where at least twenty of the team either were asleep or were pretending to be so; they gave every appearance of having no cares. VunCanon had been reading a Zane Grey novel, and he put it down and came back to the area where the two young men were reinspecting the lashings on the M-151A1 quarter tons again.

"I am trying to figure out if you guys will wear a hole in the floor of the plane or fray these lashing mounts off this equipment first." He was not being serious; they knew from the friendliness in his voice.

"Sorry, Top." Nuckles was about to apologize for disturbing the first sergeant from his relaxation. He stopped when the older man raised his hand.

"I would rather have you young guys letting me know that you are nervous rather than acting like it's no big deal and then freezing up when the time to perform comes. You'll be fine. Our whole team will do the job we have been sent to take on for our country."

"I certainly hope so, Top." Nuckles was not sure that he would get through this long plane ride, much less the drop into enemy territory that he now knew would be coming in the next few days. He had faced a lot of adversity when playing sports in school, but this was different. Not only was his life on the line, but he was aware that his teammates were depending on him as well as those men he had never met whom he wanted to help get out of that hellhole he had seen in the photos snapped from the U-2s.

VunCanon calmly placed a hand on the shoulder of each of the young men whom he had come to think of as his own men. "You four guys have adapted to so many changes without any major life-changing emotional rides. All of you will be fine when the time comes. I've watched a lot of men go out for the first time. I'm telling you I've never felt better to go with any than with this group. Our whole team has been handpicked to be the best. They would to a man agree with me. If you want, I'll wake them up and ask them how they feel."

Foster quickly interjected, "Top, we'll take your word for it. No need to wake any of these sleeping beauties." He knew that he didn't want the harassment that would come with the first shirt's kind invitation.

Foster and Nuckles soon returned to their seats and spent the rest of the flight fitfully moving in the straps and dealing with the deployment of the oxygen masks and their wearing of the equipment. When it was finally time to suit up for the jump, they were ready and soon assisting in the deployment of the M-151A1s out the back ramp. Shortly after the packages were airborne, the troops began to go off the ramp with their static lines connected to the slide to let them go into the thin atmosphere of the level they were jumping.

They never failed to enjoy the serenity of the sight of the world in its darkness unfolding below them. The vastness of what they could observe worked backward. As they approached the landing zone, the visibility decreased accordingly. Still, those few minutes were worth the effort to get to experience the grandeur of the earth as they approached it.

As they came in to the LZ, they spotted the equipment packages, once again spotted perfectly by the air force crew above them, now headed for the landing at the base on Guam. The landing maneuver came off smoothly, and the first stick of jumpers was soon on the ground, and the execution of the plan was under way. So flawless was the operation that the team was assembled at the RP ahead of schedule.

The movement to the SP was executed with the same precision. This team was really functioning as a unit should. They had achieved the optimum efficiency and just in time. This would be their final preparatory exercise. The next time would be for real, with real lives on the line. The execution by the individual elements went off without a hitch. The POWs, this time there were five of them, were rescued, and the medics moved in to tend to their physical needs. The M-151A1s were brought forward, and the passengers were loaded into the vehicles.

The vehicles then made the trek to the coastal area that had been selected as the staging site for the rubber rafts. The inflatables were manipulated and the passengers loaded into the four rafts. Each man operating an M151A1 was responsible for guiding the rubber boats to the rendezvous point with the submarine that was on site but remained submerged. When the rubber boats were in position, the sub rose a few feet so the conning tower was just over the surface, and the passengers were then discharged into the sub.

At this point, there was a major surprise in store for the team. Stidham, who had accompanied the POWs in one of the rubber rafts, informed the four operators that they would be joining the POWS in the submarine. This was not earth-shattering to the four men; they assumed the entire team would be coming aboard. Stidham informed them that they only would be boarding this vessel and accompanying the POWs to Subic Bay in the Philippines. The remainder of the team had a different exit strategy that involved the use of the boats.

Foster was the first to question the plan. Why was the team splitting up? Look around; there is not enough room on the sub for thirty-two more passengers and the POWs. Why were the medics not accompanying the POWs to Subic Bay rather than the vehicle operators? There was remaining work to get the balance of the team out of the North; their skills might become critical to achieving this. While this was a secondary goal of the mission, it was important. What would be their responsibilities aboard the vessel? They would be at the pleasure of the boat's captain. It was not expected that there would be great demands made upon them. The vessel was fully staffed. There should not be any overwhelming need for their manpower, but they were to be cooperative to any requests made by the captain.

Foster was not happy that his crew was being separated from the team. He felt they had earned the spot and the honor of being with the team when they were recognized for the work they had performed. When it was pointed out to him that his team would be the first to be so recognized, he again questioned the decision. Why would the army not recognize the entire team and all the parts equally? For that matter, why wouldn't the aircraft crew that had worked so diligently to deliver them and make their landings pinpoint perfect be part of that recognition? And the boat crew of the submarine, what about some recognition for them?

Stidham had to tell him the facts of the mission. This is your part of it. The particular skills you bring to the team are used up when the POWs board the ship. We need the medics to ensure treatment for any injuries sustained in the ongoing withdrawal from the area. In spite of their top-secret security clearances, Foster realized that they were not going to be told the details of that strategy. He was beginning to doubt that the team would be reassembled when extraction from the country was accomplished. He was having a very hard time accepting that this was the plan they had developed. He knew he had never heard it discussed, and he was sure that he had not been sleeping through meetings.

If this had been in the plan all along, it had been kept from them. That's the nature of sensitive information; simply having a security clearance for a certain level does not give you a need to know all material cleared to that level. He was realizing that there were still major areas of the army that he had little or no inkling of how they worked. This made the latest nuggets no easier to swallow.

He did know, however, that he had been given an order, and he would carry it out to the best of his ability. He would use his influence to positively affect the men under him to accept their roles as well. He was learning that leadership is not taught. The army had taught him to supervise; leading his troops would require the innate abilities that had been there all along. He could enhance them, but if they weren't present, they would not grow.

After reflecting upon the situation, he decided that it probably wouldn't be that bad—a few days in the ocean without seeing the sunshine—but the duty couldn't be that hard. He would miss the team members, but they would soon show up in Subic Bay, he kept telling himself. With that, he was ready to pursue the plan.

When he repeated the instructions to his team, there were some raised eyebrows. None of them had expected this. They had seen the discussion from a body language point of view that he had carried on with Stidham. They had pretty much adopted the view that they were going to take orders and do as instructed. He was glad that he didn't have to sell them the way that he had made Stidham sell him.

The four men were put ashore from the submarine. They were given instructions to take the M-151A1s by the road network to the air base where they were to prepare them for air travel again. The rubber rafts remained with the balance of the team; they assumed that this meant that there was a need for them in the exit strategy. The exit strategy was, of course, being practiced for the first time. At least this was the first time they knew of its existence.

On the seventh of November, Cho Dinh arrived at Duc Lo with his papers from Tran, authorizing him to supersede any orders given by the ground commander of the infantry regiment that had been sent to Duc Lo. The regimental commander was not thrilled to have this spook looking over his shoulder and "improving" on his orders to his troops. But he knew that if he wanted to survive to become a veteran leader of troops, he would make the most of this situation. He had developed a defensive posture that had it been left in place would have dissuaded the Americans even attempting to rescue anyone from the facility. In his mind, as an infantryman, this made the most sense. Debunk the enemy of the notion that coming in here was going to be easy, usually they either will not come, or they will pause to gather more resources to accomplish the job they have undertaken.

Cho Dinh immediately realigned his defenses. Moving them into more remote areas that had reduced fields of fire, they could still react to an intrusion but at greater risk of discovery and reaction by an incoming force. Still, Cho had been given the authority to countermand his orders; therefore, it was done.

On the morning of November 8, the youngest members of the team were at the assembly area assigned to them at Andersen Air Force Base. As they completed the preparation of the vehicles for the next flight, Wiznewski looked at Nuckles and said, "Through this whole thing, we have been assured that we are part of the team. Today I don't feel like I am part of the same team those guys are. They seem to be on a different team than me."

Nuckles thought about it for a minute and then slowly responded, "When I played baseball, sometimes the coach had to take out a player. For a number of reasons, pitchers were being hit, fielders were missing balls, batters would miss hitting against certain pitchers, but the coach had to decide when to remove a particular player. Maybe this is similar to that."

"Well, I see what you are saying, but I haven't missed a pitch or failed to hit, but I feel like I'm on the bench." Wiznewski was clearly upset that they had been separated from the balance of the team.

"When I played football, I broke my ankle my senior year. I couldn't stand on it during practice for three or four hours, so I didn't go to practice. When the first game came, I went to be on the sideline with the team. The coach told me if I wasn't at practice, I couldn't be at the game. I felt that was unfair then, but I think I understand his thinking a little better now." Nuckles was trying his best to make Stidham's actions make sense to all of them.

Nuckles said, "Sometimes players are put in different positions due to special circumstances. I think we are overreacting to this situation if we make a big deal out of it. Stidham has played fairly with us through this whole process. I think he will now. I wish the operation was going in a different direction, but this seems to be what we have. I plan to keep my mouth shut and see what happens."

Wiznewski turned away and continued to prepare his vehicle. Nuckles was pretty sure he had failed to convince him of the intentions of Stidham in using them. For that matter, he was certain that he had failed to convince himself, but he had arrived at the conclusion that he would do as he was ordered.

Foster walked by Nuckles a few minutes later. "Thanks for trying. I heard what you told him. A little later, I heard him telling Ash the things you said. Maybe you did get through."

"I hope I got through to me." Nuckles was not ready to celebrate that his fellow team member had accepted his advice. He was still working on getting his own mind in the right setting.

Foster thought for a moment and then responded, "We have known from the start that we are different than the others. They are all combat veterans. We are raw rookies. There had to be a reason for them to include us on the team. I believe we are about to find out what that reason is." With that, he finished the preparation of his vehicle. "Now let's get started on our personal gear."

They were soon engrossed in packing chutes and reserves. When that was finished, they began to painstakingly go through the extreme cold weather gear they had salvaged from the last jump. It seemed to be serviceable, so it was packed in the duffels they carried for that purpose. It seemed strange to them to have an entire uniform that was clearly US Army but with no identifying marks of the army, the unit, or the person.

Later in the day, the balance of the team returned to the operations area they had been assigned, and they began to go through the same ritual of preparation that the four had performed earlier. VunCanon came over to Foster and asked him to bring the four into the preparation phase.

Foster informed him that they had already done their preflight checks.

VunCanon explained, "This will not be a normal preflight. We all need to go through it together."

Foster brought the younger element into the area. They laid out their gear. There was a little bit of attitude going on in the area by the time that was accomplished. The first several minutes of the equipment check were standard as they had come to expect. Then VunCanon threw his first curveball at them. "Take off your dog tags. Place them on the floor in front of you. Empty your pockets. Section leaders will approve what can be taken. All items that can be traced to an individual will be removed." Wallets were taken. Then all items that had been removed were placed into large manila envelopes and sealed. The soldier's name was placed conspicuously on the outside. Then the individual signed across the seal of the envelope.

Representatives from the military police were waiting to receive the items, and they were quickly removed from the area. Where they went was a mystery to the men who had given them up. When all was complete, VunCanon moved them to the mess hall, where they enjoyed the air force chow. They never failed to notice that the flyboys ate better than they did.

As they were leaving the mess hall, Stidham asked Foster, "Can I see you and your men for a few minutes?"

"Yes, sir. I think they would like that." Foster was quick to reply.

Within five minutes, they had gathered in the operational area. Stidham took charge. "I know we threw some new things at you out at the submarine. "He cut straight to the chase. "There is a reason for that, and I think you deserve to know what that reason is. There will be a very public face to this exercise. Army forces who are in special operations do not seek nor are they allowed to become popularized. But we need to come away from this operation with a group of soldiers the public can identify. You are that group. You have proven you belong with the best. Now it's your turn to provide that background to pull our nation together. You have a unique opportunity. I don't have to tell you about the war protests that are going on throughout our country. This is your opportunity to set some of that right. What are your questions?"

"Why us?" Ash was the first to speak. "What did we do that we should be taking credit for what these men have accomplished? Why not let each of us say what we did?"

"I think you know from the conversations you have had with the cadre of our unit that they would never seek the publicity, and most of them couldn't or wouldn't deal with it." Stidham was resolute. He wanted them to understand what was being asked of them, but he also wanted them to know that they had no option to fail. This was the psychological side of the mission they had undertaken.

It wasn't like they had envisioned from the start, but it was the part of the stick they had their hands on.

"Tonight, while we are waiting, pick out one or more of these men and talk to them. Ask them if they resent in any way what we are asking you to do at Subic Bay. I think you will find they admire your unique abilities to do these things, but they have no desire to experience them either. They know it's time for them to become old soldiers and just fade away." Stidham made eye contact with every one of the four as he made this impassioned address to them. He knew he had to convince them of the importance of the task they were being asked to take under their wings.

Nuckles looked up. With reticence in his voice, he began slowly to speak. "Sir, if this is what we were recruited for, I would never have volunteered. But here I am. I am a soldier. If these are my orders, I will perform them. Is there not some other way, sir?"

"This is what was decided at levels way above you and me. If you would volunteer, there would be put in place this opportunity not for you but for the military to gain a level of acceptance we haven't had for a long time in our country. It's in your hands. Lead the way."

With that, he had finished his speech. The men sat and asked questions for several minutes. Stidham called for VunCanon and the senior leaders to come join them. There were assurances that the team regarded them as members, that the men with the experience had no desire to participate in the public acknowledgment of the events about to unfold. That they would never be able to accept the accolades that they could see coming their way. They knew this was the better way to handle the situation. Soon the entire team had been summoned, and the results remained the same. "You guys are the future. We are the past. Enjoy your moment. Don't worry about us."

As they returned to the area in which they had been assigned quarters, Ash noticed a small plaque in an unobtrusive area of the post. This was a commemorative reminder of the Thirteenth Seabee Battalion who had worked on this base during World War II. Thousands of men had probably walked by it without noticing it. What caught his eye was that his uncle had served with the Thirteenth Naval Construction Battalion during the war. He was indeed standing on the shoulders of the men who had gone before him.

They were soon asleep in the bunks they had requisitioned for the duration of their stay on this beautiful island. Unknown to them, this would be their only night spent here.

The next morning, November 9, they were up and about their business, doing the physical training that pervaded their lives, eating in the mess hall, and taking care of their personal hygiene. A familiar face came strolling through the area. Bringle was looking for Stidham. They had improvised a security briefing area and were about to discuss the contents of the briefcase that Bringle had, as always, carried with him and prepared to share.

Bringle asked, "Is everything ready here?"

Stidham just as briefly replied, "If everything there is ready for us."

"Here are the latest photos taken this morning." Bringle pulled the pictures from the envelope. "There appear to be six in there today."

"Does it not bother you that they always are in the open when the U-2 flies by?" VunCanon had not planned to verbally participate, but this had been irritating him for some time. It seemed all too convenient somehow that we could always get the shots that would prove the point we wanted to make. Nothing else in his life had ever come that easy; he had to wonder why this would.

Bringle dismissively smiled and said, "We don't bring you the other shots that are empty." With that, VunCanon decided to stack arms. He had come this far. Might as well see where this path led. They would fly this evening unless orders to countermand these were received. The men now knew they were indeed on the way.

None of the team noticed that the shots of the prisoners consistently failed to show any of them forward facing. The team had become so used to seeing the prisoners in the confines of the facility that they had not looked for faces. This would become a huge issue for them soon.

As the meeting broke up, Bringle looked at Stidham and asked, "How are the four young guys working out? Are there any problems?"

"No questions with the operation, but they are a little miffed about the submarine. They had given no thought to end of the game at Subic Bay, I guess."

"Do you need me to talk to them? It might help." Bringle did not seem overly enthused. He was having a hard time understanding why these guys would not jump at the chance to become household names throughout the country. He just failed to understand these members of the new generation.

Stidham thought it better if Bringle stayed away from the young guys. They had been professional and courteous to him and the team, but he had no idea how they would react to the agency man. Still, he wanted them to be prepared for the pressure they would experience when they were in Subic Bay, and he knew that he had no resources to adequately prepare them for this experience. So against his better judgment, he acquiesced.

The group was soon assembled. They had the opportunity to question why it was they who would be accompanying the released POWs back to Subic Bay. They expressed their reservations about the likelihood that the public would buy the story that they had been instrumental in affecting the release of the POWs. They did very much agree that the main story line should be the release of the POWs. They would do whatever was necessary to get these six men out of North Vietnam.

Having fulfilled their obligation to Bringle, they were engaged in the preparations for the evening's flight. When the loading of the aircraft was complete, it was time for the noon meal. This would be the last meal before they left. They had all worked up hearty appetites. Had the mess hall crew known the mission upon which they embarked, they would have taken more care in its preparation. The GIs accustomed to army chow, thought they were being treated special anyway.

After a mandatory rest period, the team was assembled for their final dry run through the operation. It was decided that the team medics would accompany the teams due to the coming evening's expected activities. The primary factors in this decision were the recent events with Stidham's "fatal injury" at Ft. Devens and the loss of balance of the element that had seen one member move to the command and control element. Everyone was reminded that the extreme cold weather gear and the oxygen canisters must be buried and hidden to ensure no trace of the unit would be found after their departure. Obviously, this was a part of the plan that had not been practiced previously due to the fact that they had always needed the gear for the next mission. There would be no next after this trip.

The team was confident of their ability to move into the area unnoticed, secure the release of the POWs, and spirit them away from the area. Their biggest concern was that the prisoners not be moved out of the facility before their arrival there. They were thoughtful as each sought any slight advantage they could secure for the success of the mission.

Finally, it was time to move to the C-141, which was ready and waiting for them at the ramp. As they approached the plane, they noticed how the B-52 bombers dispersed around the field dwarfed the plane that would carry them. Even though the C-141 far exceeded the size requirements for their mission, the massive size of the B-52s reminded them of how insignificant they were in the overall scheme of things.

Taking their seats, buckling into the straps, and feeling the plane rumble down the taxiway to the end of the runway, it dawned on them that they were on the way. Unless orders came for them while they were in the air, their next stop would be in enemy territory. They would depend upon their skills, and the element of luck to get them out of the area.

Nuckles and Foster were fighting the urge to go check the lashings on the M-151A1s one last time. They knew they couldn't be up and moving about the cabin during takeoff, but they could hardly sit still either. Ash and Wiznewski seemed to be weathering the anticipated storm better than the other two; all were headed into such a situation for the first time in their young lives.

Finally, they drew the plane's oxygen supply to their faces and managed to appear calm as the plane proceeded on its path. After what seemed like a day-and-a-half flight, the warning light was lit. They were soon in position to jettison the equipment upon the loadmaster's signal. Then it was time for them to go out from the plane. Each stick exited the aircraft just as they had practiced so many times previously. They were irretrievably on their way now. They were beyond the scope of being recalled.

As they descended through the night sky, it was amazing the difference they noted. While all their practice jumps had been made over military installations, which tended to have less lighted areas than the rest of the areas they had jumped into, they had never jumped into so dark an area as they were descending upon this evening. It was disorienting; the darkness removed any semblance of being able to judge the horizon as they came down. They were dependent upon the equipment they had brought with them totally to maintain their relationship to vertical.

Eventually after what seemed like an hour but was much shorter than that, the parachutes were popped open by the pressure devices that they had depended on for the purpose. Again, the equipment performed flawlessly. There were pops and grunts heard only above the ground as chutes opened and bodies strained with the effort to conform to the new speeds they had been slowed to accommodate. It was time to look for landing spots. They had hoped to land in a small clearing about a mile and a half from the facility itself. Given the factors of wind speed, direction, and the vagaries of getting out of the plane at the split second programmed into the landing plan, they never knew if some last second maneuvering would be necessary to keep them out of various hazards that might impede their landing.

As they surveyed, the LZ the team members were pleasantly surprised to find that they and their equipment had arrived flawlessly in the very spot they had planned to be centered. The air force was due some major kudos; Stidham was thinking as he watched the figures below him alighting in the night and beginning to secure the LZ. Soon all team members were grounded, and the details were burying the unnecessary gear. It was certain that the cold weather gear would not be missed here. In the evening darkness, it felt like it was around ninety degrees Fahrenheit as they worked. They had definitely not grown acclimated to this heat.

Completing the initial phase of the removal of the traces of the team's arrival, the men were soon moving to the RP where they confirmed that all had arrived safely and were taking positions for the move to the SP. This was a move of about a mile and was completed in less than an hour. With the restrictions of noise and light discipline, it was no surprise that the move was so arduously completed. Once again, there was no sign of enemy knowledge of the arrival or the subsequent deployment of the force.

Stidham had taken time during the move to the RP to speak to the four M151A1 operators and to assure them that they were a critical element of the team's operation. He left them with the reminder that they were not to bring the vehicles forward without his direct order. In the case of his incapacitation, it would be Captain Mizell's responsibility to order them into the active engagement area.

Nuckles had quietly remarked to him at the conclusion of his statement, "Sir, this is the smoothest we have ever moved into an area. Is this an omen?" He remembered the tales that he had heard the seasoned men relate that when things started off smoothly, they often became disasters when the operation got serious.

Stidham, recalling similar tales, spoke to assuage his concerns. "No, son, this is a sign that we are executing a well-prepared plan that is going to get these men out of here." With that, he nodded toward the vicinity of the Duc Lo facility. All four of the young men hoped that he was correct in his assessment of the situation. He quickly moved on to his other duties, leaving them to contemplate the beginning of the exercise and their participation in it.

At 0400, the lead element moved out on their way to the launch point of their part of the operation. They had the furthest movement to get into position. They were followed by the second and third elements that went off at 0415. Since they would be coming into the area from 180 degrees opposite of each other, they were synchronized in their movements. The fourth element went at 0430 and was followed by the command and control element at 0435. By 0530, all elements had reached their intermediate points, had radioed their arrival to Stidham, and were awaiting the movement to contact.

The movement to contact had been planned for 0600, thirty minutes before nautical sunrise. At this time, there would be sufficient ambient light to allow the teams to see their intended destinations and any impediments, but it would still be early enough to achieve the surprise of being the overwhelming force they planned to display to the lightly defended facility.

As they moved down the designated avenues of approach, they did so thinking that everything had gone so well. They would soon be heading for home with some homesick guys. When all elements were in position, Stidham gave the signal, and they all left the cover of the final position they had taken and moved toward the objective. Abramson's team took the first salvo, as the force watching his avenue opened up from the front with light arms and a machine gun. Reacting immediately, Sergeant First Class DeWitt tossed a hand grenade in the direction of the machine-gun nest.

At the same time, the other three elements were hit with the same surprise and ferocity. Also, at this point, the forces that had been strategically placed away from the facility came into the action as they closed from the rear upon the individual elements. Stidham had dispatched VunCanon to assist the Abramson element when he heard the firing open up from that direction. This saved his life for the time being as the rear element came under fire from the force hidden in the deep vegetation that the rangers had used for cover only minutes before.

A light flashed in Stidham's mind, and too late he knew what had bothered him about the POW photos. He had never seen their faces. These photo ops had been staged. He knew they had been set up. He realized the desperate state of their condition.

Gibson took a direct hit from an AK-47, and he was down immediately. He was fatally wounded without ever firing a shot. The balance of the team was not taken so easily. They began responding to the incoming rounds they had taken, but they were in the vulnerable positions of being on the approaches to the facility. The enemy commander had effectively preplanned the massing of fires from his advantageous positions and was pouring fire into all four elements as well as the reaction team. Through all this, the M-151A1s had remained in their position of cover. They had not been ordered forward and had held fast at the designated point.

Stidham, upon seeing Gibson take the round to his face, signaled for Sergeant Patterson to come to assist him. Patterson braved the direct fire aimed at him in spite of the Red Cross he wore on his arm designating him as a medic. Patterson arrived unscathed to assist Gibson but was only able to see him take his last breath. His wounds were too severe to be able to save him. Patterson scooped him up and carried him back to the area where he knew the four vehicle drivers would be waiting. They were eager to assist him in ministering to the wounds of Gibson, but Patterson made them understand that it was too late to help him.

Stidham had started toward Scandretti's team, but he soon realized that the team was facing overwhelming odds as they continued to absorb fire from dug-in opponents with preplanned firing lanes honing in on them. Even so, the return fire they were massing was beginning to have some effect. Stidham could see several fighting positions now, conspicuous because of the dead bodies of the inhabitants who had been caught in the return fire from his team. He also began to notice in the brush the telltale sign of movements as inhabitants of previously well-defended positions decided to move to safer ground. He had begun to get a pretty good idea of the forces that were opposing them. He knew that his men were terribly outmanned and outgunned. They had obviously not had the advantage of surprise.

As Stidham came nearer to Scandretti's position, he was spotted by one of the machine gunners who had been cutting down Scandretti's team. Firing at Stidham as he moved, the machine gunner caught the major in the legs as he crossed an open area. Stidham managed to dive into the cover of a large bushy clump of vegetation on line with Scandretti's only remaining fire team of White and Humboldt. Humboldt had started to provide aid to the team members who had been hit in the first volley of fire. The fire had been extremely effective, and four of the team members now lay in the brush, having breathed their last. Humboldt had pulled the Red Cross emblem from his shoulder and picked up a rifle and joined up with Staff Sergeant White, and they were effectively pinning down the forces directly facing them. What they didn't know was that there was a force closing in on their rear. Their position was about to become tenuous.

With Stidham close by, they were able to lock their fires and had succeeded in silencing the machine-gun nest to their front when the forces coming from the rear opened up on them. Stidham took what appeared to be a fatal wound as he went down and was not heard to fire again from the position he had been occupying. Humboldt and White decided to attempt to link up with him for the increased fire power and to allow Humboldt to assess the severity of the wounds that Stidham had sustained.

As they moved from the cover of the position they had occupied, they were exposed to the withering fire coming from their rear. They were forced back into the original position but not before Staff Sergeant White had been severely wounded. Humboldt attempted to provide him assistance, but when he saw the exit wound from the RPG that had been loosed on them, he knew that his partner was not going any further with him. He noticed a faint trail leading back around to the area they had come from. Grabbing White in a fireman's carry, he hit that trail running, the body of White shielded him from the fire that was initially directed their direction. Soon he had entered a small ravine, which shielded them from the view of the closing force from the rear. With a great expenditure of energy, he was able to carry the body of his friend into the area now occupied by the four M-151A1 operators and Sergeant Patterson. Patterson came over, and soon the two medics knew that there was nothing more that they could do for Staff Sergeant White.

After absorbing the initial blast, Abramson's team had managed to get two fire teams into position to return fire. They had effectively silenced the machine gunner who had had them in his sights when the firing commenced. They had taken out at least seven other fighters who had exposed themselves to the deadly fire the team was returning. Just when it appeared they might be able to mount an organized counter attack, a lone soldier with an RPG (rocket-propelled grenade) played an important hand in the battle. His fire had taken out the team of Abramson and DeWitt. This had turned the tide back in favor of the defenders. Subsequently, the element was left with no leader and only two members still functioning. Sergeant Brown and Specialist 4 Yount had not been hit. They had been the two least senior members of Abramson's element, but they had performed well during the training phase of the operation. In spite of being the last two members picked for the team by Stidham, they had functioned efficiently in getting the team ready for its mission. In spite of the spotty performances they had presented in the past, they had done well during the planning and practice phases of this operation.

Now they were left on their own to attempt to link up with any other survivors of what they now knew to be the doomed attack. They were still moving, so they were still trying. Instead of heading for the area they knew that the fourth element should have been attempting to make their approach from, they moved further out from the avenues of approach and attempted to reach the SP. As they came around behind the fourth element, they were able to cut off the forces that had been delivering the fatal fire from the rear of that element and silence their fires. Unfortunately, this action came too late, for the entirety of that element had already been neutralized.

As they reached the SP, they were stopped by what was now with them an eight-man team. They did not yet know it, but they were the survivors of the raid on Duc Lo. A very well-meaning group had gone in to do what had not been accomplished since World War II—the release of a large group of American POWs from an enemy-held facility. In twenty-two minutes, this fine group of American fighters had been decimated, twenty-two of them lay severely injured or mortally wounded. As they observed the area, now in full sunlight, they saw an officer of the NVA come out of the facility. Thinking they were about to be offered a chance to recover their dead and wounded, Patterson with the assistance of Humboldt, was already organizing the men into teams for the grisly task.

Brown looked at the NVA officer; he recognized Cho Dinh from dealings he had endured during his first tour in South Vietnam. He grimly nodded at the man; you won't have to worry about any wounded when he gets through. At that moment, Cho Dinh had given an order and, the deployed troops around the area had begun to gather the American bodies into a group. As they were roughly handled, some could be heard to groan. When he had counted twenty-two, he looked into the woods in the opposite direction from the SP. In very good English, he declared, "If you throw down your weapons and come out peacefully, we will treat you humanely. If you continue to resist, we will hunt you down and kill you. We know that Marty Bringle sent you here. We know there are twenty-four of you on this mission. This is your last chance. You have two minutes."

When two minutes had passed, he pulled his pistol and walked to the first American body. He calmly put a round between the eyes of First Sergeant VunCanon, and then he moved to the second body and repeated the performance. After eleven occurrences of this grisly dance; he paused and once again addressed the American troops whose location he obviously did not know since he continued to face 180 degrees away from them.

"This is your last warning. You will be hunted down and shot by the forces of the NVA. You will not survive." He again pulled out his pistol and started the execution of men who were already dead or soon would have been. Finally coming to the last body, he recognized Stidham, whom he had faced on other fields before this day. With an evil grin, he crowed, "Here's one for your dead leader."

Cho Dinh had turned to where he thought the other Americans were taking refuge in the woods. As he turned, Stidham, who had been severely wounded, was able to withdraw his .45 caliber sidearm. As Cho turned back toward him, it took a split second for him to register what had happened. As he fired into Stidham, there was no gloating, for launched from the weapon held in Stidham's hand had come a bullet straight and true. Cho Dinh joined his ancestors on that field, dead before he was on the ground. Stidham was similarly wounded and the blood spurted from his head wound.

The men under Cho Dinh's command had obviously had enough for the day. They began to go about the task of gathering their own dead from the bushes and fighting positions where so many had struggled during the short but deadly firefight. They seemed to be in no mood for further search for any remaining Americans at that time. They did send a single search team in the direction Cho Dinh had seemed so confident that the Americans would have taken.

On the morning of the tenth, after three days of silence between the co-commanders, at sunup, there had been the arrival of the Yankee team. They had been soundly defeated but not without the useless loss of fifty-eight of his good infantrymen. Before there had been time to recover their bodies, there had been the incident with Cho desecrating the bodies of the wounded and dead Americans. The field commander had started to protest when he realized what Cho had in mind, but he had not been able to stop it.

When Stidham had, as it were, risen from the dead to shoot Cho just as he had sustained a fatal wound, the commander had struggled to contain his emotions. His admiration of the invading officer, whom he assumed to be American, could scarcely be kept under wraps. He had given orders then that the bodies of the invaders be treated the same as the bodies of his men. They had all been placed in a mass grave. He was somewhat concerned about Cho's assertion that there were twenty-four Americans involved. He would have dearly loved to know the source of that intelligence. His instincts told him that he would never find out.

He had walked out to the area to inspect the bodies. He, as the others gathered about, and even Cho had assumed that the invaders were American. He was thinking of the political flak that the politicos would make of that. Upon closer inspection, he found that the uniforms were nondescript with no unit patches, rank emblems, name tapes, or even US Army tapes common to the jungle fatigues normally worn by the Americans. He ordered one of his soldiers to empty the pockets of DeWitt. Of course, he did not know that it was DeWitt. There was no identity card in any pocket, and there was no identification tags found on the body.

He had immediately radioed his higher headquarters to alert them. He had made sure to avoid asserting that the invaders were American. He suspected that they were, but he had no proof. While his electronic eavesdroppers were doing the things that they did; they had come upon a signal emanating from near the Gulf of Tonkin. Looking at the map, he surmised that the surviving party of the Americans were contacting a boat, possibly a submarine in the area for pickup. He had ordered an immediate heavy shelling of the vicinity from which came the transmission.

Immediately after ordering the shelling, he had dispatched a company of infantry to the area. They had found the four tangled M-151A1s with two bodies inside. Additionally, they had located the remains of two rubber boats that were surmised to have been for the escape. These had been way beyond any hope of repair. The jeeps, while severely damaged, would be taken to Hanoi, where they would be evaluated for salvage or repair as possible.

The young lieutenant who had been placed in charge of the taking of this portion of the American team was happy to report that the vehicles had been located, pretty much destroyed, and the remaining two Americans found dead in the wreckage. They had secured the vehicles and equipment, never noticing that much of the damage to the vehicles and the radio equipment was due to sabotage rather than the artillery barrage that had been unleashed upon them. This was the last fortunate break the Americans who were now desperately trying to depart the area were to receive that day.

The company of soldiers who were to deploy to the south within the next few days were happy to return to their base. They had no inkling that the eight Americans were now heading for the HCM trail that they would be using in a few days themselves. The Americans had been given a head start. Unfortunately for them, the trail was not closed for repairs before their arrival. While it was a wide area stretching as much as fifty miles across, there were always units under way to the south and others returning to the north. The odds of detection were great.

The regimental commander of the NVA might have been more inclined to take a personal interest in the attempt to rescue the POWs had he been included in the planning of the defense. However, he had been omitted, snubbed in front of his own troops who he was now expected to lead into combat in the south. He was in no mood to figure out the politics of the situation. There were plenty of people in Hanoi who would bend the facts to their liking. He knew that his portion of the defense had been completed, and he was already worrying about getting his troops deployed. He had turned off Duc Lo.

Indeed, when the burial detail had finished its grisly tasks, he gave the orders, and the troops were on their way back to the garrison they had left fifteen miles away. They were happy to leave the area. Some had left good friends there, but they would not be coming back to visit them.

By the time Tran had learned of the death of Cho Dinh, the military force had moved from the area and was on their way to achieve other goals in other places. Cho had never told him the name or unit of the men he had had working for him. Tran thought about the events and the political gain that could have been gotten from it and then thought about what he knew of the origin of the operation and the financial impact that he was now prepared to garner from raiding Cho's offshore accounts and decided to leave it alone. The army would have to deal with what had happened. This buck was going to stop at Cho Dinh.

Meanwhile, the eight survivors from the American team had withdrawn as far as they dared until they had made a plan.

Foster told the three sergeants, "We need to get closer to the Gulf to be able to reach the submarine. That will also allow us to erect the antenna for contacting them." Brown was immediately in his face.

"You are very junior here. We will give the orders." He indicated the other two sergeants present and then added, "Even Yount outranks you. We will follow the chain of command."

Foster shrugged and evenly replied, "I wasn't trying to give you orders. I was simply telling you what we have to do to make the equipment work, Sergeant." It was obvious to the others that this had not started well.

After some comparisons of date of rank, it was discovered that Sergeant Brown was indeed the senior man, and command would descend upon him. Humboldt and Patterson seemed relieved that they were not the senior men remaining as they had never aspired to troop leading duties. Brown then decided that it would not be safe to move the M-151A1s, and they would be blown in place. Patterson pointed out to him that without the vehicle batteries, they could not operate the radio equipment. Further, the noise of blowing the vehicles in place would be greater than the noise of starting the engines.

At about this time, Ash, who had been placed as rear guard against the possibility of the NVA catching on to their real direction from the Duc Lo facility, came into their midst with the observation that there was a large amount of vehicle traffic coming and going from the facility. If they went now, they could get out with the cover of the enemy vehicles' noise.

There was no discussion they were two-by-two into the quarter tons and rolling toward the Gulf of Tonkin in seconds. There was no indication that they had been observed. Sergeant Brown had ended up as the passenger in the vehicle operated by Nuckles.

"Why would Foster challenge my authority back there?" Brown wondered out loud.

Having seen the volatility of the sergeant, Nuckles paused for a bit before replying, "I don't think he was challenging your authority. I think he was reacting to losing our team leadership. He was, in my opinion, saying that someone needs to be in charge, and here's some information that person needs to know, and we need a decision fast."

Brown looked over at the young man. "Do you think I have blown it with the team. Will they follow me?"

"You are the only one with combat experience. We have no choice but to follow you. You have to lead us. That cannot be just a daily greeting from now on."

They rode on in silence. When they reached the forks in the road that the drivers had memorized, they quickly dispersed into the woods. Soon the antenna that would allow them to summon assistance was growing up in the wooded area. For the first time since they had heard the first burst of fire that morning, they felt a ray of hope.

When the antenna was in place, Foster looked at his watch and declared, "We are in the time window for communications with our ride home. Private First Class Nuckles, would you place the call?"

Nuckles quickly made the call with the appropriate call signs and countersigns. When the submarine commander came on the speaker, they all knew they were on the way.

"How many packages do you have?" This was the expected query from the navy captain.

Quickly, Nuckles responded, "Zero, sir."

Their hearts sank deeper than the submarine was capable of achieving when the reply came. "Then we will not make a rendezvous."

Abandoned by the navy, they realized the stark desperation of their situation. They had three days of rations, they were nineteen miles from Hanoi, and there were a bunch of pissed-off NVA looking for them.

Nuckles thought about the conversation he had held with Brown as they left the Duc Lo area. A thought was forming in his mind that just might buy them some time and allow them to get to a better area for them to survive. Brown was already inspecting the rubber rafts they had packed into the crates. They had picked up two of them before their hasty departure from Duc Lo. His hopefulness was short lived. "We couldn't have gotten to the sub anyway. Our boats were shot up. These should have been moved down here last night. They would have been away from the firefight." It was obvious from his voice how deeply disappointing this was to him. "I think I could get us to Da Nang if these worked."

Wiznewski looked at the remnants of the rubber crafts as Brown held them up. "Any chance of repairing them?" he asked this hopefully.

"No, the damage is too extensive." Brown was not able to give them any hope even though there were repair kits in each package. As he said, to get these craft waterproof would have taken much more than these meager repair kits.

Nuckles had been thinking while this conversation had taken place. "If we remote the antenna from the quarter tons, we could depress the send button. They told us in school that if we held down the send button more than ten seconds, that would allow the enemy to triangulate on us, and we would probably have a mortar or artillery round come our way shortly."

"What good is it going to do for us to get our jeeps blown up?" Specialist 4 Yount had not made any comments in the conversation. Now he added, "Can't we just drive to the South?"

"I don't imagine they are going to let us just drive through the countryside." Brown was beginning to see the logic behind Nuckles's idea. "If we put Gibson's and White's bodies into the jeeps, the NVA may think they have us and give us some breathing room. After all, I heard Cho Dinh say they knew there were twenty-four of us. They have twenty-two bodies, this would be all accounted for. But who says we are going south? Why don't we go to Hanoi? I hear that Jane Fonda is in Hanoi. Maybe we could get close enough to assassinate her. That would be worth the trip over here."

Nuckles was scared not so much that these words had come from Brown's lips but by the gleam in his eyes. Nuckles had known some crazy people in his life, and he was afraid that he was about to add another to his list of contacts. "Do you not think that eight of us walking into Hanoi would be a little bit noticeable? We would stick out like sore thumbs." He said it in a nonthreatening way, but the other six were hoping that Brown would realize the foolishness of his suggestion. None of them were really interested in taking such a chance to get close to Jane Fonda, beside which they didn't really know if she was even in Hanoi.

Brown thought about this for a minute. Then there was a visible lightening of his mood. "Well, I guess going south does make more sense. We'll hit the trail (Ho Chi Minh), but here's the deal. That trail is not just a path through the jungle. It may be fifty miles wide in places. The NVA have improved it in areas so they can move motorized vehicles down it. There may be units moving in the same area we are trying to move. I say we attack them and kill as many as we can."

No one wanted to argue with him, but the men were not eager to attack an overwhelming force either. Finally, Patterson told him, "I think we have to be careful of who we attack. We have a very small amount of ammunition. We can't afford to get into a firefight with a large unit. That would be suicide on our part."

"Yeah, it would, wouldn't it?" Again, Brown had that gleam in his eyes. Nuckles had seen it before. He didn't know if any of the rest of the survivors had or not. He was really getting concerned, but this was not the time or the place to discuss the mental state of the leader of the party. He decided to keep his mouth shut, but his eyes would be wide open.

They moved to the vehicles and placed the two bodies in the two lead ones. The antenna mast sections were erected, and Ash was about to connect the radio. Nuckles said, "Wait a minute." He went to the package of equipment that had been dropped and pulled out a long coil of coaxial cable and began to fasten the section to the lead coming from the mast. "They said this would lead to a loss of acuity in the transmission, so we should avoid doing this, but we want to get as far away from this antenna as we can when our visitors start to come in from afar." He added the last to bring the members of the team who had not attended the course on radio procedures up to date. "Since we are just going to transmit and not receive any communication, we don't have to worry about degradation of signal over the wire." He added the latter for their benefit. Foster could have kicked himself. He had been through the same course, but he had not thought of this use for the equipment. This just might save their lives, at least for the time being.

In short order, the antenna was erected, and the entire cable had been extended. Removing a roll of fifty-mile-an-hour tape from his pack, Nuckles looked around the group. "We better decide which way we're going and get started in that direction. When I depress the send button and tape it down, they say we have ten seconds. I don't know how effective these guys are in triangulating, but we have to plan for pretty good. I would say fifteen seconds tops plus a minute to order artillery fire and maybe a minute to acquire the grid coordinates. Then maybe thirty to forty seconds in flight. In three minutes, company will be arriving. We need to be a long way from here. On top of that, people will come pouring over that ridge in another ten minutes."

Sergeant Brown took charge. "We will go this direction he pointed to the southwest. For the first twenty minutes, we need to cover ground as fast as we can. After that, we should be far enough away to assume stealth mode. Yount, you and I will take the trail positions. Try to leave as few signs as possible. We will clean up what we can as we come."

"What about contact with humans?" Sergeant Patterson asked quietly.

"If they are few, take them out, observing noise discipline. If they outnumber us, try to avoid contact. Remember, if we start firing Betsy"—he indicated his M16A1—"we will be in a real bind shortly. They have all the numbers to take us out. Stealth and deception are the two best allies we have on our side right now. We do not want to lose either of them. We should be all right to head in this direction. From what I remember of the topo (topographic) map Major Stidham showed us back at Campbell, there are no houses shown for quite a way."

Brown asked Humboldt and Wiznewski to take the point, followed by Ash and Patterson, and then Nuckles and Foster, with the rear being manned by him and Yount. This was as balanced a formation as they could manage. He was considering changing the fire team partners as they came out onto the HCM trail, but that was for later. Right now they needed to hurry out of the vicinity.

Looking at Nuckles, he made a wrapping motion, indicating that the button should be depressed. Motioning to Humboldt and Wiznewski, he gave the move-out signal, and they were on their way. None of them knew the dangers that lay ahead, but they fully expected it to be dangerous. They knew the odds were they would not make it out of this country alive. They were committed to doing their best and making as much impact as possible on the enemy's ability to cross the border into their neighbor's country and wage war.

They moved rapidly through the increasingly dense undergrowth they encountered for thirty minutes. They were covered with sweat, and the exertion was beginning to tell on them. They had brought two canteens of water per man. They were forced to use some of the first canteen due to the level of exertion they were experiencing. Thankfully, Patterson had insisted that every man carry enough pills to chlorinate drinking water for four days. There appeared to be a gracious plenty of water in the area. How clean it might be was anybody's guess. Their halt was brief, long enough to get a sip of water and evaluate their back trail. There was no sign of anyone following them at this point.

Brown knew they should move on while they had this slight advantage. They were not likely to gain any further advantages, save through their determined efforts and continuous movements. The deck was indeed stacked against them.

They were ready to move now. Brown motioned Ash and Patterson to the point with Foster and Nuckles following. He and Yount split up, with Yount joining Humboldt in the third tandem and Brown and Wiznewski occupying the trail position. Again, they were paying as close attention as possible to obliterating any telltale signs of their passage. As yet, there was no sign that their presence had been detected. Brown knew very well that an experienced tracker would have followed them as if he had taken the interstate highway system. He was hoping that there were no experienced trackers in the group that they might encounter.

By 1800, they had covered about twenty miles as they had stayed in the thickest areas they could and maintained their heading. They prepared to make camp about five miles from the camp the NVA unit had moved to from Duc Lo. They had taken breaks as needed and rotated the point among the teams. Brown had been impressed with the younger men's abilities to observe and move while maintaining their headings. Since they were in for an extended, he hoped, period of movement from dead reckoning, he had to depend upon them to pull their weight. While neither unit was aware of the proximity of the other, their fates had not been completely removed from one another.

The NVA regiment was in fact due to rotate into the south within the next week. When Tran had learned of the fate of his assistant Cho Dinh, he had contacted the command center of the People's Army. He had learned of the plan to move the regiment into the South, and he had tried to find out if any intelligence had been gained from Cho Dinh. He had been able to learn of nothing that had transpired between Cho and the regimental commander. Knowing Cho, he doubted that any bonds had been formed, but he never took chances when he was stealing money from people who would miss it. Therefore, he had encouraged the immediate deployment of the regiment. However, due to the heavy losses incurred in the firefight at Duc Lo, the army was reluctant to deploy the regiment while they were so critically shorthanded. When he pointed out that they would probably have lost that many men while executing the deployment, some of the reticence had disappeared. The unit would be reinforced with reserves available, resupplied, and would move out in three days.

This would accomplish Tran's goal of getting the unit commander out of the country before he could figure out what Cho Dinh's interest in this out-of-the-way place had been, or for that matter why he, the director of intelligence, would have so much interest in such an insignificant place.

Bringle had left Guam feeling that his operation had a better than fifty-fifty chance of success. When he had heard the report from Naval Command Pacific Fleet that there was no rescue mission to be undertaken, he knew that the mission had failed. Tuning in to the North Vietnamese traffic being monitored through the NSA (National Security Agency) and the ASA (Army Security Agency), he had pieced together enough information to reach the conclusion that his team had been wiped out. That was bad for Stidham and the boys, but not necessarily bad for him. He would have preferred a successful mission, but to end up with his pockets full of money was not a bad consolation prize.

He had wondered in his mind about the willingness of Barstow to keep giving him money for the operation with very little to show for it. When he arrived back in Washington, he had received some message traffic that began to explain it to him. The traffic had been erroneously sent his way because of the nature of the information. He had been cleared for information about POW rescue missions. It had not occurred to him that there might be more than one of these missions ongoing at the time.

Reading the message he had received, he realized that there was a much bigger picture that he had not been aware existed. Barstow had been using his mission as a diversion for the Son Tay mission, which had the potential to garner a much larger take of rescued POWs. Had it not depended on outdated intelligence reports, it might have been successful.

Bringle decided not to mothball his team's mission for the time being. He had a feeling that there might be a political advantage to playing this information on the intelligence network at some time in the not-so-distant future. He had attempted to send a message through diplomatic channels to Cho Dinh. He had inquired about the status of the rice crop in North Vietnam that year. Since their cover at the peace talks had included the agricultural interest section, he thought he could get the message through without arousing too many suspicions.

When the message came back, he was not surprised. Cho had reported that the entire rice crop had been destroyed by the recent typhoon. There was no surviving area for the crop to be replenished. It would take twenty-four months to begin to recover. Bringle knew this meant that the mission to Duc Lo had been defeated. The North Vietnamese thought they had wiped out the team. They had twenty-four bodies to show for their efforts.

Bringle had no way of knowing that Cho had in fact met his fate at the hands of Stidham on the field outside Duc Lo and that Tran had assumed the monitoring of Cho's messages. Tran had suspected that Bringle or someone on the American delegation was the contact Cho had been working with for some time. He had decided to play this hand and see if he could extort some more money from the West. These men had never met face-to-face but had in fact been in close adversarial roles for many years. Had they each used operational names they had adopted in the past, they would have immediately recognized each other. As it was, it really didn't matter.

Bringle, while assuming he was corresponding with Cho Dinh, had never trusted him personally even though he had relied on the information being passed to him by the Vietnamese. Such was the nature of their business. Now Tran and Bringle would deal with each other due to the death of Cho Dinh. Bringle knew none of this nor did he know that Tran had planned the demise of Cho. The events at Duc Lo had simply saved him the need to cancel or explain the execution of his plan. For Tran, another martyr for the cause had been created.

Bringle decided to start watching the intelligence reports. He realized that there could have simply been a mistake in the body count for the team, but he knew there was a possibility that some of the team had somehow survived. The body count was not his only evidence. There was the fact that the navy had reported that the team had in fact made radio contact with the submarine. While the navy had not seen fit to come after the remainder of the team, this proved to Bringle there were some survivors, possibly eight of them.

Bringle decided he needed to know who the survivors were, how many of them were still functioning, and where they had headed. He knew they had not simply gone to ground and waited for help. He needed information, but only from Cho. He decided to attend another peace-talk session. Barstow was all for it; he was willing to try anything to keep the agency's recent debacles out of the headlines. There would be another meeting the next week.

In the meantime, Bringle went to work on who the survivors might be. It never occurred to him that there would not be an officer or senior NCO among them. He could not imagine a group of junior enlisted men having the ability to survive and function in the area without the leadership of the team. Additionally, he could not conceive of a group of leaders who led from the front rather than the rear. Given his management style, such an outlook was the expected norm. After considering the makeup of the team, he decided that most likely VunCanon had been the most senior to survive. Recalling the deployment sketches and sandbox displays he had been privy to back at Ft. Campbell and remembering how eagerly the junior officers had moved to the front of their teams as they moved, he knew in his heart that only VunCanon could have accepted his place in an area that would have allowed for his survival.

Having arrived at the deduction that it would be VunCanon who was leading the survivors, Bringle needed to think through where he would have taken them. He felt that he would have set out in the rubber rafts that had not been accounted for from the details he had so far received. He began to sort through the reports of vessels in the area. He could find no evidence that any such craft had been spotted and certainly no reports of any being picked up. If they had taken that avenue, they had been swallowed up by the sea during the typhoon, or they had managed to make it to shore and had waited out the storm.

Bringle knew this analysis was not sufficient. There were too many suppositions and not enough details to make a certain determination of the fate of the team. He had not yet decided if he hoped for their survival or if he needed to ensure their demise. Right now he needed more information.

He headed for Paris on the diplomatic plane with many questions weighing heavily on his mind. He had not decided if he wanted the team survivors found or if they needed to disappear. He did know that he needed to position himself to benefit from either outcome.

At the first negotiating session, he was surprised to see that Cho Dinh had been replaced by Hwan Chu, who eagerly came over and shook hands with Bringle as if he were a long lost brother. Bringle was immediately suspicious of the man and decided to set a trap for him. When the young Asian man was unable to provide the details he asked for, Bringle knew that he was not in fact working with Cho Dinh as he had claimed. Cho was no longer part of the team.

The first session was long on bluster, as the Vietnamese lambasted the USA for twice having invaded their territory with unfriendly attacks. The Austrian seemed slightly puzzled by the assertion of two attacks since he knew only of the Son Tay mission. He had not been briefed on the Duc Lo operation. The North Vietnamese went on and on about the sovereign rights of their country. Finally the Austrian rose and responded with a rhetorical. If we are ready to talk about border integrity, let's start with the seventeenth parallel and the repeated incursions your country has made into the South.

Of course, the response was that they had never crossed the seventeenth within the DMZ (demilitarized zone) since they were always careful to cross in Cambodia. Both sides knew this was posturing for later discussions. No real results were expected from this confrontation in any sense of the word. While much of this was posturing and expected by both sides, it was also a source of employment for analysts who would glean information from the details that were revealed in each side's presentation. If one side could be lured into an emotional response, the better chance there was for real information to be dropped into the conversation. Therefore, it was standard practice to attempt to get the other side to vary from their prepared notes.

On this day, there had been that emotional note hit when the North had accused the United States of two invasions. The United States had expected to have to deal with the results of Son Tay, but they had not expected the second accusation. The Austrian had requested documentation of the second incursion. None had been given, as the attacking team had been sanitized before their departure from Guam. Bringle had been confident that they had done a thorough job, but you never knew. The smallest oversight could be turned against you by a crafty foe.

The United States had learned that the North felt there had been a second invasion. The diplomatic corps, as of this moment, were unaware of a second incursion. The lack of an effort to really buttress this allegation led the United States to deem it propaganda for the time being, but it in no way led to the ignoring of the event. If there was something there, they needed to know. As soon as the session was ended, there would be a severe accounting session held with the intelligence portion of the team. This would not be pleasant, but it might prove beneficial to all. The United States had also learned that there was a second facility where POWs were held if a second strike had occurred.

The North had learned that the United States had made pictures of the Son Tay facility and the conditions that the men were held under at that place. This would not bode well for the Vietnamese as they sought to portray themselves as the party who had been fouled in the press. They had also learned that the United States might be conducting operations outside the official channels that they usually employed. They would have to be observant of these developments going forward.

When the session adjourned, Bringle was not at all surprised to be summoned to a meeting with the Austrian. He had in fact expected the invitation. He had made time to alert Barstow to the proceedings and had gotten the okay to brief the team's involvement as a diversionary tactic to the Son Tay operation. When considered as the scope of operations opposed to the larger mission, this was a minor operation simply designed to draw enemy resources away from the primary focal point of the larger mission. The Austrian was not happy that he had not been apprised of the operation sooner, but given the overall insignificance of the tactic, it would be swept under the rug. Since he was told that all elements of the team were lost, he assumed there would be no continuing issues. Case closed.

As a matter of fact, the issue went away and was never mentioned by either side again throughout the negotiations. Bringle and Barstow knew they had dodged a bullet, but they were sure that others would be headed their way shortly.

Bringle, for his part, was not completely satisfied with the information he had gained. He now knew that his contact in the north was no longer reliable if he was even alive. Given the track record of that regime, he now considered Cho Dinh as a former asset. He never expected to hear from him again. He had not gotten any satisfactory vibes from the delegation regarding the disposition of the remnants of the team. He was afraid to quiz anyone directly for fear that they still did not know of the survival of a portion of the unit. This would have possibly led to an intensified search for the men who may have survived. He really felt more positive that there were survivors. He was also sure that the answers to the questions he needed to ask were not to be found in Paris.

He was not an invaluable source of information for the remainder of the meetings in this session, but the Austrian adamantly refused to dismiss him from his obligations to attend. The older man had no intention of being blindsided by allegations of agency involvements in other affairs that he had not been briefed upon. He was insistent that Bringle remain throughout the proceedings. The Austrian also felt that to send Bringle home now would be a sure sign to the North of who the clandestine element of the peace talks team was, in fact. Accustomed to being allowed to operate independently and with little or no direct supervision, he chafed under the restrictions that had been imposed upon him.

He had made some calls to his friends in the field. It seemed that there was no word of any survivors turning up through any agency operation. Similarly, his MACV-SOG (Military Assistance Command Vietnam-Special Operations Group) had heard of no independent operators in their sector. His contacts from allied force nations were likewise unable to provide any information. He was beginning to think that possibly the North Vietnamese had lost the ability to count bodies. Given their propensity for expanding numbers, he doubted that they had lost out on counting. He was becoming perplexed.

Barstow had had troubles of his own. His involvement in the information loop of the Son Tay raid was leading to embarrassing questions about how an elite unit could be sent into North Vietnam to release POWs who had not been in the facility for at least four months. The total reliance on HUMINT (human intelligence), which, in this case, was severely out of date, was being called into question by the oversight committees of Congress. The black eye that had been self-administered was likely to be a slow healing one.

When Barstow learned that the Duc Lo mission had gone sour, he had not been overly concerned. He had regarded it as a diversionary tactic from the beginning. However, he now saw the opportunity to make this look like a coordinated operation rather than what it had been—two independent operations carried out with no coordination or knowledge of the other.

Brown sat them down and quietly put out his orders. They would rest until 2100 and then they would enter a new lifestyle. They would move at night and rest during the day. They had to move from here on as though they were infiltrating to the south, just as the NVA units they might encounter would be doing. It would be foolhardy to attempt to move in the daytime. The NVA would have lookouts posted and watching, and the United States would be apt to attack with air strikes any movements that were attempted. There was no future in daytime operations in this neck of the woods. The path they would take would probably lead them through both Laos and Cambodia. He doubted they would be able to make contact with friendlies in either of those areas, and due to the impunity with which the NVA operated there, they would be in just as much danger there as here. He was not optimistic about their chances of arriving safely in South Vietnam.

He established the security procedures and watch orders, and then they lay down to attempt to rest. Since they had been going for almost forty hours without sleep, the six not on watch were soon asleep. They rotated the watch every ninety minutes until it was midnight. Arising at 2400, they were refreshed but still on the adrenal edge they had experienced since the firefight had broken out early the previous morning. By 0010, they were moving out. They were not sure exactly where the HCM trail started, but they were acting as if they were on it. They moved cautiously but steadily through the early hours, utilizing the darkness to the utmost. When the first signs of light appearing began to show in the east, Brown gave the word. They found a secluded area deep in the jungle and secured the nearby neighborhood.

At 1118, Brown was awakened by Ash who had been on duty with Nuckles. He immediately heard the thrumming of motorized vehicles. "There is a motorized convoy moving about three hundred yards to the west of us," Ash whispered this information to him. "There are about forty APCs, and we counted four command vehicles. So far, their maintenance trains seem to be only two vehicles. Nuckles is observing from the south end, and I was on the northern flank. We have been using hand signals to communicate." He added the last to assure Brown that they had not relaxed their vigilance. Brown quickly awakened Yount and sent him back to the east to watch their rear. They did not need stragglers happening on their happy little enclave.

Moving up to Nuckles's position with as little motion as possible, he worked himself into position to observe the passing of the unit. They seemed intent on moving down the avenue they had embarked upon. Cursory lookouts were posted on the vehicles occasionally, but they were not expecting trouble, so they were not at full alert. Brown could not help thinking how easily they could have been taken out by even a small platoon-sized force, but he had no such force available. All he could do was watch. He sorely missed the PRC-77s that had been lost at Duc Lo. He would not allow himself to speak of that disappointment, however.

"They are moving in daylight," he finally breathed into Nuckles's ear. "We haven't reached what they consider the terminal of the trail. I bet if we were still bombing up here, they wouldn't be moving now." The United States had quit bombing the North two years earlier. There had been little advantage gained from this for the United States, but Brown knew how much easier the flow of men and materiel had become from the North. He was no politician, but he was an infantryman, and he understood that his job had gotten harder.

Even with the enemy movement around them, Foster, when he learned of the movement of the enemy, had grinned. "Well, we are in the right place to travel where we want to go," he stated. "They obviously built the road to avoid any major barriers to getting through the area. They would go around anything major. If we follow the road, we'll come out pretty good."

This had irritated Brown not because it was inaccurate but because he had not realized the importance of this piece of information. They had not completely resolved the conflict between them, and there was still a simmering lack of cooperation between them. Brown resented the younger man's intuitive grasp of the intelligence; Foster did not grasp the seriousness of the resentment festering in the more veteran man.

Brown realized he must adjust the security element to account for the proximity of a high-speed avenue of approach. This he did with thoroughness. They spent the balance of the day resting and waiting for the cover of darkness to take hold so they could continue their movement to the west and south.

On the third day, there were no convoys during the hours of daylight. However, as soon as it was dark, the first convoy was out on the road. They were operating with what passed for blackout drive conditions. As far as the team operating as observers could tell, there were no consequences for these conditions. They never heard any explosions of artillery or aerial bombardment. The movements went on with impunity. It was eating away at them to be able to do nothing about the shipments obviously headed south to aid in the fight against their brothers in arms.

The significance of the transition to night operations was not lost on the men as they watched. They had survived far longer than any of them had feared that they might when they had first grasped the severity of their situation. They were now preparing to enter one of the world's most deadly areas, and they did so not at all hesitantly, but with an added layer of caution brought on by the realization that they might be able to pull off this audacious feat they had entered upon. They had resisted the urge to take out the straggling elements of the motorized movements they had observed. While they could probably have accomplished this, there was way too much risk of those guys calling for assistance, which would overwhelm the tiny team. Better to let them go.

The first three nights on the trail proved to be uneventful. They had selected a little used portion of the trail to begin their move toward the south. They made pretty good time as they moved. Brown estimated they had covered about ten to twelve miles per night. They had their compass, and each section was assigned a pace counter, so they had a fairly accurate estimate of their whereabouts.

The fourth evening, they were faced with a dilemma. They had come to a rather sizable river flowing in the general direction they needed to go. Having no map sheets of this portion of Vietnam, they were unsure of the river or even its destination. They had been striving to reach the highlands and possibly even get into Laos. Brown thought this would be preferable to staying in North Vietnam. He knew that they couldn't follow the stream too far, or they would be heading back toward the coast eventually. Still, the ease of moving downstream had its appeal after the past three nights of hard moving in the dark jungles they had so far encountered.

He decided they would move down the stream for some distance. He knew that eventually he had to depart from the watercourse. They had probably moved three miles when the river made a sharp turn to the left and headed downhill rapidly. Brown knew they had come to the limits of the help that Mother Nature could provide them at this point. As the men came out of the river and headed up the slope on the west side of the waterway, he waited until they had gained almost the highest point of elevation in the area and called a halt.

Patterson and Humboldt began to move around the area they had secured. They had each man remove his clothing and went over them looking for and finding the black leeches they knew would be in the river water. When every man had been de-leeched, they went through the clothes that had been removed and found still more of the parasitic creatures hiding there. Removed from their free rides, the men were glad to leave their passengers at this rest stop.

When the men reached fifteen miles moved for the evening, Brown called a halt. They surveyed the area they had occupied and selected today's bivouac site. They were soon camouflaged and ready for some rest. They had slung their hammocks higher up in the canopy of the trees, so as to be almost undetectable. The trees provided shelter from the top and the foliage and the natural tendency of people to look for people on the ground combining for cover from the ground. About 1100, Foster awakened Nuckles for his two-hour guard period. They had learned to position themselves so that little or no motion would be visible to anyone passing through the area.

Foster was startled when Nuckles grabbed his arm as he was about to lower himself into his waiting hammock. The fear in Nuckles eyes told him something was amiss. Nuckles pointed behind him. On the ground about twenty feet to the rear was the largest head of a snake Foster had ever seen. Visible from where he stood was at least twelve feet of body, and it was not growing smaller as it disappeared into the undergrowth of the jungle. He guessed that it must be twenty feet long. The monster was headed directly toward Brown as he slept in his hammock.

Foster knew he couldn't wake Brown. Any sudden movement he might make in awakening would attract the attention of the mammoth snake. He motioned to Nuckles to move to the left away from the path of the snake and wake Ash and Patterson who had selected spots in that direction. Soon the four of them were considering the situation. In the meantime, the snake had moved even closer to Brown. Patterson had identified it as an anaconda. He motioned that the snake would squeeze its prey to death and then ingest it. There seemed a very good chance it thought of Brown as that prey.

All four men had their machetes at hand. Patterson, with hand motions, coordinated the attack. All four descended upon the creature at once. The power of the snake was awesome, but it could not withstand the repeated battering it took from the machete-wielding men. Still, it took almost ten minutes to subdue the behemoth that had happened upon their space.

Brown had awakened during the melee to see the struggle taking place right at his resting place. The entire team was, of course, awake by the time the struggle was completed. Brown noticed that the closest man to his position when he awoke was Foster. There was a moment of reconciliation between the two when the battle was finished. Nuckles hoped this was a sign that the two could begin to work together with less tension between them.

When the end had come for the snake, the men gathered around. Quietly, they wondered at the size of the animal. It was as thick as a man's waist. When stretched out to its full length, Nuckles, Foster, Ash, and Wiznewski, who had never seen one of these creatures before, stretched out on the ground beside it. It was about two feet longer than their combined height. Humboldt had seen evidence of a path through the jungle. He assumed that this meant people were nearby. With the assistance of Wiznewski and Nuckles, he found a long thin tree close by. He soon had cut the tree down, trimmed the limbs away, and with his crew wrapped the snake around the pole.

Carrying the load between them, they followed the path as far as they dared. As they began to see signs of usage of the footpath, they placed the pole with its load across the path and beat a hasty retreat. They had not seen anyone and hoped no one had seen them. As they returned to the site of the recent struggle, they noticed that everyone had secured their belongings in preparation to move out. Brown questioned Humboldt about what they had seen and instructed them to prepare to move. Brown reminded them that while he appreciated that they saved him from the creature, they could not afford to drop their security veil when something happened inside the perimeter. They needed to get out of the area pronto.

That was the first time they violated the commitment to move only at night. For the balance of the day, they moved rapidly, not without caution but as quickly as was feasible. By the next dawn, they had covered an estimated twenty miles. More importantly, they had gained the perceived cover of the higher elevation of the highlands. Brown, Yount, and Patterson had all spent considerable time in the highlands of South Vietnam. They assumed that this would be an advantage for them here.

They made their camp and prepared to rest for the day. Guards were assigned and sleep rotations planned. They had noticed a change in the atmospheric pressure of the area. At first, Nuckles had assumed that it was simply a result of the change in elevation. They had gained over a thousand feet in elevation during their extended movement. When he mentioned it to Patterson, he shook his head. Nodding at the sky, he said, "I was trying to avoid mentioning it, but since you noticed, I will tell you. We are in for a storm. I understand they have some doozies around here."

Week 11

Dallas 16–Green Bay 3
Baltimore 21–Chicago 20

As the afternoon wore on, the clouds continued to build from off the coast. As they came down a path in what they thought was deep jungle, they came upon a structure that set out by itself. About three hundred yards away, they could make out a rough structure from which came the sounds and smells of humanity. Investigating the first structure, they came upon a bull water buffalo. The remainder of the structure was dedicated to storage of food for the beast.

By this time, they all sensed the gathering storm. Patterson warned of the rising winds; he had been through a typhoon during his time in country previously. He did not want to face one in an unsheltered area. As the wind speed increased in intensity, they knew that this was the only shelter available to them.

The water buffalo was huge, weighing at least eight hundred pounds by Nuckles's estimate. Brown had drawn his machete as soon as he had seen the animal. It was evident that the water buffalo terrified him, and his intention was to eliminate it. Nuckles quietly began to talk to the animal and succeeded in getting it into a corner of the stable it occupied. Turning to Brown, he said, "I think you can put that away for now. He won't hurt anyone. Unless he steps on someone, he can't inflict any damage. Look at that tongue, he wants to give you a sugar." They all laughed nervously, unsure how Nuckles had become such an expert on animal psychology.

By this time, the rest of the team had gathered around. Comments were made about killing the animal and cooking him, but no one seemed to have any real desire to butcher the old water buffalo. Brown still wanted to be rid of him. Nuckles asked, "If we kill him, what are we going to do about that family up there in the house? Without their water buffalo, they can never survive on this piece of land. We might as well go in there and kill them now. It will save them from starvation."

Brown knew they could not do that. "Well, here's the deal. You stay here with the animal and keep him under control or we take him out." He indicated Nuckles. "The rest of us will bed down in the storage area. Hopefully, this thing will blow on out of here tomorrow."

Patterson, who had been through one of these monster storms, knew the storm would be with them for two or three days at least. He did not see any need to set Brown off any more than he had been already, so he kept quiet.

Brown was already establishing security procedures when Wiznewski said, "Visitor coming from the house."

Brown moved them into the storage area behind a partition. "If they come and feed the animal, good for them. If they come past the corner of the partition, we have to take them out." Such were the choices the men had to make. While they bore no ill will to this family caught in the path of the war, their instinct for survival demanded they be prepared to take extreme action if necessary. Several of them were becoming aware that the definition of necessary varied, based on the individual. They were finding that there was a defining line, which most of the team seemed to stand on one side. More and more they realized that Brown was on a different side of that line. To this point, they were unsure of where Yount stood in relationship to the line.

As the door to the shed was pushed open, they could see the young preteen boy who had come to feed the water buffalo. He petted the animal and gave him food and water. He was careful to keep his eyes away from the storage room except to pick up the forage and place it for the animal. Foster thought that he was aware of their presence and was making sure that he gave no sign of suspecting their presence.

When he finished his chores, he quickly moved out of the building and returned to the house. He didn't run, but he didn't dally around either. "Probably not the first time someone has taken shelter in their barn, given the location. He may have even thought we were NVA on the way south." Humboldt was trying to head off any thought by Brown of going into the farmhouse and committing mayhem.

Brown snorted, "You guys are making every excuse for not doing what we know has to be done." Amazingly, after that, he let it go, at least for the time being. By this time, the rain had set in, and it was coming in sheets.

Water was soon standing around the building, unable to run away from the structure as fast as it was falling. The little stream they had noticed cutting through the edge of the field behind them was running bank full within minutes and continuing to rise. Moving out of the structure was not an option.

There had been no sign of anyone leaving the house during the storm to this point. They felt relatively secure in that even if the little boy had suspected their presence, no one had made any move to report it to the local authorities. How long would their luck hold out?

There was no way for them to know that there had been a raid on the POW facility at Son Tay carried out by special forces troops who had come in helicopters to relieve a large prison population believed to be housed there. There had been no POWs found there either. The force had not been ambushed and had made it out with only a few minor incidents affecting the force. They had been a diversionary tactic to this operation; now the major thrust was providing a diversion for them. The NVA had immediately rushed troops away from this area to defend the region around Son Tay. They feared an invasion from the south was being launched.

Meanwhile, the rains continued. Water was now running through the barn. Nuckles and the water buffalo had moved to the upper end of the stable, where they had been able to remain dry for a time. Now the entire floor was under water. How long could the rain continue? The water was now up to their ankles. The balance of the team had moved into the rafters, trying to stay as dry as possible. The stability of the building was becoming an issue as the waters compromised the foundation of the structure.

As the gray of dawn welcomed the second day of the storm, they surveyed the tiny building in which they huddled. The water now was over their knees, and the force of the water against the building was ever increasing. During the night, Nuckles and Foster had thought of creating a pressure relief by opening the door at the front of the building. They had then created an opening in the rear of the building between two of the poles that had been erected to form the upper portion of the building. This seemed to be working as the pressure on the walls seemed to have relaxed a little. This now created a new issue as they had to be careful of moving around the openings and being seen from afar. So far, no one had come to investigate.

Around 1100, the winds died down, and there was a peaceful calm that prevailed. Ash and Wiznewski were on watch when the change occurred. They immediately alerted Brown. Brown informed them to keep watch; the team would not be moving right away. They had to be careful; the farm family would be coming to see about the water buffalo. Sure enough, in a few minutes, the same young man came out across what was now a lake to take care of the animal.

He did not seem surprised by the opening of the door or the wall. Indeed, he simply talked to the animal as he pulled wet forage from the store room and placed it in a mangerlike device for the huge animal to enjoy. Very quickly, he had finished his chores, and he was gone. Once again, there had been no hint of recognition of the presence of the team as they huddled out of the line of sight he had. They assumed he had not seen them or had chosen not to acknowledge their presence unless he was forced to do so.

By 1300, the eye of the storm had passed. The winds were quartering from the other direction, and the rain was coming as fast as ever. The respite had ended. The team had used the time to its advantage as Patterson had anticipated the return of the storm, seemingly from the other side. The openings in the building, improvised during the night, were improved to allow a greater flow of water through the building. Some items were moved to give greater visual sight lines to the lake now surrounding them. Working against them were the volume of water, which had already inundated the area, the inability to get to any place needing repair that would place them in visual contact with the farmhouse, and the sight lines provided by the open waters of what was now a lake covering the farm. They had yet to realize that the occupants of that structure were involved in their own struggle to survive and had not decided to involve themselves in the lives of the occupants of their barn, if indeed they were aware of their presence.

As evening came, the howling winds continued to buffet the building the team occupied. They had considered making a run for higher ground when darkness had come. However, as the rain increased, they had opted for remaining in the little structure. They knew they could not remain here for much longer. Even if the family was not aware of their presence, time would simply run out for them if they failed to keep on the move.

At about 0100, Brown was awakened by a sound he could not at first recognize. After a few seconds, he realized that it wasn't a sound, but the lack of the steady drumming of the rain that had awakened him. Crawling over to where Ash maintained his watch, he peered out the building's rear opening. Incredibly, the water had receded down to ankle depth. He quickly awoke the rest of the team. Within ten minutes, they had gathered their belongings and were moving through the water in the direction of the swollen stream. Since it seemed to head in the general direction they wished to go, he decided to follow it for a spell.

The swirling waters they passed through removed any sign of their passage, so they were able to move without worrying about back trail hints with which they might have otherwise had to concern themselves. The last man out was Nuckles, who had patted the water buffalo on the head one last time as he prepared to slip into the waters of the creek. Looking over his shoulder at the farmhouse, he knew they were getting out just in time. He saw the flicker of a light come on in the house as they turned to go down stream. The inhabitants of the house had been awakened by the silence just as the team had been. He had to think about how close the two groups had come to disaster from each other, but they had avoided that outcome by their studied insistence on not acknowledging each other.

The team continued to move well into the morning as they strived to locate a suitable area to prepare a bivouac. Finally, they selected a slight knoll that was only then becoming visible above the receding waters of the creek they had followed through the night. The canopy of the trees would provide cover, and they strung their hammocks from the limbs, making sure that the weight of the burden did not upset the root system of the trees They didn't want to be dumped onto the ground by the tree if their weight overwhelmed the ability of the tree to support the soldier utilizing it.

They moved at night for the next week without seeing any sign of anyone on the trail. Indeed, they had timed their departure perfectly from the little farm. The NVA had removed the garrisoned troops from the area to respond to the Son Tay operation, and the infiltration routes had been rendered unusable. The NVA had actually had a number of units trapped in the infamous caverns they had constructed throughout the highlands of the region. The rising waters spawned by the roaring typhoon had thinned their troop list considerably. Both these factors contributed to the team's movement into the highlands and beyond at least initially without interference from the NVA.

The surviving team members knew they had been given a slight advantage; it was up to them to utilize it to the maximum extent they could figure out. They still did not dare to move in the daylight hours when movement would have been easier. Lacking reliable night-vision devices, they were constrained to move slowly and cautiously during the hours of reduced visibility, always observing noise and light discipline and even being careful of foods they ate, which might give off noticeable odors that the NVA could detect. By this time, they had exhausted the supply of C rations that they had hoarded as long as they were able.

Yount and Humboldt had been watching the undergrowth for edible items they might use to their advantage. They were able to occasionally catch a fish in the streams they crossed, but none of them had much of a taste for it raw. Again, they were hesitant to cook over an open fire due to the smoke and smell of burning wood carrying to distant points and alerting passersby of the possible presence of someone. The berries and fruits that Yount and Humboldt had learned of during their previous time in country were becoming the staple of their diets. They had occasionally liberated the rice pouch that they had found on the few NVA they had surprised on the trail. This dried starch ingested dry would expand in the stomach and give one the sensation of having their dietary needs satisfied.

In the next few days, they began to see more signs of NVA moving in small groups. They began laying ambushes for the small units; they were actually taking out some elements of the infiltrators who were using the same portion of the trail. They had initially been reluctant to take on a unit equivalent to them in size. Brown and Yount had worked with all of them on their hand-to-hand skills during the days they had spent in the barn and at other times as the situation allowed. They did not consider themselves experts, but they were no longer shy about engaging a force even slightly larger than they were in numbers.

Brown had emphasized the use of spacing and surprise enhanced by the shock of overwhelming physical force directed at the target. They never fired the M16A1s they continued to carry. Rather, they used them as clubs and as launch points for the bayonets they extended from them. The medics were even becoming proficient in the art of self-preservation.

Brown took Patterson and Humboldt to the side one evening as they were about to begin their movement for the evening. "I believe we are nearing the Laotian border. By next week, if we keep our pace, we should be there." They both looked at the situation about them; no one wanted to ask the question they shared. Brown had shared none of his tactical decisions with any of the team, except he did occasionally confide in Yount.

Humboldt finally asked, "Why tell us this now?"

Brown rejoined with "I don't want the men thinking we are home free because we are so close, but I did want you to know that there may be hope of getting out of here." Neither of the medics was really satisfied by this explanation, but no better was forthcoming. They were becoming more and more concerned with the mental state of Brown; the stress of being placed in charge was beginning to wear heavily upon the young man. While he seemed ancient to the youngest team members, he had only celebrated his twenty-fifth birthday while they were in school at Ft. Monmouth.

Patterson and Humboldt, who were no older than Brown and less experienced in the field craft that was now so necessary to their survival, knew that vigilance must be maintained and support must be given to Brown to try to help him deal with the situation they were all in way over their heads. They began to take a more active role in the operation of the team, always seeking Brown's concurrence before taking an action but actively involving themselves in places they previously would not have ventured.

As they moved in the highlands region, they had begun to experience mountains occasionally reaching to nearly two hundred meters. These mountains were similar to the Appalachian and Blue Ridge ranges that they had performed their practice sessions on back in the States. They had not executed the types of operations they were now performing, but they had gained acclimation to the type of terrain. Of course, the vegetation here was much different than that they had dealt with back in the world.

Existing as they had with no maps and no real knowledge of the geography of this remote area of North Vietnam, they were unsure of any names that may have been given to the region's hills mountains or valleys. Taking a name from the physical appearance of one mountain they confronted, they had come to call it Ole Hunchback. They had planned to scale the crest of this old mountain, but as they worked into position to do so, they had intercepted the remnants of the regiment that faced the team back at Duc Lo. They had observed this force for two evenings and mornings as they moved down the trail.

Brown and Yount had recognized some of the soldiers who had taken an active part in the bushwhacking of the team. They particularly wanted some retribution from this group. The problem lay in the numbers. The unit consisted now of over two hundred soldiers, considerably more than they could ever hope to engage. The second day of their tailing, the NVA commander decided to split his force, sending about two-thirds of the unit to the east of Ole Hunchback and the remainder swinging to the west.

Brown had elected to keep the team together and stayed with the west-heading group. Early the third morning, the team had still not dared to engage this force of over eighty men. As they prepared for the unit to bivouac, Ash and Wiznewski reported that the unit had disappeared. When Brown heard this, he suspected there was a cavern nearby. After about forty-five minutes of careful scrutiny, he had spotted the camouflaged entrance.

Pulling his ranger knife from its sheaf, he had prepared to slip into the mouth of the cavern. After a few feet, he was stymied. His frame was too large to fit through the tight squeeze of the mouth of the shaft. He signaled for Nuckles to come forward. Being of a slighter build, he was able to penetrate deeper into the shaft of the cavern. He was enveloped in darkness. Brown had oriented him to expect that there might be booby traps and false leading shafts going nowhere. After covering about twenty feet, he sensed rather than saw something directly in the path. There was a pool of water, which almost occupied the entire shaft opening. Keeping his head up, he negotiated the pool and was rewarded a few feet further when he realized that he was encountering less and less water as he went forward. The NVA had attempted to give the impression that they had flooded their own access to the cave. As he came to the edge of the water, he sensed the presence of something thrashing about the shaft. Wearing the gloves they had all kept from the standard issue for work in the field, he had used his ranger knife to slash at the imagined obstacle. As he moved forward, he felt an object about a foot long roll under his weight.

Grabbing the object, he realized that he had three items to contend with this situation on his own—a knife, a flashlight, and a pistol that Brown had handed him before sending him up the shaft. Two of these he was afraid to use. He knew the flash from the light would draw fire from the other inhabitants of this cramped space; firing the weapon would likewise betray his position. He had a rope attached to his belt to signal back to the team. He had used less than half the length of the entire cord. Looping the rope around the body he had isolated, he signaled for the team to pull back on the rope.

They were shocked when the body of the deadly asp arrived at their position. Fortunately, he was as dead as he was deadly. Nuckles's aim with the knife had been perfect at least on one stroke. The rope was returned to Nuckles who moved a little further into the gloom. He could hear the breathing of the enemy as he went deeper into the cavern. Suddenly, he felt the warm morning air on his forehead; he had come to the back door. He thought about following the fleeing unit and realized that they would have left rear security to watch the back door. He signaled to the team that he was returning to their location and as rapidly as he could did so.

When he arrived back at the entrance, he related to Brown what had occurred. Brown told him the snake had been poisonous and intended for him as a booby trap. He had done well. The withdrawal of the enemy through the escape hatch was of more concern. If the team attempted to leave, they may have circled around and prepared an ambush for the team. They had no choice but to lay low in the mouth of the cavern during this long day. They would get what rest they could get here. At least it was cooler in the cave, giving them some respite from the stifling jungle heat they had endured since their arrival in the country.

Throughout the day, they kept a vigilant watch over the cavern opening, trying to imagine if they had done a good enough job of obliterating any trail they may have left. One factor that saved them was that Patterson had prepared two hasty two-man fighting positions near the mouth of the cavern. He had done this when they had thought they might be spending the day watching from the outside. He had done a good enough job that the NVA had expended considerable effort in taking them out. They had not realized until they were on top of the positions that they were unoccupied. The commotion of the approach was not great, but it was enough to tell the team they had company outside.

Brown decided when he heard this; his next move would not be to go out that door. They would have to traverse the tunnel of the cavern and hope for an unimpeded exit at the rear. Yount was left in the trail position as the team moved through the tunnel. Brown, not having to fear his concerted effort might give him away, was able to squeeze through the opening. Yount was left in the trail position, and as he made his way through the area, he left several presents for anyone who tried to follow. The most dastardly was the claymore mine whose trip wire he rigged into the watery trap that had been left for them. Foster, who was observing, thought, *Okay, here's a countercountermeasure.* How far would this go before someone broke?

The team waited until darkness had set in to the area firmly before making any move. They were extremely apprehensive as Humboldt and Ash moved to the opening and beyond. There was no rat-a-tat-tat from the AK-47s they had feared would be waiting for them. They quickly moved into the brush and were on their way. Brown pointed out the direction he wanted the movement to take and indicated they were to wait at the crest of the hill; he and Yount were going to pay a visit to the ambushers waiting for them outside the front door. They would be back in two hours. If not, the team was to move on without them under Patterson's leadership.

Patterson tried to protest that if they were going to set a trap for the NVA, the entire team should work together. Brown was adamant that this was a two-man job, and he and Yount were the men for the job. All Yount had to say was "Lead the way." Patterson knew he was not going to win the argument. He followed the instructions that had been given and moved the team on up the trail.

Behind them, the fire team of Yount and Brown moved noiselessly and quickly into position to engage the covering force left to observe the cavern. They had obviously not expected this maneuver from the intruders. Brown, who had chafed at not being able to use the M16A1 he had carried for weeks, spotted four positions covering the mouth of the cavern. There might have been more, but he was ready to make his move. As he opened fire on the first position, Yount

was engaging the one just to his right. They were able to eliminate these four fighters who had not fired a single shot. Brown had moved to the third position. The occupants had reacted and were returning fire when Brown's hand grenade arrived in their midst. He had not had time to hold the spoon, and the grenade was designated for return to sender pronto by the men in the position. Brown saw the returning projectile and was preparing to move when it went off in his face. He took the full force of the explosion, but he had been effective with his fire. The movement required to return the concussive grenade had betrayed the position of the enemy soldiers. He had fired three rounds and scored two kills. Meanwhile, Yount had engaged the fourth position all the way across the cave's mouth from them. The distance away had discouraged him from using a grenade, but his fire had been hugely effective. He had taken out both occupants with his accurate utilization of his weapon. Given the environmental conditions they had endured to engage with these weapons had been an enormous testament to the dedication they had shown to caring for their personal weapons. Just as Yount finished spraying the second of his targets, the returned grenade arrived over their heads. The explosion occurred directly above the two men, and they were dead in seconds. Again, the covering force had not been able to establish anything of the identity of the team. It would be days before the bodies were found, of friend or foe. The decomposition would have set in upon the cadavers, and nothing recognizable would be found of either force.

Ahead of this action, Patterson heard the noise of the firefight and recognized the sound of the 47s and the 16s. He was pretty certain that Brown and Yount would not be joining them at the designated rendezvous point. He signaled a short break and made notes in his mind of the details of the loss of these two men. He felt certain that he would be called upon to answer for their actions—if they made it to the point where accountability mattered. Even though they had often disagreed over tactics, they had both contributed mightily to the survival of what remained of the team. He wondered if he and Humboldt were equal to the task of negotiating the remaining distance. They were still not home free by any means.

Just as Patterson had expected, Brown and Yount had never made it to the rendezvous point they had established. Per the instructions he had been given before Brown departed, Patterson had put the team on the move after about a two- and one-half-hour wait. As the team of six moved forward, they began to see signs that a large unit was moving ahead of them. By Foster's best estimate, they were only a couple of hours behind this group. They began to shadow the unit that now was well into the highland area they had entered days ago. Closing on the larger unit, Foster soon returned from the OP (observation post) he had established just east by about five hundred yards of the bivouac site the NVA unit had set up.

When Nuckles and Ash had come up to relieve him, he had returned to the main body and reported to Patterson. "This is the element of the regiment we

218

observed the other day that went around that little mountain and we followed the remnant for the little excursion in the cavern. They haven't made great time. I don't think they are in a great hurry to get to the south. They are moving deliberately and not observing very good field discipline. They deserve to be taken out, but even as bad as they are, with the number advantage they have, we do not dare to engage them. I counted about a hundred and twenty when they made camp. That's way too many for us."

Patterson thanked him for his diligence and the thoroughness of his report. He had included a drawing in the dirt of the layout of the camp, the perimeter strong points, and the location of the crew-served weapons employed by the NVA regiment or what remained of it. They had to figure some way of getting at least some of the unit isolated so they could take them on in a fair fight. Patterson decided this was not the place; they would shadow the unit for a while. Hopefully, they would avoid detection while they watched for opportunity to present itself to them.

The evening came, and the NVA prepared to move out. Their shadow unit was doing the same. Throughout the evening, they maintained a somewhat erratic pace. Patterson surmised that they had slowed to give the element that had dropped back to set the trap for them outside the mouth of the cavern the chance to regain contact with the mother unit.

This would never happen as Brown and Yount had taken them out of play for any further action. Patterson knew that he already missed the expertise of the infantrymen; he really felt it was unfair to thrust a medic into such a command position as he had been. He also knew that there was no alternative likely to avail itself to the team, so he had to make the best of it. He would do his absolute best; he hoped it was enough.

Throughout the night, the unit's movements, snakelike as they worked through the rugged terrain, led them ever nearer the Laotian border. Patterson, by 0400, thought they were only ten to fifteen miles from the border. At 0530, Wiznewski, who was taking his turn as the point and trailer, signaled a stop. Patterson moved to the point to see what had happened. Wiznewski explained, "The unit was moving along this ridge. They dropped down on the far side, and now they have disappeared. But look in that area at the base of that hill." He indicated a sharp rising summit of about four thousand feet. "There are all kinds of signs leading to that hill from the south. I think we are at a trail junction. This way station is used going and coming."

Patterson sent Nuckles and Foster forward to relieve Wiznewski and watch the area. They saw no sign of anyone moving for several hours. About 1000, they saw a small squad of eight men emerge from the well-hidden entrance to the cavern cleverly hidden in the base of the mountain. The men broke into pairs, moved quickly into the brush, and soon the troops they had replaced were moving into the cavern for their rest. The ranger team now knew the strength and location of the security outpost.

Foster sent Nuckles to report to Patterson. Patterson moved forward, and Foster pointed out the locations to him. "They are dispersed enough that we could get to that one on the west without the others seeing what is going on in the fighting position." Foster pointed to the isolated post. "Nuckles and I could slip in there and take those guys out quietly and then move over to those two he indicated a position containing two men a little closer to the main cave. The four of you could make your way to come at the other two posts at the same time. If we all hit at the same time, we might be able to wipe out their security element. Then we could really have some fun." Patterson studied the area for several minutes. He then signaled for the entire team to assemble.

He explained the plan, very nearly what Foster had proposed, but he inserted a four-hour time factor to give Foster and Nuckles a chance to achieve surprise when they came at the security outpost from behind. This would give them time to come all the way around and hopefully achieve their goal with no interference. He and Wiznewski would take the post above the cavern entrance, and the easternmost post would be the responsibility of Humboldt and Ash.

Patterson gave Foster and Nuckles twenty minutes to prepare for their move. They were not accustomed to moving in the light of day, and they were absolutely cautious as they began to move. The plan called for them to hit the first outpost at 1430 and then be on line at the second point by 1500. They knew they were on a tight schedule. They were pretty sure that the Vietnamese would not change guard force soldiers before that based on the schedule they had so far observed.

At 1430, the lights went out permanently for the two soldiers manning the first target. Moving stealthily from that position, Nuckles and Foster were in position to launch their second attack at 1450. Foster was about to make the first move, which would have committed them to the plan, when Nuckles, sensing the tensing muscles of his friend, grabbed his arm and reminded him in a whisper, "This has to be a coordinated attack. If we go now, we will give our presence away and alert the other positions."

Foster relaxed and waited for what seemed an eternity for the ten minutes to pass. When the time span was right, they made their move. With vigor, they launched themselves into the NVA position, and each took out the target they had selected with the ranger knives they carried. In less than two minutes, their objective was seized.

Looking around, they noted the footpath the NVA had worn into the hillside where they had established what Stidham had called Dead Ranger Graves. This referred to the habit of fighting men to locate the position established for security by their predecessors on a piece of land and put their position in the same place. They resisted the temptation to move down the path, but they were soon assembled near the mouth of the cavern. They could see how the great pains of the enemy had successfully hidden it from view. It was a secret no more.

Glancing at his watch, Patterson observed, "The relief for the guards will be coming out in about thirty minutes. I think they will use garrison troops for this shift because the deploying and redeploying units will be moving out before the shift ends. These guys may not be as sharp as the ones who have survived the south or those who are prepared to go south. We need to use this to our advantage." He quickly outlined his plan to let the guard force emerge from the hidden innards of the mountain and then be engaged one by one from the rear by the members of his team. The plan demanded swift, efficient, and vicious action by each team member. If any one of them failed to accomplish his task, the team would be exposed and compromised. They each understood the ramifications of the tasking they were assuming.

They quickly assumed the position Patterson had indicated he desired them to take. Shortly, the guard force emerged into the daylight from the cavern. Before their eyes had fully adjusted to the bright light they were seeing for the last time, they were all on the ground around the team members, each of whom had done exactly what they had been asked.

Humboldt was the first to notice. He sniffed the air. "What's that smell?" His question was addressed to no one in particular. Wiznewski was the first to catch the odor.

"That, my friend, is the aroma of gasoline." He nodded into the cavern. "You know, when the unit was coming in from the south, each man was carrying what looked like a five-gallon can. Do you think they are hoarding gasoline?"

Humboldt snorted, "I have heard about them stealing gasoline from us in the south. I never would have believed they would carry it home in five-gallon cans. I bet there is a consolidation point somewhere near here where they put it in tankers and take it to Hanoi. You can rest assured that these poor sapsuckers carrying it in here will never get to use it back there."

Patterson had been thinking, "If we play our cards right, we might be able to get those guys who took out our team back at Duc Lo. Foster, you, and Nuckles scout up that hillside. Be careful, but see if you can find either a back door or a vent hole. If you find one, drop a little invitation to the bowels of hell in there for our friends." He indicated the grenades that the two carried on their web gear.

After a climb of twenty minutes, Foster called for a short halt. They had not seen any sign of an opening into the operation they knew to be below them. As they caught their breath, they were stopped by the aroma of gasoline fumes. For a moment, they could not locate the source. Cleverly hidden in the roots of a nearby tree, Nuckles finally pinpointed the location. Crawling as quietly as church mice, they inched toward the hole. As they neared the entrance, Foster reached onto his gear and located a concussive grenade. Pulling the pin, he kept the spoon depressed until he confirmed there were no screens in place over the outlet, and then he released the spoon and counted slowly to seven. At that point, he dropped the grenade into the hole with all the force he could exert into the downward movement. They were able to hear the metallic clank of the metal grenade striking the rock of the floor of the underground home it had found. Immediately, the sound of excited voices came in a language that neither of them understood. Nuckles removed his helmet and placed it over the opening of the vent hole. This would prevent a return to sender episode for this explosive device. It didn't matter anyway.

Nuckles looked at Foster, still crouching over the opening. "Don't you think we should run?" He got this out as he had already taken off up the hill. It took about three seconds from the clank until they heard the first explosion of the grenade. They had no way of knowing if one of the NVA had died a martyr and covered the grenade with his body. If one had done so, it would have surely meant the death of the American team.

As Foster and Nuckles continued up the hill, the answer came to them. No one had dived onto the grenade. A second growing concussive rumble began inside the mountain and continued to grow. Glancing back at the tree that had hidden the opening, they saw the helmet Nuckles had placed over the opening sent flying down the hill toward the balance of their team.

The force of the explosion grabbed the fire team of Foster and Nuckles and hurled them up the side of the mountain about twenty-five feet, depositing them against a tree that was starting to tremble from the rocking that the side of the mountain was performing. Scrambling another fifty feet higher, they turned to see the side of the mountain reconfigure itself as trees and giant boulders disappeared into the chasm created by the successive blasts still shaking the mountain. They were just in time to see eight men who had apparently been posted near the back door of the cavern ejected into the sunlight and unceremoniously dumped into a heap. They worked their way to them to complete the work the blast had started, if necessary, but no further exertion was called for. The blast had completed its task. There was no sign at this point of any survivors.

Meanwhile, Patterson and the others had been watching the primary opening into the cavern. They were aware of the rumbling below the surface. The force of the explosion had been directionalized following the cut of the cavern tunnel as it dislodged the rocks and debris it collected, which were impelled toward the opening. Among these objects were eight more bodies that were regurgitated by the earth into the late-afternoon sunlight. Again, they were ready to finish the efforts begun by the blast, but no further actions were necessary. The blast had eliminated this element also. There were no signs of any of the cavern's inhabitants having survived this cataclysmic blast.

Nuckles looked at Foster as they rested, watching the mountain seek its new configuration. "Do you think you used enough dynamite?" He was laughing so hard he had to struggle to make himself heard. They had seen *Butch Cassidy and the Sundance Kid* before their departure from the States.

Foster observed the area for a moment and then said, "Apparently not. There's no money flying around." Then he too was laughing. They did not indulge themselves in frivolity as it began to dawn on them the awesome thing that had just occurred. They had counted at least eighty-five troops from the regiment they had been interacting with since their arrival. They had counted at least sixty troops entering from the south after the arrival of the regiment. This meant they had accounted for at least 145 NVA that day. This did not include any enemy deployed to man this RON (remain overnight) site. Due to the large amount of petroleum stored in the facility, it was almost certainly a significant number of cadre was required to operate it.

Checking the bodies of the men they had taken outside the cavern, the team was able to resupply themselves with some food stuffs, primarily rice and some form of jerked meat that was tough and hard to chew, but it beat that old empty feeling with which they had come to be on such good terms.

They made their way around the reconfigured area of the mountain, rejoining the team near where they had left them. Patterson was relieved when the fire team he had sent out rejoined the main body; he had been apprehensive of dividing his force, especially considering the outcome of Brown and Yount detaching from them. Patterson had everyone up and under way. He explained that he was concerned by several things. There might be units arriving from the South or possibly the North who were near enough to have detected the rumbling sounds that had recently emanated from the mountain. There was the possibility that the transfer point for lifting the petroleum back to Hanoi was nearby, again enhancing the possibility of company coming to investigate the noises. Further, there was the possibility that the two outlets they had discovered were not the only ones. This was a well-developed complex from what they had seen; its extent was only a guess to them. These elements combined to make Patterson want to leave this area behind him. The team was quickly moving into a more covered area.

As darkness fell, they took advantage of the dusk to move out. Rather than head south, they decided to head west, hoping to reach the Laotian border relatively quickly. They had heard Brown opining that they were only forty to fifty miles away before his disappearance. Patterson reflected that they had been extremely lucky to engage such an overwhelming force and take no casualties themselves while inflicting the damage they had imposed. He knew it in no way reflected upon his leadership, but he did give unspoken credit to Stidham and VunCanon for the amount and quality of training they had insisted that every team member undergo. Even the medics had become capable warriors (the white armbands with the red crosses had disappeared some time ago—they made too good of targets), and these green troops were no longer able to be described by that term.

There was no further contact with the enemy that evening. Other facets of the HCM trail were being utilized as the word spread of the loss of the complex just east of the Laotian border. The trail was so broad that there was no bottlenecking of troops from the rerouting that had been necessitated by the events of that day. The flow of combatants to and from the combat areas of the south was not affected. The team did find the going a little easier for the next two days. By this time, Patterson and Humboldt were convinced that they were well inside Laotian territory. They now headed generally south; the mountains were a bit higher here than the ones they had encountered in the northern area they had come from. But all in all, the traveling had become a bit easier. They were physically better off now with the added nourishment they had obtained, and the emotional lift of the feeling they were out of North Vietnam was immeasurable to their spirits.

They still dared make no contact with the local population, but they had seen ever increasing signs that they were among people in a loose sort of way. The terrain was still rugged and the jungle thick, but they had seen signs that they were near to some form of population. They were about to receive a warning of how primitive the environment they inhabited was indeed.

As they made their bivouac one morning, they were discussing the distance remaining to be traversed. Humboldt, who had been in the area, opined that they were only a few miles from Cambodia; and by cutting the corner, they could emerge into South Vietnam in only a few days. Patterson, whose experience had not included this particular neighborhood, listened quietly; but making no comment, he did not join in the conversation. He thought it good they were feeling positive about the chances of getting back, but he had begun to be bothered by something as yet unspoken but still unsettling. He was concerned by the logistics of the return to the forces in the South. They had no radio, even if they were to come upon one, they had no CEOI (communication-electronics operating instructions) and obviously no knowledge of current signs and countersigns in effect for the region or the specific area in which they might need to operate. These were troubling thoughts; he had no sounding board for them at the moment.

As he pondered these thoughts, he took his place in his hammock, hoping to get to sleep before the oppressive heat and humidity of the region prevented him from doing so. The guards had been posted and the rotation worked out so that each team member stood one watch during the period of daylight. They had paid much closer heed to this since the incident had occurred with the gigantic snake. Today they had another visitor of a different nature. About 1130, Wiznewski thought he heard a cat purring from the brush, about ninety degrees from where he had positioned himself to have a good look down the most likely avenue of approach to their position. Listening intently for a few more minutes, he decided to check it out. He had extended his search into the brush when he heard the sound coming from behind him. The source had gotten between him and his teammates.

Coming around a tree, he stopped dead in his tracks. There facing him with a scowl on his face was a tiger. He had no intention of giving up his meal. He had worked hard to locate it, and now it was time to enjoy. The scraping of Wiznewski's boots on the ground was enough to awaken Humboldt, who was closest to the confrontation. Drawing his ranger knife as quietly as he could, he prepared to come to the aid of Wiznewski. Clearing his throat loudly was enough to awaken the other team members. The tiger was now surrounded but not defeated. He made a lightning-quick swipe at Wiznewski, whom he still regarded as dinner. Leaping away, Wiznewski had tried to get in a strike with the machete he had had in his hand while standing guard. This was ineffectual and only incensed the animal more.

Foster spoke quietly to the tiger, which turned and started for him. In making his turn, the animal, for a split second, left his flank unguarded. This was the opening Ash had been looking for. He moved in on the tiger, slashing viciously at the animal's right flank. His first blow struck the hamstring, disabling that leg. Still, a three-legged tiger was no pushover. The enraged animal turned toward the attacker he had just encountered, with revenge etched on his brain. Suddenly, Nuckles had struck from the other hind quarter at the other hamstring. Now the big cat was dragging both rear legs but still had plenty of fight left in him. He slashed out at Nuckles with a forepaw that was rendered harmless as he lost his balance. Wiznewski was on him in a flash, slitting his throat and opening the jugular vein. As quickly as it had started, the skirmish was over. The huge cat was dead on the floor of the jungle. None of the men had been injured more than a scratch Foster had gotten trying to position himself to lure the cat away from Wiznewski.

Surveying the area, they all realized how fortunate they were that there were no major injuries. They had never feared the majority of the animals present in the jungle because, unless trapped, most would leave rather than fight a man. This tiger had not gotten that particular memo. Nuckles had moved into a denser area of woods and found a substantial tree that had been felled during the recent rains of the typhoon. Hacking away at the limbs, he had soon cleaned about ten feet of the trunk. With the hemp rope he had carried throughout the adventure, he secured the animal's feet to the trunk with loops to the front and rear. Foster looked at him questioningly. "What are you doing?" His inquiry was for the whole team.

Nuckles replied, "If one of you gentlemen will get the other end of this pole, we will make a present of Sir Top Cat here to that village that can't be far over there." He pointed in the general direction they had noticed the most recent signs of human habitation. Turning to Patterson, he continued, "Sarge, if you think we should leave him on the outskirts like we did the snake, we can. But I for one think this is a different howdy doody. They might be friendly to us bringing them dinner."

Patterson considered what Nuckles was proposing. Slowly he shook his head. "I know there's a chance they would be friendly. But they have coexisted with the NVA. There's too good a chance that even if they are friendly, they are working both sides of the street. Even if the chief took our side, there's no guarantee that a villager won't be in an NVA camp before nightfall, reporting not only where we are, but how small we are. We just simply can't take that chance. We leave the carcass well marked at the next sign of habitation and beat feet out of here."

Hopes had risen with the expression of Nuckles's idea. As the reality of the situation explained by Patterson sunk in, the team was noticeably downhearted. Nuckles was sorry he had even thought of the offer. Turning to Foster, he asked, "Why were you trying to talk to the cat? Did you think he was going to sit on your lap?"

Foster shook his head. "I had to come up with something to get his mind off Wiznewski. If he came after me, I had a pretty good clear space to take off running."

"You thought you would outrun a tiger?" Nuckles was incredulous.

"Oh no, I didn't have to outrun him, just you, you slowpoke." Foster's response brought smiles to the team; they felt better about the situation they had encountered. Patterson had soon worked his way close to both Foster and Nuckles and expressed his thanks for getting the attention away from the possible human contact and back on the survival of the team. He thought, *Man, Stidham has worn off on these guys big-time. That was a trick worthy of the master of the art.*

The big cat was deposited on the trail after moving about a half mile toward the signs of habitation. They did not dare to remain close by to see the reaction of the villagers to this windfall of provisions. They would have dearly liked to enjoy a meal with these folk in this out-of-the-way place. "Politics," as Tip O'Neal said, "is all local." They knew this was not about to happen. With no rancor for these local people, they left their unattributed gift.

When they were out of sight and probably less than five hundred yards away, they heard a loud scream. It was a scream of joy. They didn't need to speak the language to interpret the meaning. The gesture had been welcomed.

Patterson knew this was a crucial time. For as happy as the discoverer had been for the meat of the huge cat, there was someone in the village who could not leave it at that. There would be a report made to someone on the other side. There might even be retribution against the village for the acceptance of the gift. He had seen the best intended things blow up for the givers and the receivers. He hoped that this would be the end of it.

However, Patterson knew that he could not allow the men to grow complacent on the trail. First, there was, in his mind, the certainty that the NVA would be tracking them from the spot they had left the animal. They would be seeking whoever had done this; they had not likely forgotten that a major way station on their network had been viscously knocked out a few days ago. They would be anxious to even that score. He thought, *How ironic. We think we evened the score for our loss. They think we have to give our lives to even it up, but our side will think it's uneven, so someone else has to die to even it again. It never gets to the point where both sides think it even. How sad.*

Moving along the trail, the team was becoming aware of the change in the foliage. They were leaving the northern climate and entering the monsoonal zone of the south. The monsoon season was drawing to a close, and it would be hot with less rainfall for the coming months. There was little else to differentiate between the regions. There sure weren't any welcome signs as they moved from Laotian territory into Cambodia, and in only a couple of nights, travel had moved into South Vietnam.

Patterson had spent these days and nights concentrating on the movement of the team, but in the back of his mind, he was struggling with "how do I get us safely across the wire," meaning how did the team marry up with the American forces in the area. He had held in-depth discussions with Humboldt and Foster concerning how they might accomplish this task. They had no CEOI as mentioned before. They couldn't just walk up to the gate of a compound and knock on the door.

Patterson had also been thinking about the reception they were likely to receive from the powers that ran the American forces know as MAC-V (Military Assistance Command-Vietnam). He would be surprised if that was friendly interaction. They were likely to be thought a unit gone rogue and treated with contempt if not arrested. He had little confidence in the leaders of the American forces to find out the truth before jumping to conclusions and making assumptions. He had confided some of his fears to Humboldt, especially his concern at having no paperwork to authenticate his mission or even the existence of his team within the force structure of the US Army. This concern was further compounded by the fact that they had not been allowed to carry identification cards or tags on the mission. They had thought of no likely scenario in which they came out with anything other than reprimands and other unfavorable personnel actions. As the NCOICs surviving to this point, the finger of blame would be pointed exclusively in their direction, particularly in the case of Patterson.

Furthermore, here among the Hmong of the Central Highlands, he was comfortable, having spent a significant portion of his time in country in this region. He had in fact recognized one of the villages that he had worked with during his time over here before. With a little persuasion, he thought he could make a deal with the locals and get him and Humboldt out of the area. This would leave the four younger team members on their own, but he considered them home free once he found the unit he had targeted for them to capture.

Barstow had been catching flak from the Austrian, who had seen the North Vietnamese walk out of the peace talks. They had cited repeated American incursions into their territory. It did not seem significant to them that they had repeatedly violated the territorial limits of the South Vietnamese. They had cited three separate incidents that they demanded apologies and reparations for or no further talks. The Austrian was desperate to begin American disengagement, but even more significant was the effrontery to conduct these strikes without his knowledge or permission. It never occurred to him that POTUS (president of the United States) should be the one giving permission or denial for such actions.

The Austrian had arranged for the director of the agency to be called on the Oval Office carpet and read him the riot act that such acts had to be stopped. If the agency was planning a further action, there was no doubt that it was cancelled effective immediately. The agency director had Barstow in his office waiting for him when he returned to Foggy Bottom.

In the meantime, the Austrian also had the SECDEF (secretary of defense) in for a cozy chat about what acts his minions were performing. Since only the Son Tay mission had been authorized through his office, the SECDEF was a little nonplussed at the butt-chewing he was receiving; however, there was just enough truth in what was being said that he kept his mouth shut and listened.

Long story short, there had been two raids attempting to free POWs. The SECDEF had gotten that much and had heard from General Duncan that he had a team of rangers for whom there was no accounting. The third referenced incursion was a mystery to both SECDEF and the agency director. Pouring over intelligence analysis reports, the ASA (army security agency) had noted that a few days prior, there had been a massive explosion on the North Vietnam side of the border. There was no evidence that any American unit had been involved in the explosion or whatever had occurred.

General Abrams, who had recently become commander of MAC-V, had been called into Washington for consultation. It was made abundantly clear that if this was a MAC-V-SOG operation, it was to stop immediately. General Abrams had begun an immediate investigation; he had found no evidence of any operation that could have inflicted such a devastating blow to the North. Indeed, American intelligence had not guessed that such a facility had even existed before the explosion. No one seemed to know anything about this action that had the opportunity and the wherewithal to cause it to happen. Several of those interviewed in the investigation had suggested that they had nothing to do with it, but they would have if they had known of the opportunity.

Barstow had figured he had better get someone on the ground who knew the score, at least approximately. Bringle was soon on his way. He had enough knowledge off the Duc Lo mission to brief anyone who needed to know. He had been told the bare bones of the Son Tay operation, which many of the personnel in Saigon were well versed in discussing. He had no knowledge of the third hit, but he was beginning to suspect that there might be an independent element from the Duc Lo mission at work here. It was even possible that Stidham or one of his officers had survived the massacre at Duc Lo, which the North Vietnamese had never publicly brought out since the bullet holes in the foreheads of the victims, all from the same small caliber weapon, would be hard to explain. Furthermore, they had never positively identified the remains of any of the victims of the massacre. Cho Dinh had muddied the waters there before his untimely demise.

Still, Bringle thought it might be possible that whichever team leader might have survived could have organized a resistance effort with the remnants of the team. He remembered that he had been told, "We got twenty-four of your men." That left eight team members with no accounting. He had assumed that since there had been no contact with them, there were no survivors.

Bringle hit upon the idea of contacting Naval Operations Pacific Fleet; he had not heard of any report from the submarine commander responsible for the pickup of any survivors from Duc Lo. Perhaps he could glean something from this source. He soon had the log of ship's calls for the period in question. Sure enough, there had been a call from the ranger team the next day after the jump. They had reported no packages (POWs) present, and the commander had declined to make any further contact. This was in accordance with his orders, but it was important evidence for Bringle. Twenty-four hours after arriving in country, there had been some survivors who had the ability to contact the submarine. There must have been some leadership involved in executing this phase of the operation. Still, there had been no word of any survivors or unaccounted for confrontations with any group since that day, save for this lone incident.

Thinking back to the men he had met and spent some time with who were involved in this mission, he could not begin to get a clear picture in his mind of which of the leaders might have survived. He didn't think either of the first lieutenants would have been a candidate; both were sharp but woefully short on experience. The two captains, while more experienced, had each failed to make high marks with him for innovative thinking or dominating leadership skills. They had both been more of a follower than a leader. VunCanon, he thought of him and dismissed him, had been the type man who would have been leading the mission into the compound, not sitting back where the survivors might have been. This made the thought of the four young ranger trainees come to his mind. They very well could have survived; Stidham had always held them back from the heart of the action. However, he couldn't see them surviving for this long in that hostile environment and participating in this master stroke of genius in setting back the North's war effort.

In Bringle's way of thinking, this brought him back to the intermediate leadership of the team. He now regretted that he had not gotten to know these men better. He had no feel for which may have survived and orchestrated the actions, which had had such devastating effects upon the enemy. In spite of the butt-chewing, which had ensued for the national agency heads on down, there was a growing respect for the men who had pulled this rabbit out of the hat. Bringle suspected that they would never be known for what they had achieved, but he also knew that he would be in a precarious position if it came to light that he had sent this team into enemy territory and not had a reliable, redundant extraction plan. Ever the survivor, he was thinking of an exit strategy for himself, hopefully one that allowed him to keep that pension he could now smell.

As he disembarked from the plane at Tan Son Nuit Air Base, he was well into forming his plan of action. He had to bring Barstow current on the contact with the Naval Operations Pacific Fleet. This, he anticipated, would lead to questions about survivors. He could not, at this time, speculate on numbers or names, but he could begin to formulate a disavowal plan if they turned up. There was always the chance that they had become victims in some skirmish or even in this attack; the force of the explosion could very easily have taken out the perpetrators of the attack. There was always a chance that he was chasing down a rabbit trail that led to nowhere. While he hoped for such an outcome, he could not afford to depend upon it.

He immediately began to activate his network of contacts within the country, both the formal ones and the informal ones. He wanted to know if anyone had any contact with any rogue unit or any unaccounted for personnel who might wander into an American or Allied base camp. So far, there were no reports that moved the meter on his interest. He began to mine the G-3 intelligence briefings, starting with MAC-V and working into the corps operating zones. He was finding a lot of things he didn't know but not what he wanted to know. Still, he was occupied, and he was getting the feel of the land. After having been away for an extended time, he had to reacquaint himself with the areas of operations of the various organizations involved. He assumed that any contact would come with those units closest to the border but decided not to eliminate any of the centrally located units at this time.

As of yet, no one had connected General Duncan's missing team of rangers with a CIA operation as they had been reported to be on a training mission. This mission was ostensibly being conducted in CONUS (Continental United States), and there had been no cause to connect them to the Duc Lo mission. The agency had taken ownership of that mission, but so far, they had kept quiet about the source of their personnel on the ground. Bringle believed that he might be able to keep this information quashed if no survivors showed up. If he had to contend with that, there was no telling what all might come out.

Week 12

Dallas 24–Washington 0
Baltimore 29–Philadelphia 16

Finally, they hit on the idea of watching an American unit similarly to the way they had trailed the North Vietnamese units they had observed and interacted with on the way down the HCM trail. The interaction would take on a different aspect, but the techniques could be borrowed. They began to watch units operating in the area.

The first unit they happened upon was a patrol from the First Cavalry Division. After a couple of days of tailing them, Patterson decided to move on to other units. These guys were on their toes. They moved through the central highlands, coming to the AOR that had recently belonged to the Fourth Infantry Division. The operational brigades of the Fourth had rotated out of country, and the Americal Division had moved into the AOR. They had spotted a patrol that seemed a likely subject for their attention.

They had trailed the Americal patrol for three days. These guys were marking time; Patterson would bet money that every one of them had a countdown device among their belongings on which they were recording the number of days before rotation back home. He hoped they made it, but he knew they were ripe for taking as the object of the team's search. He pulled in the four young guys that evening after they had observed the patrol going to bed; they had put out adequate security measures and were settling in for the evening.

Turning to Foster, he explained the route the patrol would be taking in the morning. He even noted where the unit would stop for their morning break. The team would be located here, and he drew the layout of the area in the dirt. He and Humboldt would be in reserve in case anything they were not expecting happened. Ash and Wiznewski would take the L-T and the platoon sergeant, while Foster prevented help from coming from the front of the column, while Nuckles took his position to the rear. They were not to use fatal force but just let them know they had been had.

Then they were to arrange to give themselves up to their captives. Patterson mentioned that they might not expect the captives to be thrilled at how easily they had been neutralized but expected their disposition to improve upon realizing they were not in mortal danger.

He had not mentioned anything of his plan to disappear. He did not want the young guys to be burdened with information that they either could not divulge or that would have led to his and Humboldt's being taken into custody. He had another plan for their removal from the area. He had not yet gotten Humboldt's agreement to this plan, but his reading of his peer's disposition told him he had an accomplice. Still, he felt responsible for getting the four younger men into a position that they could successfully negotiate. He thought to himself this was ever so much more than Brown had taken care of before he had departed. Of course, he was not ready for the radical departure that Brown had engineered for himself and Yount.

The team was growing weary as they were tracking the Americal patrol as well as watching for VC or NVA activities in the evenings. This was high-energy activity, as they had not one but two prime targets not only to watch but also to carefully avoid contact with until they were ready to make their move. This task was made somewhat easier by the actions of the Americal patrol; these guys seemed more anxious to avoid contact with the enemy than to locate the source of the annoyance that had led to their dispatch into the area.

Finally, Patterson felt that they were prepared to make their move. That evening, he had Ash and Nuckles watching the VC group operating in the area. These guys were pretty good craftsmen of the trade but not quite so good as they thought themselves. They had not seen or sensed the presence of the American team shadowing them for the past four days. They had, however, spotted the Americal patrol. This evening, they had decided to take them out.

As the VC moved into position to lay a hurting on the Americal patrol, Patterson realized that he had to intervene, or his hard work and planning was going to go up in smoke. He and Humboldt had moved up to the front of their formation and were side by side with Nuckles and Ash. He would really have liked to have an M60 machine gun, but none of these had survived the first action at Duc Lo. He would have to make do with the M16s that the team had carried for almost seven weeks through the forests and jungles. Besides carrying an M60 through the jungle without using it for seven weeks while subsisting on limited rations would have been a real bummer. He would find out if they had really been maintaining them or just going through the motions. Some of them had not been fired since that first day.

As the VC formation moved into array preparatory to engaging the Americal patrol, he saw his opportunity. It was not a great advantage, but there was a slight break in the line as they moved into position. He thought he could take advantage and maybe get them to fire on one another if he created some confusion among them. He worked his way through the small gap and took up a position to the rear of the VC formation. It was none too soon; the VC commander had noticed the gap and repaired it by deploying a fire team into the thicket Patterson and Humboldt had just vacated. Fortunately, in the haste to move to contact, the VC team did not recognize the signs that they were occupying a recently held position. Patterson signaled to Ash and Nuckles when he was in position. The VC were only minutes from engaging the Americal patrol when Patterson and Humboldt opened up on them from the rear. As Ash and Nuckles poured withering fire from the front, the VC unit began to take casualties from both sides.

Pulling the pin on the first grenade he had in his possession, Patterson lobbed it into the fighting position he was sure contained the commander of the VC unit. Now they were not only taking casualties, but also they had sustained the loss of their leader. The remaining elements of the attacking force, assuming they were surrounded, began a hasty withdrawal from the area. Patterson and Humboldt followed them into the brush and headed toward a Hmong village not far away. Neither of them was heard from again. No bodies were found in the area when the action had ceased. These two Americans had simply vanished into the night. They were never accounted for as POWs taken by the VC or NVA, and no bodies were ever discovered.

Meanwhile, Ash and Nuckles had turned their attention to continuing the rout of the VC force, which had taken heavy losses. Additionally, Wiznewski and Foster were engaged across an opening in trying to keep the Americal patrol out of danger and in a safe posture for their purpose later that morning. As the sun came up, the Americal patrol was deployed around their perimeter, weapons loose and safeties off. The four Americans, hoping to link up with them, were extremely concerned that they would either shoot themselves up or that the VC would realize the lightness of the opposing force that had hit them and return in force to take out this unit. Fortunately, the VC unit did not figure out the true composition of their opposition.

As Foster watched the Americal's perimeter, he was startled to see that when the sun came up, they stood down. They were having their breakfast. The patrol leader was bringing his team leaders together to review the action. Incredibly, after finishing breakfast, they began to search the bushes and surrounding area. Foster realized they were getting a body count. He was flabbergasted. These guys were asking to get knocked off.

He watched for a while longer and saw his opportunity. The lieutenant in charge of the patrol had dispatched the platoon into the operation, keeping only himself and three others in the CP (command post). Foster quickly moved his team into position to cover the evenly manned post and, quietly, when they were in position, gave the command, "Just nice and easy. Lay your weapons down. We want to talk to you." When the lieutenant reached for his M16, a bullet kicked up dirt beside it. "Remember, we want to talk." Again, the voice came from the bushes. Now they had to move quickly before the outlying elements of the patrol reacted to the sound of the gunshot.

The NCO in the group slowly turned toward the voice. "Okay, we hear you. What do you want?"

Foster began to explain their situation, "We just saved you from some really bad guys. They had high hopes for you. Maybe they won't be back. Maybe they will. We want to help you, but we need to turn ourselves in to you so we can get back with our unit." Slowly they came out of the bushes. Nuckles first and then Ash and, seeing that they had not been accosted, Foster and Wiznewski.

The young lieutenant introduced himself to them. His name was Edward Fischer, and he was incredulous when he saw the condition of the four. He repeated over several times, "You guys in this shape were able to take on that unit?" His troops had accounted for twenty-three bodies in the brush already and thought there were more. This ragtag outfit had saved their bacon. But now he had to explain why it had been necessary to his superiors. He didn't think that was going to be a pleasant conversation.

Foster noticed his discomfort and, in his disarming best down-home imitation of Nuckles, spoke to the lieutenant. "If y'all hadn't of pitched in there at the end, I don't know if we could have held them off much longer. When that M60 of yours opened up, they knew they were outgunned. We surely do thank you for the help, sir."

Seeing his opportunity, Fischer took the bait. "Why, I do see what you mean. Of course, we have to report in to headquarters." He began to get his platoon in some semblance of order. He got his RTO (radio telephone operator) on the horn to his company and filed a situation report (SITREP). He was, of course, a hero when they heard of the body count. Choppers would be dispatched to return the patrol to base camp, and coordinates were exchanged for the hookup. When he mentioned the four men who had joined them, there was a pause on the other end. Finally, they were told to bring them in with them.

Foster and Nuckles were growing more incensed by the minute. They had not been able to find any trace of Patterson and Humboldt, who had gone off to keep an eye on the VC in the area before they launched at the Americal unit. The Americal guys were proving deaf when it came to searching for the two missing sergeants. This remnant of their team had come this far together, and they were not about to leave the two behind if they had been wounded or injured during the action that had taken place. The four young members of the ranger team had finally gone out to search the area for any sign of the two men. They had found signs of them, but not the men nor their bodies. They had positioned themselves in such a way that they had poured withering fire into the VC as they moved toward the Americal unit. But there was no sign of where they had gone when the engagement was complete. The two men were not accounted for, and they were not heard from again as long as the American presence lasted in South Vietnam.

In about forty minutes, the choppers, Hueys as they were known, arrived and transported the patrol back to base camp. The lieutenant was whisked into a briefing tent where the brigade commander Col. Norman Sportscoat waited for him. Sportscoat was livid. He had surmised that the patrol had been taken unaware and that, if not for the actions of the four Americans who had reached out to them, would have been annihilated. Now he had to figure out who the four were and get them out of his hair. He thought, *These guys woke up this morning and thought, "What can we do to screw up Colonel Sportscoat's day?"* He was certain that this as everything in his life was all about him.

Meanwhile, orders had been given. The four young men were given a hut, issued fresh uniforms, and the filthy, tattered jungle blacks taken from them. They had the first showers they had enjoyed in almost two months and were soon freshly shaved. It surely did beat bathing in the streams they availed themselves of during their journey down the HCM trail. Nuckles was first to notice that there were two armed soldiers standing outside the hut. He noiselessly motioned to Foster, who came to the window. Without showing themselves, Foster whispered, "What's going on here?"

"I just noticed this myself." Nuckles reply showed the perplexing emotions he was experiencing in his voice. "Why would they be guarding us? Do they think we are going to commit suicide or something?"

In truth, the guards had been ordered to keep other soldiers away from the team. They had been quite a sight when they came off the choppers. The men who had been on the patrol had, of course, in spite of warnings to the contrary, immediately began to relate to their acquaintances the actions that had taken place on the patrol. These guys had saved their bacon that morning. A group of American grunts would know and appreciate the actions that had been taken to get them out of a tight spot. When they had performed the body count of the VC and seen the positions they were in, the grunts knew they had been in imminent, mortal danger.

There was soon the whirling of chopper blades overhead, and the arrival in the compound of the division G-2, Col. Fred Goins, was confirmed, when one of the soldiers with the arms politely knocked on the door of the hut. "Col. Goins would like a word with Private First Class Foster." It was an announcement, not a statement or a request, just an order couched in polite terms.

Foster turned and gave the palms-up sign to his team as he headed to the door. He was treated courteously, but he noticed that none of the soldiers he spotted as he crossed the compound made eye contact with him or spoke even when he nodded to them as they went by. Something strange was going on.

As he entered the briefing tent where Col. Goins waited for him, he was about to learn some of it firsthand. Of course, as with all things regarding military intelligence, they would never tell him what they knew or suspected, but they expected him to give them all he knew. That's just how it worked. At first, Goins was nice and polite, asking questions about the mission he had been on, the unit he was assigned to, and the commanding officer. Foster was equally as nice as he endured the debriefing, asking why they were being held under guard and when could they get some real chow. He found Goins to be pleasant and efficient in getting the obvious information that the army would need to establish that they were who they said they were and had been doing what they said. Goins explained that he would need to talk with each soldier individually and that they would not be able to communicate with each other until all had been debriefed. He explained that this was common military procedure in these cases. It did not occur to Foster to ask how frequently these cases arose in the military.

When Goins had finished with Foster, he was taken to a different holding area, where he was indeed given a scrumptious meal. He thoroughly enjoyed the first few bites before he realized that his system, having been deprived of this type of nourishment for such an extended period, was not going to be able to handle it well now. He had to get to the nearest latrine.

Meanwhile, Wiznewski had been the next one summoned to the briefing tent. His answers had been substantially the same as Foster's, but he had not quite the detailed explanation that Foster had provided. Goins, at first, thought he was holding back, but eventually it was mentioned that Foster had been an acting supervisor for the group. Goins appeared to be satisfied with that explanation. He had soon completed the debriefing of Private First Class Wiznewski. It took him all of eighteen minutes to fully debrief what had taken almost two months to complete.

Ash went next. Nuckles was getting concerned that they were being taken by the unsmiling guard to the briefing tent one by one, but they were not being returned to the hut they had been given the run of when they had arrived. Being the territorial animal that he was, he began to look around for any sign of anything that might have been left in the hut by the other three when they left. There was nothing he could spot, but he was certain that when he was taken, the premises would be thoroughly searched and all belongings checked. He was getting nervous about what was going on. He had never been arrested, but he felt like he was about to be. It took only sixteen minutes until the knock on the door announced that they wanted Private First Class Nuckles.

As Nuckles entered the briefing tent, he was courteous to the senior officer who greeted him. Goins asked if he was being treated okay. Nuckles replied that he was and then asked, "Is there a reason that I would not be treated okay?"

Goins was startled that this junior enlisted man had picked up on this nuance so quickly. He would be careful of his questions to this man. Again, he went through the standard questions he had asked three times previously. The only significant variation he received from the man before him now and the others was that when he questioned the unit they were assigned to, Nuckles's reply was that they were part of the prototype ranger school at Ft. Campbell, Kentucky, which was organized as part of the Second Ranger Battalion, Company H, Team 7 as augmented for the tasking and with authorized attachments. As he gave this answer, he searched his memory because he had only heard the full explanation once from Stidham, and that had been quite a while back. None of the others had mentioned this piece of information to Goins. This would become critical to the disposition of the unit in the military fashion. Due to this unexpected windfall of information, Goins spent twenty-two minutes with the debriefing of Private First Class Nuckles. Goins was beginning to see his way out of the sticky wicket he had found himself stuck inside.

At the completion of Nuckles's session with the Division G-2 (intelligence and signal section), he was taken to a fourth place where he was treated in much the same fashion as had been the other three. The only difference was that they were now all being held in solitary conditions. It had been explained to them that this was to ensure that they were not collaborating on their stories but telling the whole story. They were beginning to doubt that this explanation was sufficient since they had all completed their interviews. Nuckles was the first to be aware of this, as he had been the last interviewed.

Colonel Goins had mentioned that he would be talking to the individuals involved in the rescue of the team. Nuckles had chuckled at this categorization of what had transpired earlier that day, but it now seemed like a week ago. It seemed to Nuckles that the colonel found it incredulous that the team members could not only survive but also thrive with their entire leadership element wiped out. He had tried to explain that this was a testament to the leaders of the team, but the colonel seemed set on the absolute essential presence of leaders for any team to not only thrive but also to simply survive. Nuckles was finding that many of the military leaders apparently did not buy into the premise that soldiers were trained to survive rather than trained to follow. He was beginning to appreciate the efforts that had been made to train his small group from a whole new perspective.

Goins completed his cursory interviews with Fischer and his platoon sergeant, receiving their sanitized version of how they had rescued the ranger team who had been fully engaged and receiving the worst of a beating from the VC force that morning. Fischer had already been put in for a Silver Star for his part in the rescue. The platoon sergeant would have to get by with a Bronze Star. Of course, Bringle had not gotten involved with those commendations yet.

Nuckles had unknowingly provided Goins with the "out" he needed to pass this issue on to someone else. The assignment of the team, if confirmed, would make it the property of the Fourth Infantry Division since Company H was detached to their command. He had figured out a way to weasel out of the direction this had been taking since its arrival upon his desk. After all, why would he want to deal with something he could give to someone else? Still, he was intrigued by this unique story; and now that he knew he would not be making any politically sensitive decisions in regards to the matter, he wanted to hear the entire story before he shucked and jived out of the area.

He continued to question and record on tape the answers he was getting from the team members. He was beginning to see a chance that they were telling the truth. He also felt it prudent to interview a representative sample of the patrol that had picked them up. Of course, the patrol members were not sequestered during the questioning, and amazingly enough, their stories were all consistent with how they had rescued the ranger team element from certain disaster. When it came to accounting for their ammunition, it was discovered that they had indeed performed well. They had expended fewer rounds than the number of bodies in the body count. With a little encouragement, that number was increased to a reasonable excess of rounds to bodies. Goins was definitely trying to help Fischer get that Silver Star. He had no opinion in the matter of the young rangers and refrained from any acknowledgment that there might be legitimacy to their claim as to how they had gotten to this point.

Goins completed his interviews, with the feeling that he had covered the trail for Colonel Sportscoat, who was now an acknowledged water walker. He felt reasonably certain that the patrol leaders would be justifiably rewarded with recognition for their heroic performance. He had talked to only two patrol grunts; they had been well-coached in the details of the patrol that had been invented. How was he to know that rumors were already swirling through the base camp compound? Fischer had been such an overachiever when it came to getting people to dislike him. Within the compound, there was rumored to be a lottery as to how long it would be before he was fragged (the practice of tossing a fragmentation grenade into the fighting position of a particularly loathsome young officer during a firefight).

Goins was in a hurry to get back to the division HQs, and he knew how he was going to make this mess disappear. He called his boss, the division commander, and explained that while the Americal unit had taken custody of this ragtag element from the jungle, they were really apparently the property of the Fourth Infantry Division, as they claimed to be an element of that unit, which had been detached without benefit of paper as far as he could determine. His strongly worded recommendation was that the Fourth, which, by the way, had recently seen its brigades rotate home, and the division HQs would soon follow and would benefit significantly by straightening out the mess they had apparently created. Within twenty-four hours, Goins was instructed to turn over to the Fourth Division G-2 the findings of his investigation and the personnel at question from the patrol's rescue of them.

Goins was only too happy and, as authorized, made voice contact with Col. James Wilsong, G-2 of the Fourth. Wilsong was thrilled, of course, to hear that he had to clean up this mess before returning to the United States where the Fourth would be residing at Ft. Carson, Colorado. Goins made arrangements to fly the men by Huey helicopter to Pleiku, where they would be formally turned over to Wilsong. The records of his investigation were placed on a second Huey, which was dispatched to Pleiku four hours after the one containing the men.

Week 13

Dallas 52–Houston 0
Baltimore 35–New York Jets 20

This four-hour head start with Colonel Wilsong was to prove pivotal to the men. They were flown as a group to Pleiku, which was the first time they had been allowed contact with one another since the questioning had begun. They were able to compare notes. All had come away with the feeling that the American personnel they had encountered were not friendly, nor were they likely to believe the story that the four men were telling. This was incredulous to the team. They had been drilled and drilled to develop survival skills. When they were demonstrated, no one believed it possible that they could have made them work. They had the feeling that a great deal of distrust had gone into the investigation, and a lot of plate cleaning had come to bear for the men of the Americal. It seemed to the young men involved that the investigation to this point had had a definite slant that had been orchestrated to reach a particular conclusion. They were beginning to understand the reticence of the more senior guys to come back to this reception.

Upon arrival at Pleiku, Colonel Wilsong, who had few other chores to clean up as his division headquarters prepared to depart the country, met the chopper when it landed. He immediately had the four men brought to his office, where he had them made comfortable. He asked to speak to them as a group. He listened to their stories, made notes, and explained that he would need to talk to them individually as well as in a group. They asked if they were under arrest. He replied that "No, you are not under arrest, but we have no record here of your unit. We have to ascertain whose orders you were following and if those orders were indeed valid." Foster did most of the talking for the team, but it impressed Wilsong that when a topic came up that he was not the most familiar with, he would turn to the team member who had the most salient knowledge to explain. He thought, *How many senior field grade officers never learn that little trick?*

By the time the records of Goins investigation arrived, he had debriefed the team and was attempting to contact the Flight Control Center at North Field in Guam. He had placed a call to ascertain if a C-141 from there had indeed flown to the area of North Vietnam on November 10, 1970, as the men claimed. He also felt that there would be a good chance there was no record of that flight or that it existed in another form, such as an alternate destination or some such tomfoolery.

He also requested records of the air force regarding the fuel dump explosion that had taken place in early December, exact date unknown. He further requested MAC-V records of body counts for any such incidents of that time frame. He was very impressed with the young men he had met and had a hard time believing they were part of any rogue operation that may have been instigated. He had indeed found already that the unit had been identified as the parent organization of the school for rangers that General Duncan had authorized much earlier. These men were located in that DODACC (Department of Defense Accounting Code Center). He had made more headway in four hours than Goins had in three days. It was amazing what could be done if one actually tried.

The call to MAC-V headquarters was the break that Bringle had been searching for with the greatest of diligence. He now knew there were survivors of the raid on Duc Lo. He soon had the location and was on the way to Pleiku. He demanded that Wilsong give him access to the four men, whom he referred to as prisoners. When Wilsong informed him that they were not prisoners, he demanded they be placed in confinement immediately. Wilsong informed him that the men were restricted to post, but they would not be placed in confinement. Wilsong then demanded to know what Bringle knew about the origin of the team and its mission.

Bringle had seen his fate boomerang on him in a few short minutes. He had gone from holding the trump cards to this colonel looking him in the eye and asking him pointed questions. He decided to play the national security card. He informed the colonel that the men had in fact been a part of a plan to free POWs from the NVA. Things had gone awry; now there were lives at stake. He could not reveal the details of the lives, but it was in the national interest to keep this under wraps. Barstow confirmed this when prompted by Bringle for the benefit of Wilsong. A little truth wrapped in a blanket of obfuscation seemed like the way to go.

Suddenly, Bringle hit upon a new strategy that might work just as much to his advantage as getting these men released to him. There were still areas where heavy fighting was occurring. Why not suggest that these men be placed in an area that they might be exposed to heavy fighting? They might not survive such activity and give their all for their country while preserving the secrets of his involvement in their previous mission. After all, they might survive. Faced with this sudden cooperation, Colonel Wilsong opted to keep the men in his line of sight. He had never been much for writing letters of condolence to families back home. He didn't see any point in putting these men in such a situation. He was beginning to share some of the feelings that Stidham and the team leaders had felt for Bringle; he just had not suffered from the degree of exposure they had.

Ash had been on his way to the mess hall when he spotted a man in civilian attire heading to Wilsong's office. He had had that instant of recognition, but then couldn't place the man. When he returned to his quarters, he mentioned to Foster, "I saw a man I thought I knew crossing the compound. He went into Col. Wilsong's office, but I know him from somewhere else."

Foster nodded non-committedly. "I don't know who it could be. Maybe someone you knew before the service."

Later, Foster and Nuckles were sitting outside their quarters when Bringle left Wilsong's office. They both instinctively turned away from the agency man as he came out of the office. With the level of things he had on his mind, he paid them absolutely no attention. Foster immediately told Nuckles, "We need to get out of sight. That was the man who used to come see Stidham back at Ft. Campbell. I never got the feeling that Stidham had any use for him. If he's been in talking to Wilsong, we need to be careful of what we say to him." They were in the hooch by now. Foster approached Ash, "Was the guy you saw earlier that civilian who would come to Ft. Campbell frequently to see Major Stidham by any chance?"

"Yeah, that's who that guy was. But you know he didn't just come to Ft. Campbell. We saw him at every place we did dry runs, including Guam, by the way." Ash was finally feeling good about remembering the face.

"We all better be careful." Foster was deadly serious. "I don't know what his connection to us is, but I betcha that if it was good, we would have been sent for by the colonel. They haven't asked us over, so I'm thinking he's up to no good."

Within fifteen minutes, a young specialist 4 knocked on the door of the hooch and informed them they were requested to be in Colonel Wilsong's office in ten minutes. They politely thanked him and convened a council. Wiznewski was all for running immediately. Nuckles spoke for "let's see what they have to say," and Ash said, "Well, Wilsong seems to shoot straight. The fact that they didn't ask us over with Bringle in attendance could be good or bad, but I don't want to spend any more time running."

Foster summed it up, "Well, let's see what the good colonel has to say."

With that, they were on the way to the meeting they had not requested. When they walked into the room, Colonel Wilsong sensed a difference in their demeanor. He had carefully instructed the specialist 4 he had sent to get them to not tell them anything about the reason for the meeting. Still, he sensed a reticence that had not been present earlier. He decided to see where this new attitude led. After all, first impressions were not always bellwethers of what someone was.

He started out slowly, "I've been doing some checking on the story you told me."

Foster, for the first time since assuming leadership of the team, grew impatient. "Sir, we knew you would check us out. That doesn't surprise us. What does surprise us is that the man who was constantly visiting our team commander in the States and even in Guam is in this vicinity. While we are restricted to post, he has the run of the country. We don't understand what is going on. We never felt that Major Stidham trusted this man, and we don't either. And by the way, sir, everything we told you is the truth."

Wilsong, with no emotion showing on his face, produced the statement about the mountain containing the petroleum dump. He laid it on the table before them. "The air force says their bomb set this little racket off." He deftly slid photos of before and after the explosion toward Foster. Foster felt as though he had been punched in the gut. Here was proof that they hadn't blown up the dump even though they all knew they had.

Nuckles simply bent over the after photo. After studying it for a few minutes, he said, "Where's the crater?" In his haste, he had neglected to add "sir" as required by military protocol.

"What are you talking about, soldier?" Wilsong did not comprehend the question.

"If this destruction was caused by a bomb, there would be a crater. I have looked this photo over, and there is no crater. Furthermore, I was on the side of the mountain right against this tree. If this had been taken from the nose of a bomber, there would be evidence of Foster and me up there. As a matter of fact, our helmets were left beside the vent shaft, which is clearly shown here, no helmets. I know for a fact that no air force planes flew over this mountain on the day this happened." He tapped the photo for emphasis. He suddenly remembered where he was and added, "Sir. Further, this mountain is in North Vietnam. We haven't bombed there in over two years."

With this, Wilsong knew he was through. The other details of the story had checked out; there were discrepancies in the story of Fischer and the rescue of the team and the team's accounting of that final event in their odyssey. He believed their version due to the part about searching for Humboldt and Patterson. Fischer had never mentioned this aspect of the rescue, but this tracked with the creed of "no man left behind." He realized these men were living out the creed far more than the soldiers assigned to his unit had.

Meanwhile, Bringle had been busy. He could not afford to have these four men tell their stories to the American public. His first order of business had been to let Barstow know that there had indeed been survivors at Duc Lo. However, they had not liberated any POWs. On top of this, there had been no survivor who held a rank higher than E-5. He wasn't actually sure if they were sergeants or specialist fifth class. These were not the makings of heroes, beside which they hadn't gotten anyone released. He could at least assure the Austrian that the mayhem the North Vietnamese had been complaining of on the HCM trail would not be an ongoing concern from these guys.

He followed that with a request that the mission and all relevant documents be classified top secret. Justification was national security and ongoing operational security concerns. This was quickly acted upon and the affected documents and records amended to reflect the change.

Bringle wasted no time in getting in touch with the G-1 at the Americal Division. The rumor mill had said that there was a Silver Star and a Bronze Star in the process for the heroes of the rescue. These awards were quickly quashed with the assignment of the security classification.

Additionally, Bringle contacted the G-1 at Fourth Division and informed him that there was to be no record of the four men having been assigned, attached, or augmented to the team that had never existed. All thirty-two personnel files were to be expunged. There had to be notations of service time; these were blacked out except for the one copy kept permanently at ARPERCEN (Army Personnel Center in St. Louis). While this tactic succeeded partially in erasing the existence of certain aspects of the ranger team that had been performing at Ft. Campbell, he was not successful in totally destroying the evidence of the existence of the team. There were redacted copies of the documents that remained in the army official files even though they were classified and not eligible for release.

The effort to redact their files of the four surviving members of the ranger team had produced mixed results as well. The evidence that they had been in Vietnam could not be totally removed and still get them orders to come home. So while some references to their service were removed, some weren't.

Wilsong was able to turn the handling of the case over to the Fourth Infantry Division G-1, who quickly cut orders to bring the young men back to Ft. Carson, Colorado, where they would be reassigned or discharged depending upon the decision of ARPERCEN in the disposition of their military obligation. The officers involved assumed that due to the nature of the service rendered, the four would jump at the chance to have their service obligation wiped clean. None of them had ever been assigned to a ranger team, not did any of them discuss this with the young men involved.

Wilsong did call the young men in for a final debriefing before sending them on their way. He thanked them for their efforts and shared with them a memo he had received through channels from Gen. Creighton Abrams, commander MAC-V, concerning the Austrian's repeated efforts to control the mayhem on the HCM trail. General Abrams acknowledged that he had been unaware of the existence of the remnant of the ranger team but upon reflection had determined that if he had been given 350 troops such as these, the war would have taken a different direction. This memo was never shared with Gen. Duncan, who was making the decision about the location and content of the new ranger school that was about to be launched.

Wilsong informed the four that due to the fact that none of the events they had performed on the HCM trail having been witnessed by officers or senior NCOs, no military awards or honors could be issued. He stated that each man would have undoubtedly received at least a Silver Star for the acts that they had performed and confirmed by one another's accounts. Foster asked if it was possible for any of the deceased members of the team to receive recognition of the acts that they had performed posthumously. Wilsong wasn't sure. He didn't think it would be able to happen, but he would check it out.

Then he delivered to them the news that they had been members of a top-secret operation, which they were prohibited from discussing with anyone who had not at least a TS clearance and the need to know any details of the operation. As an added bonus, he threw in that had they been awarded any honors. These would have been suppressed so that they would not actually be able to wear them.

Nuckles asked if this requirement stemmed from the visit of the civilian to the compound the day of their arrival. Wilsong truthfully replied that he didn't know if the civilian had any bearing upon the decision to place such a high level of security clearance upon the mission. He was not certain if Mr. Bringle was capable of making such decisions or of affecting the decisions of others who could. Without realizing it, he had given the four men before him an important piece of information. They had never known Bringle's name. Now they would never forget it.

They were hardly surprised to learn that their records were being redacted to reflect that they had never been in country, at least the version that would exist in files that would be public information. They were being returned to Ft. Lewis, Washington, for processing and being assigned to Fourth Division at Ft. Carson, Colorado, as previously mentioned. Foster was glad to hear this, being that he was from that area. His face fell noticeably when they were informed that they were to be discharged from the military upon their arrival at Ft. Carson.

"Is there any way to appeal this decision?" he questioned the colonel who had been very kind to them up to this point.

"I thought you would want to get out. Most of the men who come through here are chomping at the bit to leave the service." Wilsong's response surprised them. Ash and Wiznewski replied that they were appreciative to have no further obligation; they would be happy to exit the military. Foster looked at Nuckles with a question in his eyes.

Nuckles's response was not what Wilsong or Foster expected. "What kind of reenlistment code will we receive? Will we have the option to reenlist later if we want to?"

"Well, be sure and ask that question as you go along. I will alert G-1 to your concerns." Wilsong was well into his song-and-dance routine when Foster held up his hand.

"Sir, this is not a concern. This is a deal breaker. We are being asked to act like twenty-eight men who gave their lives for this mission never existed, and you can't tell us if we are eligible to reenlist at a time when the army is losing the highest percentage of first-term soldiers ever?" Foster threw his hands up when he delivered this. "I personally will not accept any such compromise."

Wilsong simply lifted the phone from his desk, called the division G-1 colonel Raymond Freeze, and informed him that the four men were ready for him. He turned to the four and crisply informed them that they were dismissed and to report to Colonel Freeze down the hall on the left. With that, he had the MP who had been waiting outside the door escort them from his office.

Colonel Wilsong was not happy with the outcome of his debriefing, but he had a plane to catch. Orders had just been issued for the Fourth Division Headquarters to join their brigades back in the states at Ft. Carson. He was glad to be rid of this potential political football, which was now being buried in a mountain of red tape. He for one hoped his role in this decision might never come to any further light. Watching the young men leave, he was aware of the feeling that they were not likely to let this issue go lightly.

Colonel Freeze greeted the team amiably and began to ask if they had questions of him. Immediately, they all wanted to know about the reenlistment code. Very few people were aware of the codes, and even fewer knew the meanings of the codes that were placed on all departing soldier's DD-214, the discharge paper. He had to wonder how they had become aware of it. He was pretty sure that Colonel Wilsong had not brought the matter to their attention.

He thought about the matter and studied the instructions he had received from MAC-V headquarters. There was no mention of reenlistment coding. He decided he was in charge of that and unilaterally made entries into each man's 201 file, which he had had sent to him. The subject was the code to be assigned. He looked up and smiled at the men. "I have entered the codes to be assigned. You will not be given a DD-214 until you reach Ft. Carson." He closed the files and asked, "Any more questions?"

Nuckles looked him over coolly and asked, "Sir, I personally would like to know what the reenlistment code is, and I would like to see a master list of the codes and their interpretations."

Freeze thought this guy is like a bulldog. He doesn't let go. He simply nodded and said, "The list is classified. You may not make copies or take notes from it, but since you have just been told that your last five months of service are top secret and each of you has that level of clearance, I can show you the list." He provided the list and the code that would be assigned to them. According to the list, they would have no trouble reenlisting. His opinion was, here were four young men who had performed an enormous mission. They were being silenced for some political reason even he did not know. Who better to serve in the armed forces of our country if they still so desired?

Freeze looked around the room. "Everybody satisfied now?" His query was met with nods. "Then you will be catching a chopper flight down to Tan Son Nhut Air Base the first thing in the morning. He gave them the contact information for the passenger terminal at the air base and told them, "By the way, you are no longer restricted to the post here. You can go off-post if you want for dinner or whatever."

This was meant as a peacekeeping move. He had never been happy with the decision to restrict these young men to start with. They had not done anything wrong, and they were being treated like criminals, while a good portion of the force was in fact smoking pot and staying drunk a large percentage of the time. That didn't sit well with him, but he had not been the one who made that decision.

Foster looked at the other three and spoke for them all. "Thank you, sir, but I don't think we can see a representative sample of the country in one evening. I'll be staying in this evening, sir." The others all nodded their assent. They spent the evening in their quarters, together with their thoughts of the team members who were not present that evening.

Bright and early the next morning, they were picked up by a Huey helicopter that flew them to the Ton Son Nhut Air Field, where they were directed to the passenger terminal area. There they were issued tickets on the 0800 Lion Air flight heading to the United States.

Meanwhile, Bringle had been at his very busiest. He could not afford to have anyone start looking into the expenditures of the Duc Lo mission, considering that most of these monies now resided in his offshore accounts. He had every intention of keeping them there. Using his considerable contact list, he soon had arranged the delivery of a Hawk Missile firing system by an ADA (air defense artillery) unit to a little used point in the Vietnamese countryside. He had also arranged for the presence of a VC unit in the area through other contacts he had on the other side.

The perimeter of the site had not been thoroughly secured when the VC hit the compound hard. They had soon overrun the post, compromising the integrity of the command center. Orders were given for the withdrawal of forces to a secure location where the call for reinforcements was answered and a return in force organized.

Unfortunately, while the VC had control of the compound, they had been able to activate the Hawk Battery and fire four missiles. Three of the missiles had been aimed at armed air frames, which had taken evasive actions, and those missiles had fallen harmlessly to the earth. The fourth missile had been fired at another target and had achieved its deadly goal. After firing the four missiles, the VC unit withdrew from the area, leaving it to be reclaimed by the ADA unit, who were no longer an effective fighting force since their arsenal of Hawks was now strewn about the countryside.

Bringle had taken precautions that there would be no reporting of the base overrun, having Barstow arrange with the MAC-V intelligence section to classify the actions that had taken place. Eventually, the press would discover the source of the fourth missile, but there would never be confirmation of the first three rockets. These became subject to the no-harm-no-foul doctrine, which was rampant in that part of the world at that time. He had achieved all of this with no paper trail and, in his mind, more importantly, no money trail.

The team members, with their tickets in hand, would have a wait of three hours for their flight to the USA. Foster suggested they hit the latrines early as there would be little other activity for them in the terminal. As they entered the latrine area, Nuckles was surprised to hear a loud discordant voice bemoaning the fact that he had been promised a seat on the 0800 flight, but his ticket had been pulled, and he would have to wait for the next flight. He was loudly protesting to the walls the unfairness of having done his year in country and then being bumped from his flight. He was sure it was the most unfair thing he had encountered in his time in the service. Nuckles noticed there were three others with him who were similarly upset over losing their seats.

As he and Foster returned to the waiting area, he related to Foster the details of the overheard conversation. Foster looked at him. "Want to bet on who the four tickets went to?" Foster thought about what he had been told for a while.

"You know these tickets have no names on them, just an assigned seat number." He thought about the ramifications of his next statement and then decided to go ahead with it. "We've seen this shadowy character hanging around. We know he knows us, yet he has never acknowledged us. He could have made our debriefing sessions a lot easier, yet all he did was cause doubt about our story. He could be planning something bad for us. He was in thick with Stidham and the team leaders on planning this mission. He may have been the setup man."

Nuckles thought about what he had just heard. He had been troubled by the appearance of the civilian since their debriefings had begun at the Fourth Infantry Division Headquarters. The fact that he had not made an appearance at the Americal compound had been the one thing that had thrown him.

Foster, as if he read Nuckles mind, continued, "He couldn't have been at the Americal compound because he didn't know we had survived, not until the first reports from Fisher got sent up the chain would he have had any way to know. He may have arranged for us to go to the Fourth. Anyway, I know tickets have been pulled to get us on this flight." He looked down at the ducat he held. "I am going to go see that old boy who was complaining about losing his seat and see if he wants to trade back. The rest of you can do as you please. I would like us to all go back together, but if you want to stay on the first flight, I understand."

Nuckles moved over beside him. "I think what you are saying makes sense. I will find his partner and make the same offer."

Ash hesitated and then stated, "All I want is to go home. I think I will keep this ticket. There may be tracking devices we don't know about. I don't want to get into trouble now for getting on the wrong plane."

Wiznewski nodded and added, "I wish you guys would come with us. We've been through a lot together. It would be nice to go back that way."

Foster grabbed the two men's hands and said, "As I said before, no hard feelings. I just have this feeling that there is something up with this flight. It may be nothing, but I am willing to take the later flight just in case."

Ash and Wiznewski then headed for the boarding waiting area. Foster and Nuckles headed for the area they had seen the disgruntled specialist head for earlier. They soon spotted him and another of the bumped soldiers off to one side, holding court with some of their associates.

Approaching the group, Foster respectfully asked the disgruntled leader if he could speak to him privately. "They get you too?" the bitter young man asked as they walked away from the group.

Foster nodded toward the latrine. "Let's take our business in there."

Once inside the confines of the latrine, Foster looked around to make sure there was no one else in the area. "I am one of the people who got the benefit of your ticket." Foster began slowly. "I would be willing to swap it back to you since I see how upset you are. But the plane is ready for boarding. You will have to hurry to the gate. Your duffel will probably not make this flight, but I guess you could pick it up later when the next plane comes in at Ft. Lewis. I wish you wouldn't tell anyone about this before you get on the plane. The other guys may be angry because they didn't get this chance."

"Partner, I won't tell a soul." The specialist grabbed the ticket from Foster's hand and was out the door, leaving his ticket for the later flight lying on the sink of the latrine. Foster snatched it up and was out the door. Seeing Nuckles still standing with the group that he had detached the specialist from, Foster gave him the thumbs-up signal and loitered about the area.

Nuckles turned to the other man and asked, "Would you be available for a private conversation like the one your friend just had? He looked awfully happy when he ran out of that latrine, especially for someone who was so pissed off a few minutes ago."

"Why should I?" Suspicion was rampant in the voice and on the face of the young man.

"You might come away just as happy as your friend. Never know unless you try," Nuckles answered evenly, but he was becoming desperate. The first call for boarding had just come over the intercom system. His time to consummate the deal was running short. He turned and began to walk away. He felt a hand on his shoulder, and the second young specialist nodded toward the latrine.

When they walked into the latrine, Nuckles noticed that the young soldier was bristling as if he expected to be attacked. He grinned and tried to ease the situation. "I am one of the guys who got you bumped from the first flight."

His beginning was almost his end. The specialist drew back his fist and said, "I hate SOBs like you."

Nuckles backed away slightly, still grinning. "I wanted to tell you I see how upset you are over the delay. I can offer you the seat back. These tickets have no names on them, see?"

The specialist was coming around to his way of thinking, but Nuckles wasn't sure if it would be fast enough. The second boarding call was echoing through the terminal. "All right, I reckon, how much do you want for this seat?" The specialist was still suspicious.

Nuckles just said, "No money, just give me your ticket for the later flight, and we'll call it even. OK?" The specialist reached for the ticket, but Nuckles said, "I get yours at the same time."

"OK, here." The specialist had grabbed the ticket and shoved the other one at Nuckles and was out the door. Grinning, Nuckles scooped the ticket from the floor and headed for the door. Seeing Foster outside waiting for him, he headed in that direction. They arrived in the boarding area just in time to see Ash and Wiznewski going on board the plane.

"Having some trouble making a deal?" Foster was needling his friend as they strolled through the concourse.

"He was just having last-minute jitters about flying," Nuckles replied with a grin. "By the way, what do you think they have in store for us when we get back?"

"I don't know. I've been giving it some thought," mused Foster. "I don't think we could be arrested. We haven't broken any laws, but they could take us into custody and hold us for a while. I don't think they would try that since we signed the security arrangement not to talk about what we were up to while on this little excursion. Let's watch them board and see if they seem to be receiving any special treatment." With this, they moved over to a better vantage point of the tarmac around the plane. They could see no evidence of anything special going on as the plane was loaded. The duffels were brought to the plane and secured in the cargo area. There was nothing unusual that caught their eye there either.

The doors of the plane were made secure, and the plane pushed back from the gate and began its taxi to the end of the runway. A few minutes later, the brightly colored private plane was streaking down the runway, under way to take another load of American soldiers home from having done their duties in this Southeast Asian war.

Foster and Nuckles returned to the benches on which they had waited for the first flight. It would be another two hours before their new flight would be called for boarding. Nuckles couldn't resist asking once more, "Do you think Ash and Wiz are being taken care of like everyone else?" He couldn't fathom what the concerns that had led Foster to take the actions he had taken to this point. He did know that if his friend sensed something foul about the situation, he was well ahead of the game to take on those same concerns. Therefore, he wanted to get as much information as possible about what they were dealing with.

Foster responded, "I don't know. Something felt all wrong about that flight. There were too many strings pulled to get us on board. I just feel better coming in unannounced. Everything seems to be going well." He nodded in the direction the plane had left. "That should be them right there." He pointed to the glint in the sky where a plane was banking left and heading for the South China Sea. At that exact moment, there was a bright flash, and the airplane appeared to disintegrate before their eyes.

A few moments later, the intercom in the airport became active with instructions for all passengers on the 1000 flight for Lion Air to report to the departure area. This flight would use a different gate from which what they had just seen would not have been visible. Soon an announcement was made that there would be a delay before the 1000 flight took off. Nothing had been mentioned about the 0800 flight.

Bringle was positioned in such a way that he had a perfect vantage point as the Hawk missile flashed across the sky, seeking the heat of the Lion Air plane's exhaust. It was an awesome sight to see the impact with which the missile made contact with the plane. There was soon a meteor shower of plane missile and people parts upon the ground below. His thought was, *I'm finally rid of those four meddling fools. Now I can close the book on Duc Lo. No one will ever know what a disaster that was.* Even so, he hoped none of the passengers or crew had suffered after the explosion.

He walked into the hooch he was working from and picked up the phone. Dialing the number of the Airfield Arrival and Departure Group responsible for Ton Son Nhut, he inquired if all the passengers scheduled for the 0800 flight had indeed made the plane. Since the operations people at the airfield were not yet aware of the fate of the flight, the operator, after a brief pause, confirmed that there were 137 passengers scheduled for the plane, and all 137 had in fact gotten on for the trip home.

Bringle, Foster and Nuckles were not the only people to witness the downing of the 0800 flight. Soon there were multiple reports of the downing of the airplane. At first, it was reported that a bomb had gone off on board. Eventually, reports began to come of individuals who had spotted a trail of a missile. Being in a war zone, it was not long until someone knew the missile type. Bringle had every confidence that the army was not going to confess that one of their units had lost an entire battery of Hawk missiles. He was not disappointed.

The story was soon put out that the missile had been fired accidentally during operational procedure testing. An investigation would be conducted to determine the origin of the mistake, place blame, and correct the possibility that such a mistake could reoccur. Of course, nothing ever came of that investigation.

Bringle was on the secure phone to Barstow within the hour, confirming that all evidence of Operation Duc Lo now existed only on some lonely army reports that had been designated top secret and would be relegated to the back drawers of some filing cabinets that probably would never be opened. Additionally, no mention of any related activity would be mentioned in any DA-201 personnel file. The recommendations for medals and honors had also been expunged.

Bringle told Barstow to proceed with the paperwork he had left for his boss to process his retirement. He would not be returning to the DC area. He had arranged his retirement home on a small lonely South Pacific island, one where he could inauspiciously monitor any coming and going by strangers to him or the islanders.

Foster and Nuckles meanwhile kept their tickets for the next plane headed toward the USA. They were huddled in the terminal, quietly discussing the ramifications of the shot-down plane, when they heard that the passenger list for the flight manifest had been released. They were amused to find that their names had indeed been listed among those who were feared lost on the flight. Nuckles looked at Foster and said, "You know we were not feared lost. They hoped we were lost."

Foster nodded somberly. "I am afraid that that's how it looks to me also. When we get back—if we get back—they'll come after us again, I believe. I think we should split up and make it where they have to come after both of us individually."

Nuckles pondered this for a while. "You mean I can't spend the rest of the winter in those lovely Rocky Mountains you are always talking about?"

"Yes, and I will never get to eat that red clay you always tell me about making you Carolina boys so ornery," Foster playfully added.

After a moment, Foster thought, "I think I will reenlist as soon as they will let me. That was a smart thing you thought of, making them give us good reenlistment codes. Can you think of a better place to watch if anyone is watching us?"

After thinking that over, Nuckles replied, "No, I hadn't given it much thought, but I think I will check out the army reserves. We need to be in opposite places. I don't think I want to shoot at Americans, so the guard is out for me. But I would like to keep my hand in the pot, so to speak. I really think we better watch our backs. Do you really think we are better off by ourselves than together? We might cover each other if anything comes up."

"We might make a much better target that way too. I just think we make it harder to come after if we split up. I know that's against every survival lesson we were ever taught, but they never taught us to prepare for our own coming after us." Foster was deadly serious as he considered the ways that this could play out.

Their flight was called for boarding, and as they went aboard, they both paused briefly and said a short prayer not only for Ash and Wiznewski but also for the other servicemen who had been aboard the ill-fated flight they had so nearly been on themselves a short time ago. They were soon strapping themselves into the seats they would occupy for the next several hours until they landed in Alaska for refueling, and then they would go on to Ft. Lewis, Washington. There they would process out of the MAC-V portion of their lives and be reassigned to the Fourth Infantry Division. They would then move on to Ft. Carson, Colorado, where they would be discharged from the army, and their civilian lives would resume.

Week 14

Dallas 5–Detroit 0
Baltimore 17–Cincinnati 0

When they were ready to in-process in the welcome center at Ft. Lewis, they made their first discovery. They were reported as tentatively KIA (killed in action) since they were listed on the flight manifest in Vietnam for the flight that had not made it home. The look on the face of the sergeant who made this discovery was one that neither of them would ever forget. "But you can't be here." He kept repeating it as if the more he echoed it, the more likely they were to disappear. Then the real fun and games began. The army never allowed passengers to travel on the plane with their own personnel files. Then if something tragic occurred, the records and the personnel would not both be destroyed at the same time. The records carried on their flight had been those of the personnel manifested on the previous flight. Nuckles and Foster had flown home with their records.

It was going to take some doing to get them off the rolls of the deceased that they had been placed upon. They could plan on several days passing, while the army figured out how to account for them and tried to learn exactly who had been on the ill-fated Tiger Air flight, which had in fact gone down in Vietnam.

After three days of waiting around for the resolution of their status, it was decided that they should proceed to Ft. Carson, Colorado, where the Fourth Infantry Division would become responsible for dealing with their status and reinstating them from the dead. Orders were cut, and they were placed on a military transport that was going to that vicinity. Since the ranger team was part of Fourth ID, it was assumed that they would be able to resurrect their records from the state they had been placed in by the MAC-V personnel center that had proclaimed them on the downed aircraft.

When they had arrived at the AFB near Ft. Carson, they had discovered there was a randomly scheduled shuttle bus that operated occasionally to transport passengers to the fort from the AFB. After a wait of about six hours, they were able to get seats on that shuttle. In fact, they were able to get any seat they wanted since they and the driver constituted the total personnel making the trip.

Upon being dropped off at the Welcome Center, they were assigned quarters in the transient barracks and retired for the evening. Bright and early the next morning, they reported for in-processing. They were anticipating the end of their travels coming quickly. They were soon to learn that nothing could go that well for them. As they began the out-processing procedure, the first discovery was that their records had not made the trip with them; and therefore, had not yet arrived at Ft. Carson. It was likely to be three days before the records would arrive. They were beginning to get the hang of hurry up and wait as it was performed in the Rockies.

Play-Offs First Round

Dallas 17–San Francisco 10
Baltimore 27–Oakland Raiders 17

There would be no game the following week as there was a week off before the Super Bowl. For that reason the following chapter will deal with two weeks filled with waiting, indecision, and more changes of direction than any of the teams had yet to endure.

With the arrival of their records at Ft. Carson, their hopes were renewed of being allowed to resolve the status of their recent demise and out-process and go their separate ways. In fact, for four days, they were required to check into the personnel center to discover that their status had not yet changed from the previous day. Apparently, the military really had problems with the resurrection piece they were being required to perform. It never occurred to the two young PFCs that this was something that might have happened in other instances and that somewhere in the bureaucracy that ran the military, someone knew how to handle the situation.

Nuckles, on the morning of the fourth day, looked over at Foster as they completed their easy four-mile run that they had taken both to keep their conditioning but also to ease the tension caused by the unsettling effects of not knowing their status or the procedures necessary to resolve it. "I'm thinking of just reenlisting and trying to get back into the school I originally was going to attend. That might be easier than what we are doing."

Foster thought for a while and then answered, "I doubt they will let you take any action until they resolve our status." This reply drew Nuckles up short.

"Then we really are in limbo." This thought had not fully sunk into his thought pattern until this moment. "I wonder if they have notified our next of kin as to our status." He had not thought of calling home before this moment. Nuckles absentmindedly started to the pay telephone bank they had just arrived in front of to make a call.

Foster half-jokingly called to him, "Let's at least go to the in-processing point and see if they will let us call on their dime." They were soon standing in the line of soldiers who were arriving at the fort to become part of the revamped activities associated with the Fourth ID. When they made their request, the same friendly lady who had been keeping them posted upon the lack of change in their status informed them that not only were they not allowed to use the phones for making a call home, but they also had been instructed not to allow them to call home, period. This was not earthshaking news for Foster, who really did not have any close relatives alive or any distant ones that he would want to talk to. For Nuckles, this was a little different.

He had been close to his grandparents and his brothers and sisters, and even though he had proclaimed to Stidham that he never intended to go back to his hometown, he had no wish for them to suffer any distress from being mistakenly informed of his untimely demise. "I'm beginning to think our shadow has followed us here. There seems to be more and more things that make no sense that are popping up on our watch." Nuckles watched Foster's face for his reaction. Foster considered the statement for a few moments and then pronounced, "Well, we haven't seen our shadow back here. If he is pulling these strings, it appears he is doing so from a distance."

Nuckles said dismissively, "Well, it just seems like too many people are trying to control what we say, think, and do. I for one do not feel comfortable here."

The following Monday morning, when they reported to the incoming personnel processing center, they were greeted by the news that new orders had been cut for them. They were to proceed immediately to Ft. Campbell by commercial means. They had two days to report to their new duty station. When they questioned how they were to out-process from Ft. Carson, they were told that since they had not completed in-processing, there would be no need to out-processing.

Through this entire operation, it never occurred to either of them to disobey the instructions they had received and call home. So deeply had they been trained to obey orders that they could not conceive of disobeying them, even in this environment. Besides, they really didn't have anyone to call.

Super Bowl V

Baltimore 16–Dallas 13

Foster and Nuckles had flown commercially from Denver to Atlanta. The details of their trip had been orchestrated by the travel office at Ft. Carson. They had flown to Atlanta's Hartsfield Airport and made a connecting flight to Nashville, Tennessee. They had then been picked up by the routine shuttle between there and Ft. Campbell.

Arriving at Ft. Campbell, they went to the area that had been their home for the weeks of training they had endured there. It came as quite a shock to them to find the old buildings standing empty and the notice affixed to them that they were to be torn down shortly to accommodate the space needs of the 101st Airborne Division (air assault upon their return from Vietnam). The aviation brigade would need additional space, and they could not be placed in such working conditions. They didn't want to get involved in any debate over what was occurring. They simply needed to find Cansler and Ms. Cross. When they came upon several people in the area, they discovered that not everyone appreciated the destruction of the old World War II–era buildings for the new modern editions. After standing there in wonderment for a few minutes, they hit upon finding an open building where they could use the post directory.

Eventually, they were referred to the post headquarters, which Nuckles knew exactly how to find, owing to his trip there earlier to straighten out his mom's complaint. Upon entering the building, it took them several minutes to discover the section to which Cansler had been assigned. While he had never been detached from the school, Ms. Cross had seen to it that he had not been abused in the transfer and had kept him gainfully employed.

Foster and Nuckles were soon explaining to Cansler and Ms. Cross the fate of the team, which had gone out from this location. Using her contacts, she was able to confirm that they had been listed as killed in the crash of the transport plane taking off from Vietnam. Apparently, everyone into whose jurisdiction they had fallen subsequently was unable or unwilling to begin detangling the mess that this had created. At every stop, they had discovered a way to hand it off to someone else.

Perhaps more troubling to her were the trip wires she discovered in their personnel files. While the new-fangled computer system, with its punch cards, could be intimidating to work with, she discovered there were two sets of reports generated every time she touched their personnel files. There was no trace to where the second set of reports was going, but she suspected based on what they had told her someone in the clandestine agency was being informed every time their file was touched.

Now Ms. Cross was on the job. She had them back among the living before the first day was over. Then she went to work on the other members of the team. With Cansler's records and the accounts of the survivors, she was able to handle quietly the balance of the team. Then it was time to handle the files of the four young men who had been trained at her beloved Ft. Campbell, by her own Major Stidham. Even if she had only known him briefly, he had become one of her boys.

After some experimentation with the files of Wiznewski and Ash, she discovered there was a notation on all their files to alert the agency if any personnel transactions were attempted. Keening her memory, she drew upon Nuckles's and Foster's accounts of their experiences with Bringle and remembered the creepy feelings she had encountered during their brief meetings when the team had first been formed. She packed the three of them off to lunch while she considered how best to deal with this situation. She now had no doubt that Bringle had instituted the watches on those four files in particular. To what purpose he would use any information gleaned from the trip wires, she was uncertain. But she was adamant that it would not be good for the two young men.

While these thoughts were racing through her mind, it suddenly dawned on her to check on Cansler's file. After all, he had been identified by the same talent search that had generated the woes of Nuckles and Foster. She was soon convinced that his file was not contaminated by the influence of this man she did not trust and was beginning to hate for the things she was finding in the files. For all the years she had worked in the system, she had never seen personnel files manipulated in this manner, and she was determined to put a stop to it.

Suddenly, the thought hit her. What if she created parallel files for these two. It would not be required that the personnel actions required to clear them of their present entanglement process through their original files. She then could create a file almost identical to the original for each man, with just enough changes that the computer would never recognize that there were not two people holding those characteristics. She had heard that this new computer system frequently had enough keypunch errors to create multiple personages for some soldiers. In this case, she felt there was a good chance that the duplication would never be discovered.

When the two young soldiers arrived at her office the next morning, she had already received confirmation from her source at ARPERCEN (army personnel center) in St. Louis that the new files were up and running with all entries confirmed. Unless someone at the agency stumbled upon them from another angle, she thought these files would stand the test of scrutiny. The old files were just to confirm that the dead were in fact dead. As long as she never touched them again, there would be no reason for them to be disturbed.

Now she embarked upon the task of building the appropriate details into the new 201 files. She meticulously repeated the entries from the original files. She finally called the two young men into her office. Just as she suspected they arrived clean-shaven and freshly washed after their morning workout, which they had certainly been under no compulsion to complete but which had become part of their routine. When they were seated in her office, she explained that the new files were them now and why it was important that the old files not be disturbed. They would be able to access the veteran benefits to which they were entitled with the new files, but she emphasized that everything they had done had been classified as top secret.

She was not able to remove such a classification, but she was able to layer other entries over the blacked-out portions to give a plausible explanation of their time and how it had been spent. Judging from the details they had confided in her to this point, she was somewhat concerned for their safety if the wrong parties were to discover her efforts to reconstruct their carefully laid plans for these two. She felt comfortable that these new records would pass the eye test, but she did not want them to attract undue attention to them, as possible links might be discovered, which would lead back to the originals.

Cansler had, in the meantime, remembered the envelopes that had been completed by the team before their final deployment. Retrieving them, he handed Nuckles and Foster their envelope and discussed the disposition of the other thirty with Ms. Cross. Those envelopes had been opened, and the inside envelope prepared for mailing to the indicated party.

When Cansler returned the letters to Foster and Nuckles, they thanked him for keeping them. Then it occurred to them there were four letters that they were not sure should be mailed. They had no idea definitely that those members of the team had paid the ultimate price. Here was another opportunity for the leaders of the military to shine. She sent the letters to the G-1 for disposition.

While she had been busy preparing their records for their new lives, Nuckles and Foster had been acclimating themselves to the Ft. Campbell scenery. They were seeing it for the first time from the perspective of having wheels of their own to take anywhere they chose to go on post. Cansler had taken possession of Nuckles's vehicle as mentioned before. Now the three of them were discovering the life available in the greater environs of Ft. Campbell. Of course, Cansler had

257

achieved a considerable head start on the other two during the time they had been away.

Indeed, for the first few days, Nuckles had declined to take possession of the keys that had been offered by Cansler. He had simply informed his friend, "When I'm ready for it, I'll let you know." Secretly, he was having trouble adjusting to the faster pace of life, which he was encountering after the extended time they had been in virtual isolation on another continent.

After three days of riding around with Cansler, Nuckles felt he was ready to take control of the vehicle. That evening, he and Foster went into Clarksville, Tennessee, by themselves. This was another new experience for them. The few times they had been off post since arriving for basic combat training, they had been with someone else driving or in a commercial or military vehicle. The world was fast changing for them.

Cansler had confided to them that before the team departed from Ft. Devens, he had been instructed by Stidham that if anything happened to the team, he should forward all team records to TRADOC at Ft. Monroe, Virginia. He was preparing to send all units files to the address he had been given. Foster and Nuckles thought about this news and finally decided not to try to persuade their friend to not follow his instructions. While they were apprehensive that this may open a new trail to them for the likes of Bringle, they could not stand in the way of the inclusion of their training into the official development of the ranger school.

This newfound independence was beginning to take effect on their thought patterns by the fourth day. When Ms. Cross sat them down for a long talk, it was somewhat sobering for them. They had both enjoyed the training and the regimentation they had experienced. They had made friends with men, who, had they survived, would have formed lifelong bonds. However, due to the loss of those men, they would have only each other and, to a limited extent, Cansler and Ms. Cross to rely on in the days to come. Ms. Cross suspected that those days would be tough enough for them, just knowing what they had been through.

What really concerned her, however, was that the trip wires she had discovered in their original 201 files were worrisome. If someone was that eager to monitor their activities, she could only hope her efforts to allay these preparations would be successful in escaping detection. She could not overemphasize the need for them to lay low, at least until the top-secret classification should be removed from their files and from the logs of the detachment they had accompanied upon their mission.

When she had sternly informed them of her concerns for them and the seriousness of the situation in which they had been placed, she smiled and informed them that they would have three days to clear post and prepare for their post-military lives. She was floored when she inquired as to their intentions for those lives.

Foster very calmly informed her that he intended to reenlist in the United States Army at the earliest moment he could achieve this goal. Nuckles indicated that he would like to go to college, but that he intended to enlist in the United States Army Reserves. She smiled when it dawned on her how much these two young men had been influenced by Major Stidham and the team he had assembled to train them. She informed Nuckles that if he were sure that was his intention, she could arrange for him to simply transfer to the US Army Reserves and gave him a list of units close to his home of record to decide from for assignment. Nuckles, when pressed by Foster as to why the reserves, responded simply, "I want to go to college. I can remain in the reserves and go to school at the same time." She explained to Foster that he would be assigned to the US Army Reserve Control Group or inactive reserve as it was known, and he would simply need to see his local recruiter when he was ready to reenlist.

With this, she sent them on their way to begin their post-clearing odyssey. The idea of having four days to clear post seemed extravagant to them until it was explained that they had to take a physical, and there was a three-day waiting period for the tine test for tuberculosis. The days didn't seem so outlandish after this. During the initial physical, Nuckles was having blood drawn for testing by a seasoned first-class sergeant who openly sneered at him because he was being discharged in what the older man considered less time than was honorable. When the older soldier failed to get blood with his first two sticks, Nuckles simply looked at him calmly and informed him that "This is your last try. If you don't get blood this time, I'll draw some from you and submit it." When the first-class sergeant started to get loud in his response, the officer-in-charge responded to the area. His intervention soon calmed the situation, as cooler heads prevailed.

They discovered that they had to clear numerous activities that were consistently unknown to them. Usually, they were able to simply find the offices on the post-locator and get a quick signature. At the Central Issue Facility, they observed a soldier trying to turn in equipment he had been issued upon arrival at the base had never removed it from the packing material. He was informed he would have to clean the equipment before it would be acceptable for turn-in. They were certainly relieved that they had not been issued anything from that facility.

Moving on through the checklist, they divided up the stops so that there were about the same number for each day. On day 3, they had closed out all of the items except the reading of the TB test, which would be the next morning. Stopping in Cansler's office, they were approached by Ms. Cross, who had really taken a liking to the two young men.

She drew them into her office and explained the actions she had taken to keep their activities from triggering any trip wires that may have been hidden in the system by anyone from another agency. She reminded them that she couldn't overturn the classification of the mission in which they had been involved.

Therefore, they would have to abide by the restrictions placed upon such material. She reminded they were prohibited from discussing these matters with anyone unless they were asked by someone with the appropriate clearance and the need to know. Of course, they had no intentions of discussing them with anyone else anyway.

That evening, Foster had a present for Nuckles. It was a copy of Lewis Carroll's *Alice in Wonderland*. Regarding it dubiously, Nuckles wondered aloud about his friend's selection of reading materials. Then foster explained to him that he had been thinking about the need Ms. Cross felt to continue their awareness of the possibility that someone might not have their best interests at heart. He had devised a plan to utilize the book as a source document for any conversation they might need to carry on. After a few trial runs, they both seemed comfortable with the use of the code. Foster then told Nuckles, "We need to keep our distance. Never get anywhere that with one action we both could be reached. I think that west of the country fits me, and the east seems to be where you are best suited."

Neither of them spoke of the matter again, but both knew they would say good-bye the next morning, never to see each other again. They went to dinner and enjoyed it greatly. As they returned from their evening of good-bye, as they approached their rooms, they noticed a young man in civilian attire lounging in the lobby. It was soon apparent that he was studying them but not approaching them. As they passed through the lobby, he had unobtrusively followed them into the elevator. Looking at Nuckles, Foster observed, "I just remembered that I need some gum. I am going back down to get it."

With that, he had exited the car and gone into the stairway. Quickly, he had sprinted to the landing where Nuckles would disembark. Remaining in the shelter of the stairwell, he observed the arrival of the car and the exit of Nuckles. When Nuckles went into his room, the young man had written something on a notepad he held. Foster would have bet on a room number. He was flabbergasted when he saw the young man take out a passkey and enter his (Foster's) room.

Striding quickly and purposefully down the hall, he was soon at the door to his room. He had rapped three times on Nuckles's door as he passed and had sensed rather than seen Nuckles join him in the hall. He indicated his room and got a nod.

Throwing open the door with a quick and violent opening motion, he was surprised to see the young man sitting in a chair facing him. There was no visible weapon within his reach.

The stranger spoke. "Hello, my name is Lewis Hudson. I have been assigned to replace Mr. Marty Bringle, who I believe you know."

It only took a moment for Foster to respond, "Look here, you SOB (same meaning militarily as civilian), the only thing you can replace him for is a target in my sights. If you know his whereabouts, now would be good time for you to share that with us."

"Well, you see, I really do not know his location, but I can assure you that he is no longer affiliated with the agency. We had hoped to offer you the opportunity to engage in some further activities with us when you have had opportunity to recuperate from this one." His reply was delivered crisply and professionally. "We will be in touch."

Just as nonchalantly as if they were in a college dorm breaking up a study session, he stood and went to the door. Touching the bill of his imaginary hat, he opened the door and was gone.

"Well, what do you make of that?" Foster looked at Nuckles who was deep in thought.

"I think we better check him out closely." That muttered response was all that Nuckles could manage. The impact of what the visit of young Mr. Hudson would mean to them slowly began to dawn upon them. Each seemed to grasp different straws from the overall bouquet of information they had just been presented.

The next morning, both reported to the medical facility for the reading of their TB tests, which were negative. From there, they returned to Cansler's office, turned in their clearance papers, and received their DD214s and were on their way back to their homes of record.